Courtesy Hudson River Day Line

THE HEADLESS HORSEMAN

Junior English in Action

❖ *Book One* ❖

BY

J. C. TRESSLER

Head of the Department of English
Richmond Hill High School
New York City

AND

MARGUERITE B. SHELMADINE

Vice-Principal and Supervisor of English
Jefferson Junior High School
Rochester, New York

D. C. HEATH AND COMPANY

BOSTON	NEW YORK	CHICAGO
ATLANTA	SAN FRANCISCO	DALLAS
	LONDON	

Copyright, 1933, By
J. C. TRESSLER
And
MARGUERITE B. SHELMADINE

No part of the material covered by this copyright may be reproduced in any form without written permission of the publisher.

3 F 4

PRINTED IN THE UNITED STATES OF AMERICA

PREFACE

The purpose of Books One, Two, and Three of *Junior English in Action* is to help boys and girls to find in play, in work, at home, and at school things they want to say, and to enable them to express their ideas easily, naturally, correctly, effectively. Not by accident is *In Action* a part of the title. We have tried to make English an active, dynamic subject and to stimulate, entice, and help young people to live on paper and in speech.

Book One, which is intended for the first year of the junior high school or for the seventh year of the elementary school, provides abundant material for the normal pupils of the grade. Slow pupils in a class may omit exercises or the more difficult sentences at the end of exercises; slow classes may omit one or more units — may, for example, postpone the unit on verbs until the eighth or ninth year.

Because conversation is more natural than writing, the starting point in teaching English is conversing. The conversation unit, the first one in each book of the series, makes the pupils speech conscious, helps them to form desirable language habits, and prepares for other types of speaking and for writing.

True to its name, *Junior English in Action* has a maximum of examples and practice and a minimum of theory and rules. Moreover the explanations are simple and informal and are commonly based on the illustrations. In the presentation of a topic in composition there are regularly three steps: (1) a brief explanation; (2) the discussion of an example, preferably from a pupil's theme; (3) practice based on such a large number and wide variety of suggestions that every pupil will find at least one topic of interest to him. A usual procedure in explaining a grammatical point is to ask a question about three or four sentences; to help the pupil to answer the question; to derive a simple rule, definition, or generalization; to add a model to show the pupil just how to go to work; and then to give him an abundance of practice.

Ten planks in the platform on which *Junior English in Action* is built are —

1. Explanation without illustration and practice is valueless.

2. Good speech and writing habits are more to be desired — and harder to secure — than a knowledge of correct forms.

3. Because arousing pupils to undertake enthusiastically, energetically, and systematically the job of breaking their bad speech and writing habits and forming good ones is in many schools half the English problem, a text should suggest varied motives, show the practical value of the work to be done, and touch a variety of boys' and girls' interests as a basis for oral and written language.

4. Major emphasis should be placed on the types of speech and writing most frequently used — conversation and letter-writing, for example.

5. As models, pupil themes are more stimulating than literary masterpieces. A teacher should not "hold up a picture of the Colosseum and say, 'Go make a woodshed like it.'"

6. The aims in grammar teaching are to help pupils (1) to write and speak correct sentences, (2) to construct varied, effective sentences, (3) to punctuate correctly, and (4) to extract thought from the printed page. Grammar should therefore be reduced to the lowest terms compatible with learning to speak, write, and read.

7. A good way to study grammar is by applying it. Pupils learn grammar rapidly when they use it in building varied sentences.

8. The criteria for the selection of drill material and the determination of how much emphasis should be placed on

each point selected are the frequency of use and the frequency, persistency, and social seriousness of error.

9. "Written composition in the junior high school should be thought of primarily as a tool to be used in meeting real expressional demands in school and outside."

10. The best way to help pupils to learn what they need to know about grammar, spelling, punctuation, capitalization, and the effective sentence is to "test, teach, test, teach, test, teach to the point of mastery." Half-knowledge is of little value.

Because testing is an essential part of teaching, the text contains many varied mastery tests so constructed that either the teacher or the pupils can score them quickly and accurately. To provide an opportunity for retesting after reteaching we have included two equally difficult forms of every mastery test. Teachers who like to begin with a diagnostic test may give one mastery test when pupils start the unit and the other when they complete it, and thus measure achievement and progress.

Inside the back cover is a model for a progress graph. The teacher may have every pupil, using this as a guide, draw a progress graph and enter on it his per cent in each mastery test.

Believing that no two teachers will wish to present the work in exactly the same order, we have divided the book into two distinct sections: "Writing and Speaking" and "The Sentence and the Word." This arrangement and a full index and table of contents make it easy for the teacher to find the drill exercises which the class most needs at the hour and to sandwich them between the speeches and the themes.

To Miss Maude E. Mitchell, teacher of English in Jefferson Junior High School, Rochester, New York, sincere appreciation is expressed for constant assistance and helpful suggestions and for careful testing of exercises in the classroom. Miss Kathryn Tressler, a teacher of English in the Lambertville (New Jersey) Junior High School, made valuable contributions.

Grateful acknowledgment is made to the English teachers of Jefferson Junior High School for their coöperation, especially to Miss Ethel Dunn and Miss Dorothy Mount, and to Miss Marie M. Ball, teacher of speech correction.

J. C. T.
M. B. S.

CONTENTS

UNIT   PAGE

    Preface iii

PART I. WRITING AND SPEAKING

1. Conversing 3
   - Why Learn to Converse? 3
   - Speaking Distinctly 7
   - The Habit of Speaking Correctly 9
   - Courtesy 12
   - Accuracy 14
   - Sales Talk 16
   - Sharing One's Books 17
   - Over the Telephone 18

2. How a Composition Should Look 23
   - Guide Posts for Written Work 23
   - A Handwriting Scale 26

3. Story-Telling 29
   - Holding the Attention 29
   - Voice 30
   - Posture 31
   - Pronunciation and Enunciation 31
   - Good Listening 33
   - Retelling a Story 33
   - How to Write Conversation 39
   - How to Prepare a Dictation 43
   - The Anecdote 47
   - Checking Your Composition 49
   - Telling Experiences 50
   - How to Tell a Story 51
   - Account of a Red Letter Day 56

4. The Paragraph 58
   - Why We Have Paragraphs 58
   - What a Paragraph Is 58
   - Topic Sentence 59

CONTENTS

UNIT		PAGE
	Unity	62
	How a Paragraph Is Built	63
	Beginnings and Endings	65
	Paragraphing Conversation	68
5.	THE FRIENDLY LETTER	71
	Why Learn to Write Friendly Letters?	71
	Heading	72
	Salutation or Greeting	73
	Complimentary Close, Signature	74
	Body	75
	Envelope	78
	Appearance of the Letter	79
	Informal Notes	81
	Invitation, Acceptance, Regret	82
	Directions	83
	Thanks	84
	Postcards and Postal Cards	86
	Travel Letters	87
6.	EXPLAINING	91
	Why Learn to Explain?	91
	Being Clear	93
	Accuracy	95
	Outlining	96
	How to Do Something	101
	How to Make or Build Something	103
	How to Play Games	105
	Complete Definitions	109
	Intelligent Answers to Questions	110
	Explanation and Illustration of Proverbs	112
7.	THE BUSINESS LETTER	114
	Heading	115
	Letterheads	116
	Address	117
	Salutation	118
	Body	119
	Complimentary Close, Signature	120
	Envelope Address	122
	Paper and Folding	123
	Change of Address	125
	Request for Catalog	127

CONTENTS

UNIT		PAGE
	Order	128
	Correction of an Error	131
8.	READING AND MEMORIZING	134
	Reading for Pleasure	134
	Magazine	135
	Newspaper	141
	Directions	143
	Letters	145
	Memorizing	146
	How to Memorize a Poem	147

PART II. THE SENTENCE AND THE WORD

9.	SUBJECT AND VERB	151
	Sentence	151
	Verb or Simple Predicate	151
	Two-Word Verbs	153
	Separated Verbs	155
	Verbs in Questions	156
	Verbs of Three Words	157
	Simple Subject	160
	Introducing Word *There*	162
10.	THE PARTS OF SPEECH	165
	Nouns	165
	Nouns and Verbs	167
	Pronouns	169
	Modifiers	171
	Adjectives	172
	Pronouns and Adjectives	174
	Adverbs	176
	Prepositions	179
	Beginning Sentences with Prepositions	182
	Prepositions and Adverbs	184
	Conjunctions	185
	Interjections	187
11.	PARTS OF THE SIMPLE SENTENCE	191
	Predicate Adjective	191
	Predicate Nominative	193
	Object of Verb	196
	Predicate Nominative and Object	199

CONTENTS

UNIT	PAGE
Indirect Object	200
Appositive	203
Nominative of Address	206
Adding Modifiers	207
Complete Subject and Complete Predicate	209
Inverted Order	211
Simple Sentence Having Compound Subject or Predicate	214
Other Compound Parts	215
12. SENTENCE SENSE	220
Half-Sentence	220
Comma Blunder	224
13. PUNCTUATION OF SIMPLE SENTENCES	233
Why Learn to Punctuate?	233
Kinds of Sentences	233
The Period after Abbreviations	236
Comma	236
Apostrophe for Contractions	245
Exclamation Point	246
14. NOUNS	252
Capitalization	252
Plural	259
Gender	263
How to Form the Possessive	264
15. PRONOUNS	271
Personal Pronouns	271
Case	272
The Personal Pronouns Grouped	274
Correct Case	275
Word Order	277
Double Subject	278
Them, Those	279
Compound Personal Pronouns	280
Interrogative Pronouns	280
Indefinite Pronouns	282
Pronouns and Adjectives	283
Agreement with Antecedent	283
16. VERBS	289
Transitive and Intransitive	289
Tense	294

CONTENTS

UNIT	PAGE
Correct Use	298
Principal Parts	299
Ain't and Other Errors	305
17. THE RIGHT WORD	310
Why Learn New Words?	313
The Dictionary	314
Use of Guide Words	316
Finding Out How Words Are Pronounced	316
Studying a Word	323
Finding a Definition That Fits	324
Use of Hyphen	325
When to Use Capitals	326
Finding the Plural of Nouns	327
Common Abbreviations	327
Words Often Misused	328
18. SPELLING	333
Why You Should Be a Good Speller	333
How the Words Were Selected	333
Notebook	333
The Ten Hardest Words	334
Four Groups	335
Adding *s* and *ed* to Verbs	335
Final *y*	335
Possessive Singular	338
One Hundred Demons	339
New York State Spelling List for the Seventh Year	340
INDEX	345

LIST OF ILLUSTRATIONS

	PAGE
The Headless Horseman	*Frontispiece*
A Lynx of the North Woods	38
An Auto Trip in the Far North	52
His Pets	55
Seeing Herself	85
Fishing Smacks at Nantucket	89
Good Enough to Eat	101
Building a Model Signal Tower	102
Children Casting Their Work in Plaster	105
Away Up There	138
Pupils of People's Valley School near Kirkland, Arizona	154
Girl Scouts Raising Old Glory	159
A Monkey with Two Adopted Kittens	163
Getting Ready for a Ski Race	168
Happy Days	175
Canoeing on Lake Placid	183
A Good Shot	197
Trout Fishing in Lake O'Hara	198
Friends	206
A Milkman in Holland	216
Babe Ruth at Bat	289
Feeding a Woodchuck	290

JUNIOR ENGLISH IN ACTION

Book One

Part I — Writing and Speaking

UNIT 1

CONVERSING

Why Learn to Converse?

"Why doesn't somebody say something?" thought Fred frantically.

When his mother had given him permission to have this party, he had hoped it would be great fun. Now here they were — six girls and six boys including himself — sitting around the room as stiff as though they were in church.

Realizing his duty as host, Fred made a brave remark, "It's cold, isn't it?"

"Y-yes," came a feeble response.

Silence! Another attempt. "When do you suppose the skating rinks will open?"

No answer for a minute. Then a half-hearted murmur from someone, "I don't know."

Desperately he raked his mind for another topic. Finally he recalled a picture he had noticed in the paper that evening of two lion cubs that had been born a few days before at the city zoo. Forgetting for the moment his embarrassment, he asked eagerly, "Have any of you seen the new lion cubs?"

"You bet I have," replied Jack Snow. "My father took me out to see them Sunday. They play just like little puppies. One cub was chewing and biting his mother's tail for all he was worth. The old lady would stand it just so long. Then she would lift that big tail and swing it over to her other side, and that cub would go right after it."

"What was the other cub doing?" someone asked.

"Oh, he was chewing the first cub's tail."

Everyone laughed at this, and the ice was broken.

How would you have helped had you been at Fred's party? Have you ever been embarrassed because you could think of nothing to say? Do you realize how much pleasure in your life comes from your ability to talk and another's ability to understand? Both pleasure and business depend largely on these abilities. The engineer must be able to tell others what to do, and the workmen must be able to follow directions. The successful counselors at scout camp are the ones who can give directions which others can follow and who, at the same time, can listen to others' opinions.

Do you realize how much of your life is spent in conversing? In a day of twenty-four hours you usually sleep about nine hours and have fifteen hours for eating, work, and fun. Let us suppose that you spend even eight of those fifteen hours in talking, or in taking part in conversation. That means that about a third of every day — or a third of your life — is spent in conversing. Is it strange, then, to say that *learning to talk well is vitally important?*

Learning the Game

No one learns to skate merely by watching others or by talking about doing it. One learns to skate by skating — that is, by constant practice. The league baseball players do not become famous merely by playing baseball a few weeks or a few months. They learn the rules of the game, pay strict attention to what they are doing, and practice continually. Likewise, to speak good English one must learn the rules of that game and practice constantly.

Playing the Game

Conversation is like a game of baseball. There are several players: a pitcher who starts the conversation, a catcher who listens and sends the conversational ball back, and basemen who are on the alert to catch the ball if it comes their way. Every member of the group must keep his mind on what is being said, just as every player must watch the ball.

Attentive listening shows intelligence and courtesy. When someone is talking to you, do not keep looking away; do not fidget. Look at the speaker and keep your mind on what he is saying.

Just asking or answering questions does not make a good talker. You must have something entertaining to say. This may be your own experience or something you have read or heard. Many interesting events are taking place all the time, and comment on such topics may be both enjoyable and worth while. Watch the newspapers and magazines for unusual bits of news about discoveries, peculiar places, and famous people, for strange stories of animal life, for new inventions, and for amusing happenings.

Practice 1

Read the conversation between Jo and Laurie and answer the following questions:
1. What information did Laurie give?
2. What part did Jo take in the conversation?

"Abroad!" cried Jo. "Oh, tell me about it! I love dearly to hear people describe their travels."

Laurie didn't seem to know where to begin; but Jo's eager questions soon set him going, and he told her how he had been at school in Vevay, where the boys never wore hats, and had a fleet of boats on the lake, and for holiday fun went on walking trips about Switzerland with their teachers.

"Don't I wish I'd been there!" cried Jo. "Did you go to Paris?"

"We spent last winter there."

"Can you talk French?"

"We were not allowed to speak anything else at Vevay."

"I suppose you are going to college soon?"

"Not for a year or two: I won't go before seventeen, anyway."

"Aren't you but fifteen?" asked Jo, looking at the tall lad, whom she had imagined seventeen already.

"Sixteen, next month."

"How I wish I was going to college!"

— LOUISA M. ALCOTT, *Little Women*

Practice 2

Divide the class into groups of three or four each. Appoint a chairman for each group. Have each group choose one of the suggested topics and prepare to talk about it before the class.

The chairman will start the conversation by asking one member of his group a question. The one answering will, in turn, ask a question of another member, until each member of the group has had a part in the conversation. The class will decide which group had the most interesting discussion.

1. Why do you think boys should learn to cook?
2. What kind of movies do you like?
3. On what occasions have you seen dogs show intelligence?
4. What part of the United States would you like to visit? Why?

5. What foreign country would you like to visit? Why?
6. How did you happen to start collecting stamps?
7. What kind of radio programs do you like?
8. What kind of vacation would you like best?
9. How can we improve our school spirit?
10. What do you like best about camping?
11. What kind of books do you enjoy most? Why?
12. What assembly program did you enjoy most this term?
13. Did you ever take any prize at a county or state fair? For what?
14. What interests you most about a farm?
15. Why do you enjoy roaming through woods?
16. Why do you like summer better than winter?

Speaking Distinctly

When you are talking, you do not like to be interrupted. Yet if you are speaking so that you cannot be understood, how can you expect others to listen? To speak distinctly open your mouth, enunciate the words clearly, and pronounce every syllable of each word. Say *doing* (not *doin*), *get* (not *git*).

Do you ever listen to the sound of your own voice? The radio has made us conscious of the differences in voices. You like the tone and clear enunciation of one speaker's voice, and you do not like another's broadcasting because his tone is rasping and his words are not distinct.

If your voice is high-pitched, harsh, or nasal, practice to make it pleasing. Your voice should not be harsh but should be loud enough to be heard in every part of the room.

Practice 3

Practice the words on the next page until you can pronounce them clearly and distinctly.

this (*not* dis)
arithmetic (*not* rithmetic)
library (*not* libary)
history (*not* histry)
something (*not* sumpin)
geography (*not* jogfry)
thousand (*not* tousand)
not yet (*not* notchet)
last year (*not* las year)
give him (*not* givum)

Would you? (*not* wouldjew?)
Don't you know? (*not* don cha know?)
Yes (*not* yeah or uh-huh)
Because I want to (*not* cuz I wanta)
What are you doing? (*not* wa cha doin?)
What did you say? (*not* wa je say?)

Pet Word

What are your pet expressions? You can tell what peculiarities your friends have, but perhaps you do not realize what yours are. Do you have just a few words to describe everything? Try to count how many times a day you use *very, awfully, nice, great, grand.* If you are telling a story at home, how many times do you use *said?*

Do not be one who begins each sentence with *listen, why,* or *well.* Avoid ending your sentence with *see, see the point, you know what I mean, don't you know.*

Pause at the end of a sentence. Then begin a new sentence. Don't tie sentences together with *and, so, and so,* and *and then.* Perhaps you are in the habit of saying *ur-r* when you hesitate for a word or a thought. Show that you can talk without using the words *and-ur, now-ur, why-ur, but-ur.*

Practice 4

Said is a word which you overwork. Copy the following sentences, substituting for *said* a suitable word chosen from the list given below the sentences.

Model

"It's time to get up, John," said Mother.
"It's time to get up, John," called Mother.

1. "Hurry!" said the fire chief. "Put the ladders on the right side."
2. "Where are we going?" said the Red Queen.
3. "Please give me that box," said John.
4. "Be very quiet; the baby is asleep," said Mother.
5. "When does the train leave for Chicago?" said Mr. Brown.
6. "Quick! Quick! Call the doctor," said the captain.
7. "Three cheers for our team!" said the boys.
8. "The clouds are getting darker," said Mr. Pitcairn. "Row faster."
9. "I got here just in time," said the scout as he dashed in breathlessly.
10. He bent over Danny and said sharply, "Drink this, sonny."
11. Danny's face glowed. "Oh, sir, you are so good," he said.
12. "Save me! I'm drowning!" said Eric, as he sank for the second time.

Words which may be used instead of *said:*

answered	remarked	cried	pleaded
demanded	exclaimed	called	replied
questioned	whispered	roared	insisted
groaned	requested	shouted	gasped

The Habit of Speaking Correctly

If you play with a boy who has the mumps, you will doubtless have them yourself in a few days. Just in the same way you can catch good or bad habits in conversation. Ungrammatical expressions make you appear ignorant even though you know better. Correct your own mistakes. Good English is a habit. Acquire the habit of speaking correctly. Say *I did* (not *I done*); *I saw* (not *I seen*); *I am not* or *I'm not* (not *I ain't*).

Practice 5

On your paper copy the number of each sentence, and after each number write the correct form chosen from the parenthesis:

1. I —— book like that. (ain't got no, haven't a)
2. I could have —— if I had been home. (gone, went)
3. He —— what I told him. (did, done)
4. She had —— them often. (seen, saw)
5. Tom —— going with the team. (ain't, isn't)
6. He asked whether the guests had ——. (gone, went)
7. When he ——, the crowd had gone. (came, come)
8. She —— think she'll pass. (doesn't, don't)
9. She said she —— the man enter the shop. (saw, seen)
10. The boy had —— better than they had expected. (did, done)
11. He —— the crowd as he flew over the park. (saw, seen)
12. She —— ready to go swimming. (ain't, isn't)
13. As John entered the room, Jim called, "Where —— you last period?" (was, were)
14. I —— been home since morning. (ain't, haven't)
15. John called, "Has the bell ——?" (rang, rung)
16. "Yes," answered Mary, "and I haven't —— my lunch yet." (ate, eaten)
17. Have you —— the story for the school paper? (wrote, written)
18. What —— you doing when the fire broke out? (was, were)
19. —— you going to see the game this afternoon? (ain't, aren't)
20. He —— the boys a few minutes before they —— him. (saw, seen)

Practice 6

Correct the following conversations:

1

"I haven't no pencil."
"Here, take Jack's. He don't need it."
"I ain't got no paper either."
"Where did it go? I seen some on your desk last period."
"Here it is."

2

"Are you going with me?"
"I ain't asked my mother yet. Tom don't think he can go."
"How do you know?"
"I seen him last night and asked him."

3

"There isn't nobody at home."
"Have you rang the bell?"
"Yes, but there isn't no answer."
"It's funny that Mary isn't never at home."

Practice 7

If you were correcting proof of a story for your school paper, you would have to watch carefully for errors. In the following there are five mistakes. After the story is corrected, it may be dictated by your teacher.

IT PAID

"Are you going to play baseball this afternoon?" called Tom as he dashed up on the porch.

"No, I never can do nothin'," mumbled John disgustedly. "Mother says I gotta watch the baby."

"Let's take the baby with us. Father sometimes takes my little brother when he goes to the games. I went with him once when he done it."

They pushed the carriage quietly off the porch and hurried down the street. Just as they turned the corner, John said, "Oh, I guess I'd better go back. They might worry about the baby."

"All right for you," called Tom, as John turned toward home. "You're no good. You never do nothin'."

As John pushed the carriage slowly toward the house, his mother called, "Hurry, John, your father is going to take you to the ball game this afternoon."

"Boy, I'm glad I didn't go no farther," thought John as he quickly wheeled the carriage into the hall.

Courtesy

Courtesy is necessary in conversation. You have noticed that often one person does too much talking, while another seldom gets in a word. Take only your share of the time; give everyone a chance.

Do not ask too personal questions. Such questions may be embarrassing and are apt to hurt someone's feelings.

Interrupting another's conversation or attempting to find words for the speaker is a common fault. This usually happens when one is not paying attention or is impatient to give his own opinion.

Conversation is most interesting when every member of the group is taking part. Each should consider that he has three duties: to add his share to the conversation, to listen attentively to others, and to bring into the conversation those who have not yet taken part.

Practice 8

Read the following conversation and answer the questions:

1. What part did each take in the conversation?
2. What shows that each listened to the others?

The tower clock was striking eight as Sam turned the corner into High Street on his way to school. Rain or shine, the three friends met there each morning.

"Hello, Jed," Sam called. "Have you been waiting long?"

"No, only a few minutes. There's Jim running through the alley. Hi, Jim! What was the score yesterday afternoon?"

"Our team won 15 to 14," answered Jim breathlessly. "It was a tie of 14 to 14 until toward the end of the last inning. Then Phil made the extra score. It was a real game. You fellows should have been with me."

"I couldn't, you know," answered Jed, "for I had planned to meet my uncle. We had a wonderful time. We went to the store and my uncle bought me this sweater. Isn't it a dandy? Then we had dinner at the Blackstone Hotel and listened to the music. After that we saw a hair-raising movie."

"What did you see?" asked Jim.

"It was the kind you would have liked. It showed people taking pictures of wild animals in Africa. I was sure they would get killed, but of course they didn't."

"I'd like to see it. I wish I had an uncle like yours, Jed. But you weren't the only ones that had a good time. You'd never guess where I was. Dad and I went to the airport, and while he was seeing a man, one of the pilots took me up for a few minutes."

Practice 9

Choose a chairman and divide the class into groups of three or four. Each group will select one of the following scenes and dramatize the conversation which might take place.

1. Three boys are walking home together after school.
2. Several girls walk home together and plan a hike.
3. Mary and Janet are walking home from school and meet Mary's sister, who tells her of company at home.
4. Several boys or girls from different classes are talking about the class soccer games.
5. John or Mary, who has been out of town for two weeks, meets two friends on the way to school.

6. Three girls plan a surprise party for Jean's birthday.
7. John and Jim are telling a new boy in the neighborhood about the school, which he will attend on Monday for the first time.
8. George tells two friends how he learned to swim.
9. Anne and Dorothy invite some new girls to become members of the Girl Reserves.
10. You try to interest two new members of your class in some after-school games.

Accuracy

A great deal of one's conversation consists of explaining or giving directions, such as locating places and telling how to play games and how to do or make ordinary things.

Interest in what you are saying and accuracy in the information given are requirements in such conversations. A good explanation is clear, courteous, and complete.

Read the following example of such a conversation and answer these questions:

1. How do the boys become acquainted?
2. What does the newcomer want to know?
3. Are Alec's directions clear?

Example:

"Hello," called Alec. "When did you move to our street?"

"Yesterday," answered the stranger. "Where do you live?"

"I live in the house on the corner. My name's Alec Brown. What's yours?"

"George McCauley."

"What grade are you in in school?" asked Alec.

"In the seventh," replied George. "Where are you?"

"I'm in the seventh, too," answered Alec.

"Where's the school I'll go to, Alec?"

"You'll go to the junior high school in the park. I'll tell you exactly how to get there. Go down Seneca Parkway to Lake Avenue; turn right on Lake Avenue and go to Phelps Avenue; turn right on Phelps and go through the park to the school. But pshaw! I'll take you Monday morning."

"That'll be fine," answered George. "What time do you start?"

"Oh, I'll be along about eight o'clock," called Alec, as he rode off on his bicycle.

Practice 10

Divide the class into groups of two each. Each group will choose one of the following suggestions and give the conversation which might take place. This requires clear thinking and the careful use of words. The class will decide which conversation gives the most accurate directions.

1. A new boy or girl moved next door on Saturday. Explain clearly how he or she may reach the junior high school. Don't waste a word.

2. Tell a new pupil how to reach the lunch room and what the regulations are for the lunch period.

3. You meet a stranger who asks how to reach the library. Give definite directions.

4. Explain to a new pupil the rules about tardiness.

5. Instruct a new pupil in your grade about the procedure during fire drill.

6. A boy who has recently moved to your neighborhood does not understand the marks on the report card. Explain them to him and his father.

7. A new pupil asks how he may become a member of the band, orchestra, or glee club. Give him the necessary directions.

8. Direct a passing motorist to the post office. Give accurate directions. Don't use unnecessary words.

9. While you are going to class, you meet a visitor who asks for the principal. Direct him to the principal's office.

10. A cousin who is visiting you wants to attend the ball game. Tell him how to reach the baseball park.

11. Tell a stranger where and when to get the bus to the lake.

12. A neighbor wants to get some books at the library. Tell her when and how she may draw them out.

13. A stranger asks how he may find a doctor's office.

14. Sam tells a new friend how he made a bird house.

15. Betty gives her cousin her recipe for making fudge.

Sales Talks

Have you ever tried to sell booster-tags, newspapers, magazines, books, or baseball gloves? This is your chance. Here are some general directions which apply to the selling of anything from a can-opener to a Rolls Royce.

1. Show the usefulness of the article you are selling.
2. Prove that it is worth the price.
3. Make the buyer feel that he cannot be without it.

You must believe that the article you are selling is worth the price and show interest and enthusiasm. Half-hearted conversation will not be convincing.

Practice 11

Divide the class into groups of two each. Each group will select one of the following and dramatize it before the class. Remember to speak distinctly and to use correct English. Do not use pet expressions. Don't waste time and words. Get to the point.

1. Sam goes to the door and tries to sell a magazine to Mrs. Smith.

2. Jim tries to sell a good baseball glove to his neighbor, Tom Stewart.

3. Mary has a tennis racket which she would like to sell.

4. Jean is moving out of town and will not need her new gymnasium suit. She offers it to a friend at a reduced price.

5. John is moving to a state where textbooks are furnished and tries to sell his seventh-grade mathematics book.

6. George finds that he has outgrown his roller skates and offers them to a neighbor at a reduced price.

7. You are selling tickets for an entertainment your school is to have.

8. Eric has a reputation for making kites that will fly. He promised to pay you twenty per cent on all you sell for him.

Sharing One's Books

Sharing a book with your friends is like giving them gifts. In some books you open up a new land to them; in others you introduce them to new people who may become lifelong friends, like Tom Sawyer or Robin Hood.

In sharing books, one does not give the whole story away at the beginning. It is more fun to tell interesting bits about a story and to arouse another's curiosity, so that he will want to hurry to the library to get the book.

In the following conversation between two seventh-grade girls, does the one arouse the other's interest?

"Have you ever read *The Legend of Sleepy Hollow?* I've just finished it and liked it."

"No, I haven't read it but we'll have it in class."

"It's the kind of book I'd like to read twice. One girl I know said she'd read it three times and didn't get tired of it."

"How could she read the same book three times? What is interesting about it?"

"It gives such funny pictures of some people. You can see fat Mr. Van Tassel, and laugh at thin Ichabod Crane.

I love to read about the party, about Ichabod's being so frightened, and of the ghost that followed him."

"Did a ghost really follow him? What did Ichabod do?"

"You'll have to read the book. I'd spoil it for you if I told you the most exciting part." — PUPIL

Practice 12

The class will choose a chairman. He will divide the class into groups of three or four. The pupils in each group will then choose a book they like. Imagine that only one has read the book. The others will ask him questions which will bring out the most interesting points. At the close of the class period judges may decide which group gave the best-prepared review. Some questions which might be asked are: What are some interesting facts about the author? What other books has he written? Where does the story take place? What characters will you remember? Why? What is the most thrilling part of the story? What other books are like this one?

Over the Telephone

A telephone conversation is a substitute for a business or a friendly call. As in ordinary conversation, one should pronounce correctly and use his most pleasing tones and best English. It is not the loudness of the voice, but the distinctness in enunciating which makes speech easy to hear.

Forms of Call and Answer

We are accustomed to answering the telephone by saying "Hello." Because this answer gives no definite information, questions must follow, such as, "Is this Smith's residence?" or "Is this Stone 1836? Who is speaking?" One can save time by using one of the three answers recommended by the telephone company:

1. "This is William Smith's residence, Harriet speaking."
2. "This is Wiliiam Smith's residence."
3. "This is Stone 1836."

Example of a telephone conversation:
Mary. Stone 1836.
Miss Hill. This is Stone 1836, Jane Hill speaking.
Mary. Hello, Miss Hill. This is Mary Johnson. May I come for my music lesson at 10:30 Saturday morning instead of at 10 o'clock?
Miss Hill. I'm sorry, Mary. That will not be convenient, as I have a pupil at that time. Could you come earlier?
Mary. Yes, I could come at 9:30. Would that be all right?
Miss Hill. Yes, I'll expect you at 9:30.
Mary. Thank you, Miss Hill. Good-bye.
Miss Hill. Good-bye, Mary.

Practice 13

Divide the class into groups of two each and dramatize some of the following telephone calls. Let one be the person calling and the other the person who receives the call.

1. Call your mother from Jack's home, asking whether you may stay for dinner.
2. Ask the librarian to reserve a book for you.
3. Ask the dentist for an appointment to have your teeth cleaned.
4. Invite two friends to go to the circus with you and your father on Saturday afternoon.
5. Call the store and order groceries to be sent to your home.
6. Ask Betty's mother whether there is any school work you should bring to Betty, who has been ill.

7. Call the Bus Terminal and ask when the next bus leaves for a neighboring town.

8. Invite your music teacher to come to an assembly at which you are to play.

9. You have been out of school for a few days. Call Jack and ask him the results of the basketball game Monday afternoon.

10. You have just returned home after a week's absence. Call a friend and tell him that you will be ready to go to school with him in the morning.

11. Invite a friend to go to a movie with you and give directions as to where and when you are to meet.

12. Call your mother, who is visiting out of town. Tell her some interesting home news.

13. Call your home when you are visiting out of town.

14. Call Betty, who is quarantined with scarlet fever, and tell her some school news.

15. You have just arrived at the railway station after having spent a week with your grandmother, who lives in another town or city. Call your mother and tell her when you expect to reach home.

Practice 14

Imagine the conversation which might take place between the following characters familiar to you in your English and history stories. Arrange for different groups to dramatize some of the following incidents. Make each dramatization entertaining and as true to the story as possible. Remember to speak distinctly and to avoid pet expressions.

1. Tom Sawyer makes a game out of painting the fence.
2. Huckleberry Finn visits Tom Sawyer's relatives.
3. Columbus tells Queen Isabella about his plans for reaching the East Indies.
4. Ulysses escapes the enchantment in Circe's palace.
5. Jason tells how he secured the Golden Fleece.
6. Robin Hood christens Little John.

7. Sir Walter Raleigh tells Queen Elizabeth about the strange people he found in the New World.

8. John Alden gives to Priscilla the proposal from Miles Standish.

9. Miles Standish quarrels with John Alden.

10. Washington talks with two of his soldiers at Valley Forge.

11. Two men try to influence a third to sign the Declaration of Independence.

12. Rebecca and a new friend discuss her life at Sunnybrook Farm.

13. Robinson Crusoe and Friday find footprints in the sand.

14. A group of villagers discuss former residents who were thought to resemble the Great Stone Face.

15. Katrina Van Tassel discusses with her father the strange disappearance of Ichabod Crane.

16. Rip Van Winkle returns home and inquires about his wife and friends.

17. Gluck's brothers scold him for cutting the roast.

18. Dramatize a conversation between two characters in a book you are now reading.

Never Again

Write NEVER AGAIN at the top of a page in your notebook. When anyone points out an error in your speech — a wrong pronunciation, a wrong word, or a mistake in grammar — write the error and the correction on this page. Your list after a week might look like this:

(Right) That isn't right.
(Wrong) That ain't right.

(Right) Drowned.
(Wrong) Drownded.

(Right) My mother went with me.
(Wrong) My mother she went with me.

Better Speech Campaign

Plan a Better Speech Campaign, the purpose of which is to discover outstanding speech errors, to devise plans for overcoming them, and also to become accustomed to using correct grammatical forms and words that paint pictures.

The teacher appoints a chairman, who in turn appoints two detectives for each row. The duty of Detective A is to make a list each day of the serious errors made by pupils in his row. Detective B is to make a list of the most descriptive words and best sentences, together with the names of the pupils in his row who have a good record each day. The chairman makes the same kind of record of the English used by the detectives.

At the end of each day the detectives turn their lists in to the chairman. He in turn hands them to the teacher. The teacher discusses them with the class, and the pupils record in their notebooks the corrected forms of the most frequent errors and also picture-making words.

Remember that you should —
1. Always use your best English.
2. Speak clearly and distinctly.
3. Avoid pet expressions.
4. Choose companions who talk well.
5. Be a courteous listener.
6. Cultivate a pleasing voice.
7. Become speech conscious.

UNIT 2

HOW A COMPOSITION SHOULD LOOK

"One would never have guessed when John Henderson first entered our class that he was so good looking," remarked Adeline, as she and Ada were walking home from school.

"I should say not," answered Ada. "Wasn't he the messiest person you ever saw?"

"Do you remember," continued Adeline, "how spotted and wrinkled his clothes were? I honestly think that he slept in them."

"I don't believe he ever washed his neck," laughed Ada.

"But look at him now! He's so particular about his appearance! I think he's handsome," declared Adeline.

Blotted, dirty, and carelessly written compositions make the same impression John did. A story that is scribbled on a ragged piece of paper attracts no one, even if it is well told. Boys and girls should take pride not only in their personal appearance but also in their written work.

Guide Posts for Written Work

1. Use black or blue-black ink.
2. Use white paper about 8 by $10\frac{1}{2}$ inches.
3. Leave a one-inch margin at the left. Keep the margin even. Have about a one-half inch margin at the right.

4. Indent the first word of every paragraph one inch from the margin.

5. At the end of a line divide a word only between syllables. Place the hyphen at the end of the line.

6. Write your name, your class, and the date according to your teacher's instructions. One place for them is close to the top of the paper.

Edwin Frees   7B²   February 3, 1934

Good Sportsmanship

Being a good sportsman in school means more than being

7. As in the example, place the title near the center of the line.

8. Capitalize the first word of the title and all other words except articles, short prepositions, and short conjunctions.

9. Use no punctuation mark after the title unless a question mark or an exclamation mark is needed.

10. Leave a blank line after the title.

11. If you use more than one sheet of paper, number each in the upper right-hand corner.

12. Do not use the sign & for the word *and*.

13. Do not hand in a blotted, untidy paper. After writing a composition, revise it and then copy it neatly.

14. Make your penmanship easy to read. Form each letter, join the letters of a word, leave a space between the words.

Practice 1

Check a paper which you have prepared for English, social studies, or another subject.

1. Are the following correct: Ink? Paper? Margins? Indentions? Title? Your name and class?
2. Is the penmanship easily read?
3. Is the paper neat enough to hand in?

Penmanship Test

In about half a page, tell of something interesting you saw on the way to or from school yesterday or to school this morning. Then grade your penmanship, giving yourself ten credits for every question you can answer "Yes" and zero for other questions. Place your mark at the top of the page.

1. Do I leave enough space between words?
2. Do I leave a double space between sentences?
3. Is a good forward slant shown? Is the slant uniform?
4. Are the letters of a word joined together?
5. Do I close the tops of *a*, *o*, *g*, and *q*?
6. Do I place a dot above *i* and *j* and cross *t* with a short line and *tt* with a longer line?
7. Do I write clearly *a* and *o*; *b* and *l*; *h* and *k*; *e* and *i*; *r* and *s*; *u* and *w*; *u* and *n*; *It* and *W*?
8. Do I always open the loops of *l*, *h*, *k*, *b*, and *f*?
9. Do I avoid flourishes and elaborate capitals?
10. Is my writing easy to read?

Practice 2

After grading your penmanship, rewrite the composition. Make it neat and easy to read.

Using Handwriting Scales

The study of a handwriting scale will help a poor penman to make his writing more legible. To grade your penmanship, place a sample in turn under the POOR, GOOD, and SUPERIOR specimens in your book, and find which of the three it resembles most closely.

Practice 3

Study the following handwriting scale which has been prepared for the seventh grade and check your writing by it frequently. Do not be satisfied until your writing compares favorably with the upper specimen on the scale.

A Handwriting Scale [1]

SEVENTH B GRADE STANDARDS

7B — SUPERIOR

It is better to suffer a thousand reverses than to run away from battle. It is better to suffer a thousand reverses than to run away

7B — GOOD

It is better to suffer a thousand reverses than to run away from battle. It is better to suffer a thousand reverses than to run a

7B — POOR

It is better to suffer a thousand reverses than to run away from a battle. It is better to suffer a thousand reverses than to run away from

---

[1] Taken by permission from *The Mills System Handwriting Scale*, written and published by Edward C. Mills, Rochester, New York.

SEVENTH A GRADE STANDARDS
7A — Superior

Work is given to men not only because the world needs it, but because the workman needs it.
Work is given to men not only

7A — Good

Work is given to men, not only because the world needs it, but because the workman needs it
Work is given to men not only

7A — Poor

Work is given to men not only because the world needs it, but because the workman need it.
Work is given to men not only

Practice 4

What are the faults in the following specimens? What are the good points?

1

One Saturday last April four of us went fishing down at Spring Brook. The water was deep and swift and the fish seemed to be waiting to be caught

2

was deep and swift and
the fish seemed to be waiting
to be caught.

3

The wind howled and the rain came
down in torrents. We crowded into our corner
and tried to keep warm but the rain

4

The girls dashed into the house, found
their skates and had reached the door
when the telephone rang.

5

The score was four to ten to seven in favor of the
Greyhounds. Our home team had possession of the
ball and they tried every hard to advance it down the
field. Sometimes

6

His companion went up ten
miles and broke the world's
record by ten thousand feet.
They had to spend the night
on a glacier

UNIT 3
STORY-TELLING
Holding the Attention

Everyone in class was delighted. Miss Catherwood had asked two of the boys to tell some of their most interesting experiences. As each had driven last summer with his family from the East to California, had camped, climbed mountains, and seen many thrilling sights, the class expected an entertaining half hour.

Edward was the first. He described the fun they had getting all their baggage into the car, a terrifying thunderstorm, two punctures within an hour miles from a garage, a midnight hold-up at an auto camp, the friendly thieving bears at the Yellowstone, a chicken-pull in an Indian village, and the thrill of watching Will Rogers play polo. His stories were interesting, but his unpleasant voice and slouchy manner annoyed the class. He made frequent grammatical errors and connected sentences with *so-ur, but-ur, and-ur, well-ur*, until his account seemed like one long sentence.

When Stephen began his story, the class was restless, but after a few words there was perfect attention. The incidents he told were no more interesting than those Edward had related, but he had a pleasing voice, stood erect, spoke correctly and distinctly and with so much enthusiasm that everyone was sorry when the bell rang.

The Manner of Speaking

The purpose of telling stories is to entertain. One not only must have a good story and be interested in it, but he must tell it well. Both Stephen and Edward told interesting experiences, but only Stephen really entertained his audience. Telling a story well is an art. Some boys and girls are natural story-tellers; others require a great deal of practice. Good story-telling includes having a pleasing voice, standing erect, and pronouncing each word correctly and distinctly.

Voice

Have you ever heard anyone say, "What he said was good but his voice spoiled it"? Such a statement shows the importance of pleasing tones. Pay attention to the voices of men and women who speak over the radio. Listen attentively to someone whose voice you like to hear. Why does it attract you?

Practice 1

Change your classroom into a broadcasting studio by arranging a screen as a booth at the back of the room. Pupils chosen by the teacher will read a paragraph which has been selected. The others in the class, who will not know the order in which pupils read, may choose the best broadcaster. They will base their decision on these four points:

1. Is the voice harsh? Shrill? Pleasing?
2. Can each word be heard in the farthest corner of the room?
3. Is the pronunciation correct?
4. Are the words enunciated clearly and distinctly?

Posture

What difference does posture make? Do you ever notice how a speaker stands? Of course you do. Sometimes you become so interested in his posture and gestures that you forget to listen to what he is saying. Here are three suggestions:

1. Stand erect and at ease, with the weight thrown forward.
2. So far as possible forget your hands and arms.
3. Do not make the desk or table support your weight.

Pronunciation and Enunciation

Correct pronunciation and enunciation are essential to good speaking. The most entertaining story may be spoiled by carelessness in pronouncing words. You cannot expect your audience to be interested if you do not speak distinctly. Follow these suggestions:

1. Enunciate both vowels and consonants clearly.
2. Pronounce *ing* and *th*.
3. Cut your words apart.
4. Do not say *and-ur, why-ur, but-ur, so-ur*.

Practice 2

Read the following groups of words vertically, then horizontally.

1

tan	than	Dan
tine	thine	dine
ten	then	den
toes	those	doze
tie	thy	dye
tense	thence	dense

2

tin	thin	din
two	through	do
true	threw	drew
tick	thick	Dick
trash	thrash	dash
tear	there	dare

3

bath	bat	bad
death	debt	dead
faith	fate	fade
fourth	fort	ford
path	pat	pad

4

wet	whet	wine	whine
wail	whale	wile	while
weather	whether	wen	when
wit	whit	wear	where
watt	what	witch	which
woe	whoa	wig	whig

Practice 3

Read the following, being especially careful of the sound of *th*:

A family of fashion were gathered together,
All of them deeply considering whether
They ought to stay in on account of the weather.
"Rain," said the mother, "would ruin my feather."
"Dust," said the father, "would dim my shoe leather."
"Sun," said the brother, "though out but an hour,
Would probably wither my buttonhole flower."
And thus they concluded, agreeing together
There's danger to clothing in all sorts of weather;
So they then bought a big bandbox, together climbed in it,
Shut down the lid, and they're there to this minute.

Read aloud. Notice the *ing* sounds.

There was a rustling that seemed like a bustling
Of merry crowds justling at pitching and hustling;
Small feet were pattering, wooden shoes clattering,
Little hands clapping, and little tongues chattering,
And, like fowls in a farm yard when barley is scattering,
Out came the children running.
— ROBERT BROWNING, "The Pied Piper of Hamelin"

Good Listening

The audience has an important part to play when any oral work is given. Even though pupils may not be intensely interested, courtesy demands that they listen attentively. They should be ready to commend the good points of the speech as well as to suggest improvement.

Retelling a Story.

There was excitement in Mary's home. Her uncle who had just returned from a trip to Alaska was coming on the 9:15 train and would stay for two or three days. Such thrilling tales as she would hear! Of course Mr. Johnson, who lived next door, had told some interesting stories about his trip to Alaska. But no one could make you see the places and people as Uncle Park could. Even Father forgot how busy he was when Uncle Park began with "Now that reminds me." How did he do it? He was interested in what he was telling, remembered details which other people seemed to forget, talked directly to his audience, and didn't hesitate and drag out the story.

You can be entertaining if you are willing to practice. One of the ways of learning is by retelling stories you have read. Try this on your classmates. Choose an interesting story which you think they do not know. Read it over and over until you know it. Tell it to the friends with whom you walk to school; then tell it to your family. Here are some suggestions which may help you:

1. Be interested in what you are telling. If you are not, do not expect others to be.
2. Talk directly to the class, not to your desk, the blackboard, or the window.
3. Speak distinctly.
4. When you stop to think, do not let your voice run on with *and-ur, but-ur, so-ur*.

Practice 4

Read the Indian legend, the Russian fable, the pioneer story, and the hunting story. Prepare to retell one of them in class. Be enthusiastic and make the story interesting.

THE INDIAN AND THE WOLVES[1]

The hut of an Indian was threatened with wolves. His trembling wife hugged her baby close, for the wolves were lean and hungry and the walls of the hut were thin. It was bad enough that her husband had very few arrows, but to make matters worse, his eyes had been injured by the cold of his last hunt. What could be done? The question was urgent, for the beasts were scratching at the door. The hunter searched in his medicine bags, while his wife shook her head. This was not time for magic; a good aim and plenty of arrows were needed, not charms. Nevertheless the hunter fumbled in his pouch and drew forth several objects which he wrapped in chunks of fat. With a cry he flung the chunks out of the window toward the wolves.

[1] Reprinted from *The Indian How Book* by permission of the author, Arthur C. Parker. Doran Publishing Company.

Scenting food, the pack dashed forward and began to lick up the fat. One pack leader grabbed a chunk in its mouth and began to chew. Suddenly blood began to spurt from the mouths of the wolves that had snatched the fat. The smell of this drove the whole pack into a fury of madness. They pounced upon the bleeding wolves and tore them to pieces, while others pounced upon those who were sinking their fangs in the first victims. The yelping was terrifying but soon the entire pack had exterminated itself. Magic had been performed, and the hunter smiled at his wife as he tied up his medicine pouch.

What had he done? Simply taken thin sharp blades of flint, enclosed them in fat, and lured the wolves into cutting their mouths. Blood excites wolves, and they have no love for their wounded comrades. Once blood flows the whole pack goes mad.

A FABLE: UNCLE MITYA'S HORSE

Uncle Mitya had a very fine bay horse. Some thieves heard about the bay horse, and laid their plans to steal it. They came after dark and crept into the yard.

Now it happened that a peasant who had a bear with him came to spend the night at Uncle Mitya's. Uncle Mitya took the peasant into the cottage, let out the bay horse into the yard, and put the bear into the enclosure where the bay horse had been.

The thieves came in the dark into the enclosure and began to grope around. The bear got on his hind legs, and seized one of the thieves, who was so frightened that he screamed with all his might.

Uncle Mitya came out and caught the thieves.

— LEO TOLSTOI

MEETING THE INDIANS [1]

The Indians were all around us, and every settler had a collection of hair-raising tales to tell. I was about twelve

[1] Reprinted from *The Story of a Pioneer* by Anna Howard Shaw, with permission of Harper and Brothers, publishers.

years old when I had my first encounter with them. I was alone in the woods at sunset with my small brother Harry. We were hunting a cow James had bought, and our young eyes were peering eagerly among the trees, on the alert for any moving object. Suddenly, at a little distance, and coming directly toward us, we saw a party of Indians. There were five of them, all men, walking in single file, as noiselessly as ghosts, their moccasined feet causing not even a rustle among the dry leaves that carpeted the woods. All the horrible stories we had heard of Indian cruelty flashed into our minds, and for a moment we were dumb with terror. Then I remembered having been told that the one thing one must not do before them is to show fear. Harry was carrying a rope with which we had expected to lead home our reluctant cow, and I seized one end of it and whispered to him that we would "play horse," pretending he was driving me. We pranced toward the Indians on feet that felt like lead, and with eyes so glazed by terror that we could see nothing save a line of moving figures; but as we passed them they did not give us a side-glance. They were, we realized, headed straight for our home; and after a few moments we doubled on our tracks and, keeping at a safe distance from them among the trees, ran back to warn our mother that a group of Indians were coming.

As it happened, James was away, and Mother had to meet her unwelcomed guests supported only by her young children. She at once prepared a meal, however, and when they arrived she welcomed them calmly and gave them the best she had. After they had eaten they began to point at and demand objects they fancied in the room — my brother's pipe, some tobacco, a bowl, and such trifles — and my mother, who was afraid to annoy them by refusal, gave them what they asked. They were quite sober, and though they left without expressing any appreciation of her hospitality, they made her a second visit a few months later, bringing a large quantity of venison and a bag of cranberries as a grateful return. These Indians were Ottawas; and later we became very friendly with them and their tribe, even to the degree of attending one of their dances.

HUNTING A COON [1]

The firelight reached far up into the night, and once or twice the boys thought they saw the shining eyes of the coon in the tree above them.

"Now who wants to climb?" asked the Scout.

"I will," "I will," several voices shouted at once.

"You're mighty keen hunters, but I want you to know I can't tell what it is that's up that tree. It may be a powerful, big coon, but it seems to me the dog acts a little like it was a wild cat. Judging by the actions of the dog, I think it's something dangerous. Now who wants the job?"

For a while no one spoke. Then Yan said, "I'll do it if you'll lend me the revolver."

"So would I," said Wesley, quickly.

"Well, now we'll draw straws" — and Yan won.

There was an absence of joking and there was a tension that thrilled the climber with a weird sense of venturing into black darkness to face a fearful and mysterious danger. The dancing firelight sent shadows in a dozen directions with fantastic effect. A little higher and he was out of sight of his friends below. The danger began to appall him. He wanted to go back, and to justify the retreat, he tried to call out, "No coon here!" but his voice failed him. As he clung to the branch, he remembered Caleb's words, "There's nothing ahead of grit, and grit ain't so much not bein' scairt as it is going straight ahead when you are scairt." No, he would go on, come what would.

"Find anything?" called a cheery voice below.

Yan could not answer but continued to climb into the gloom. Suddenly he thought he heard a coon snarl above him. He swung to a higher branch and shouted, "Coon here, all right!" The moment he did so a rattling growl sounded close to him, and looking down he saw a huge, gray beast spring to a branch between him and the ground. As it leaped to a still nearer place, Yan got a dim view of a curious, four-cornered face, shaggy and striped. It was an enormous lynx.

[1] Taken by permission from Ernest Thompson Seton's *Two Little Savages*, published by Doubleday, Doran and Company.

Yan got such a shock that he nearly lost his hold, but, quickly recovering, he braced himself in a crotch, and got out the revolver just as the lynx, with a fierce snarl, leaped to a side branch that brought it nearly on a level with him. He nervously cocked the pistol, fired, and missed. The lynx recoiled a little. The boys below raised a shout.

"A lynx!" shouted Yan, and his voice betrayed his fear.

Courtesy Canadian Pacific
A LYNX OF THE NORTH WOODS

The lynx was growling ferociously. Yan put forth all his will power to control his trembling hand, took more deliberate aim, and fired. The fierce beast was struck, but leaped wildly at the boy. Yan threw up his right arm and the lynx buried its teeth in the flesh. He knew that in a moment he would be dragged off the limb and thrown to the ground. He clutched for his revolver with his left hand but found only the fur of the lynx, and the revolver dropped from his grasp. Dark fear fell on him. But the beast was severely wounded. It loosened its hold of Yan and struggled to get on to the limb. A kick from his right foot upset its balance; it slipped from the tree and flopped to the ground below.

A surge of reaction came over Yan. He might have fainted but again he remembered the trapper's words, "Bravery is keeping on even when you are scairt." He pulled himself together and very cautiously worked his way back and slid down the tree. A giddiness came over him; he trembled and reeled, and sank down on a root.

"What's the matter, Yan?"

"I'm sick — I —"

Caleb took his arm. It was wet.

"Hullo, you're bleeding."

"Yes, he had me — he caught me up the tree. I — I — thought I was a goner."

All interest was now turned from the dead lynx to the wounded boy.

"I'd have been scared out of my wits," said Sam.

"Well, I was scared — just as scared as I could be," admitted Yan.

Practice 5

Imagine that you are one of a group seated around a camp fire. Each has agreed to tell a story. Retell one of the following which you have read or heard:

1. A fable — one of Æsop's. 2. A myth. (See Herzberg's *Myths and Their Meaning,* Haaren and Poland's *Famous Men of Rome,* Gayley's *Classic Myths,* Baker's *In the Light of Myth,* Sabin's *Classical Myths that Live Today,* Hawthorne's *Wonder Book.*) 3. An animal story. 4. An Old Testament story — Moses in the Bulrushes, Daniel in the Lion's Den, David and Goliath, Samson and Delilah, Noah and the Ark. 5. A ghost story. 6. A humorous story, such as an incident from *The Adventures of Huckleberry Finn* or *Tom Sawyer.* 7. A story about a baseball or football hero. 8. A story about a famous aviator. 9. An Indian legend. 10. A historical incident, such as Paul Revere's ride, the Boston Tea Party, the landing of the Pilgrims, the making of the first American flag. 11. A story about George Washington, Benjamin Franklin, Daniel Boone, Thomas Edison, Kit Carson, Clara Barton, Helen Keller, Theodore Roosevelt, or any other famous American.

How to Write Conversation

When you are selecting a book in the library, do you choose one with long solid paragraphs or one that contains a good deal of conversation? Everyone agrees that conversation adds to the interest of a story, but it must be natural and lifelike. Correct punctuation and paragraphing make a conversation easier to read.

Practice 6

Read the conversation between Robin Hood and the Bishop and answer the questions given below. Write in your notebook three rules you should remember for punctuating and paragraphing conversation.

1. What punctuation mark is put before and after each speech?
2. How are the direct words of the speaker separated from the rest of the sentence?
3. When is a new paragraph begun?
4. What words are used instead of *said?*

ROBIN HOOD AND THE BISHOP

"This is the Bishop of Hereford," laughed Robin to Little John, "and no pardon shall we have from him."

"Cut off his head, master!" growled Little John.

Upon hearing this the Bishop was dreadfully frightened, and his fat face went as white as paper.

"Pardon! Pardon!" cried the Bishop. "If I had known that it was you, I'd have gone another way."

"I dare say you would," replied Robin, "but no pardon do I owe you. You must come with me and go to the forest."

Practice 7

Rewrite the following sentences, making each into a direct quotation. Punctuate correctly. Avoid using *said* too frequently. Use a word which describes how the person spoke — *whispered, exclaimed, laughed, sighed, observed, shouted, stammered, warned, called, cried, growled.*

Models

1. Lawrence laughed and told them not to mind him and to stay in the garden as long as they wanted to.

"Don't mind me," Lawrence assured them laughingly. "Stay in the garden as long as you want to."

2. Elizabeth told Marjorie to get her racket and come along to the park to play tennis.

"Get your racket, Marjorie," called Elizabeth, "and let's go to the park to play tennis."

1. He said that his name was Theodore but that he didn't like it, as the fellows called him Dora.
2. The game warden told them that fishing without a license was against the law.
3. The stranger asked where he would find the forest ranger's cabin.
4. The doctor encouraged us by saying that all danger was past.
5. The guide informed them that all roads through Yellowstone Park were in fine condition.
6. Mother said that she was very tired and wanted to go to sleep.
7. Father asked John to telephone Mr. Brown that he wanted to see him as soon as possible.
8. Her mother told Mr. Lawrence how much her family had appreciated the fruit he had sent them for Christmas.
9. The explorer surprised them by saying that beautiful flowers can be found in summer in the arctic circle.
10. The little girl told Mrs. French that she was lost and couldn't remember her name.
11. John said that he had had no luck all day with his kites.
12. The art teacher said that any pupils could earn extra credit by working Saturdays at the Art Gallery.
13. Her brother told her that this was a secret and that she must not tell Joan.
14. Mary told her little sister that unless she was good that afternoon she could not keep the kittens.

15. Margaret told her mother that the day had started wrong, as she had already upset the inkwell and sat on her hat.

Practice 8

Read the conversation which was overheard by a boy who was visiting his cousin, and answer the following questions:

1. How is it true to life?
2. How is the conversation punctuated?
3. Why are there so many paragraphs?
4. How has the writer avoided repeating *said?*

GETTING OFF FOR SCHOOL

"Donald! Donald! It's time to get up."

"All right, Mother," he mumbled sleepily. "What time is it?"

"Ten minutes past seven. Hurry up!"

A few minutes later she called again, "Donald, are you up? Do you hear me? It is almost 7:30."

"Yes, I'll be down in a minute. Say, Mother, where is my clean shirt? Oh, never mind! Here it is."

There was a brief period of silence. Then the stair door opened. "Donald, your father is ready. I'm not going to call again."

"Here I am," answered Donald, running downstairs.

"Donald McLean, go upstairs and comb your hair."

"Oh-h, Mother!"

In a few minutes he reappeared with his hair plastered down. "Is my lunch ready?"

"Yes. Eat your breakfast."

"Do I have to eat all this cereal?"

"Every bit of it and drink your milk."

"There, I'm through. Where are my books?"

"On the table in the hall."

"Oh, Mother!" he called from the door. "Did you see my baseball mitt?"

"Here it is behind the kitchen door, just where you threw it. Now, you have everything, haven't you?"

"Yes, I guess so. Good-bye."

"Good-bye, Donald. Be a good boy." — PUPIL

Practice 9

Write a conversation which might take place in one of the following situations. Make it lifelike and natural.

1. A boy tries to persuade his mother to let him get a bicycle.
2. A girl tells another about plans for a Saturday hike.
3. After a girl gets on the street car, she finds she has left her pocketbook at home and a friend comes to her rescue.
4. A stranger asks to be directed to the station, the post office, or the city hall.
5. A boy or a girl is applying for a position.
6. Several boys or girls are discussing plans for summer vacation, for a Christmas party, for a skating or skiing party.
7. A newsboy talks with a customer.
8. You hear two people talking at a bargain counter, at a ticket window, at a movie.
9. You explain your report card to your father.
10. A boy tells at the dinner table of an incident at school that day.
11. Two boys from different schools discuss the basketball teams of the two schools.

How to Prepare a Dictation

1. Notice the division into paragraphs. In a conversation each speech is a separate paragraph.
2. Note the division of each paragraph into sentences.
3. Study the punctuation, especially the marks before and after speeches.
4. Look at the spelling of new and hard words.

5. At home have someone dictate the selection to you. Correct your work with the book. When you make a change, think what your error was and how you will avoid making it again.

Rules of the Game

In class write the passage dictated, then exchange papers, and with your book open place a number over every error:

Word omitted
Word added
Wrong word
Misspelling
Punctuation or capitalization error
Mistake in paragraphing
Mistake in the division of a word at the end of a line
No margin or a narrow margin

1. Count a misspelling two and each other error one.
2. Omission of a pair of quotation marks is one error.
3. If a comma ends a sentence, omitting the period is one error, and beginning the next sentence with a small letter is another.
4. Each word omitted or added is one error; three words are three errors.
5. Failure to indent a paragraph or indenting in the middle of a paragraph is an error.

Model for Scoring

[1] [2]
Notebook, paper pencil, and pen were all where I had placed
[3]
them the night before. My poem book alone was missing,
[4] [5] [6]
what had I done with it. I had looked on the table on the

mantel, in the bookcase, and[7] in the wastebasket. As it was getting late, I hurried to school. Their[9] on my desk was the lost book.

Practice 10

Study the model for scoring the first paragraph; then prepare to write the eight selections from dictation:

1

Notebook, paper, pencil, and pen were all where I had placed them the night before. My poem book alone was missing. What had I done with it? I had looked on the table, on the mantel, in the bookcase, and even in the wastebasket. As it was getting late, I hurried to school. There on my desk was the lost book.

2

When Kit Carson was a small boy, he decided to be a hunter and trapper. When he got a chance to join a party of traders who were leaving Missouri, he went with them.

With no paths and no guides the party pushed westward toward New Mexico. They traveled over great level plains that were the hunting grounds of Indians. At last the party reached Sante Fe. There Kit left the others and went farther west. He journeyed on to the Rocky Mountains. During those days he acted in turn as guide, teamster, and even as cook.

When he was not yet twenty years old, he was brave, self-reliant, and quick to act in time of need. Men had already begun to look up to him as a valuable guide.

3

"John," asked Miss Field, "how do you find the lowest common denominator?"

"I didn't know it had been lost," exclaimed John in astonishment.

4

The Joyce Kilmer Public Camp is located in the Bald Eagle State Forest in Union County, Pennsylvania. It is named in honor of the American boy poet who was killed during the World War.

At the entrance is a sign saying, "Gypsies Are Welcome to Camp Here." Kilmer once wrote his mother that he wished he owned a woodland where gypsies could camp. Though he did not live to get his wish, the state has fulfilled it for him. Near this welcome to gypsies stands a stone tablet on which is written his beautiful poem, "Trees."

5

Clara Barton was only five years old when her brother David taught her to ride.

"How can I learn to ride a horse, David?" quavered the child as the animal came to the pasture bars at her brother's call.

"Catch hold of his mane, Clara," said David, as he put her on the back of a colt and sprang on his favorite. He held the reins of both horses in one hand, and steadied his sister by seizing one of her feet as they galloped over the pasture.

6

Tom's books were carefully piled away. His lessons were all prepared, and he planned to read his sister's library book. Its mysterious title, *Twenty Thousand Leagues under the Sea*, appealed to him. "It's a good thing I worked hard," he thought. "I'll have time to enjoy myself now."

Just then he heard his father's voice calling, "Tom, I'm ready for you to help me clean the furnace."

7

"May I go and help carry the things to the poor little children?" asked Beth eagerly.

"Yes," Mrs. March replied, "you shall all go and help me."

They were soon ready, and the procession set out. They found a bare, miserable room, with broken windows, no fire, ragged bedclothes, a sick mother, a wailing baby, and a group of pale, hungry children cuddled under one old quilt, trying to keep warm.

"It is good angels come to us!" said the poor woman, crying for joy.

"Funny angels in hoods and mittens," said Jo, which set them laughing. — LOUISA M. ALCOTT, *Little Women*

8

Dr. E. C. Stewart opened the door of his office. It was five o'clock on a Tuesday afternoon, and he was tired. There sat a little girl and her dog. "My dog Ginger is sick," she said. "Do you think you can cure him?"

The doctor looked at the dog's tongue and felt his pulse. Then he produced a stick of candy. "This," he said, "is for Ginger's mistress, and a wee piece is for Ginger."

"What a nice doctor!" she exclaimed. "I'll be back again soon."

The Anecdote

The anecdote is a story which has three outstanding characteristics.

1. It is brief, yet clear and complete.
2. It has a pointed and surprising ending.
3. It is suited to the occasion and the audience.

Practice 11

Read the anecdotes; then answer the following questions:

1. What is the point of each story?
2. How is each anecdote helped by the use of direct quotation?

BORROWING

Mark Twain once asked a neighbor if he might borrow a set of his books. The neighbor replied ungraciously, "You are welcome to read them in my library, but I have a rule never to let my books leave the house."

Some weeks later the same neighbor went over to ask Mark Twain for his lawn mower.

"Certainly," said Mark, "but since I make it a rule never to let it leave my grounds, you will be obliged to use it here."

DIDN'T SEE HIM STEAL

Josh was brought before a country squire for stealing a hog, and three witnesses swore that they had seen him steal it. A humorous fellow who realized the squire was rather stupid volunteered to act as counsel for Josh. He addressed the squire as follows: "May it please your honor, I can establish this man's honesty beyond the shadow of a doubt. I have twelve witnesses ready to swear that they did not see him steal the hog."

The squire rested his head for a few moments upon his hand, as if in deep thought, and then with great dignity arose, and pushing back his hair, said, "If there are twelve who did not see him steal the hog and only three who did, I discharge the prisoner."

WHICH WAS RIGHT?

Hans was subject to fits, and his wife had always been able to help him with her home remedies. But it happened this time her remedies had no effect, and so she found it necessary to call a doctor.

The doctor worked over him for some time without results and then looked at the wife and said, "I'm afraid, dear woman, I can't help him. He is dead."

Hans revived just in time to hear the words, "He is dead." He shrieked in terror, "I am not dead!"

His wife looked down on him in amazement, and said firmly, "Hans, lie still. The doctor knows best."

Practice 12

Prepare to tell an anecdote to the class. In choosing your story, be sure that it is suitable to the occasion and that it will be interesting. You may refer to the following books:

WHITING, R. R.: *Four Hundred Good Stories*
COBB, Irvin S.: *Pros and Cons*
HENRY, O.: *Postscripts*
MASSON, Thomas L.: *Tom Masson's Annual*

Checking Your Composition

What sort of composition work are you in the habit of handing in to your teacher? Does it represent your best effort?

Automobile manufacturers don't put new engines in old car bodies. Instead, they set the engines in attractive new bodies. The engine of your composition is the content or what you say. The body is the form or the way you say it. Take care that the form doesn't spoil the effect of the content.

The form consists of sentence structure, paragraphs, punctuation, spelling, correct grammar, margin, and general appearance.

Copy the following table of reminders in your notebook and form the habit of checking your compositions by it. Be sure that all details are correct.

Reminders

SENTENCES	PARA-GRAPHS	PUNCTUATION CAPITALIZATION	SPELL-ING	GRAMMAR	APPEAR-ANCE
No half-sentences (see page 220) No comma blunders (see page 224)	Indented	Capitals Commas Apostrophes Quotation marks Periods Question marks Exclamation points		Pronouns Verbs	Margin Hand-writing Neatness

Telling Experiences

Example:

SARAH ANN'S RIDE

It was a beautiful October day in the year 1833. Twelve-year-old Sarah Ann, dressed in her new red calico and with her yellow curls flying, raced to the pasture and threw a blanket on the old black mare. This was no ordinary event but one she had looked forward to for days. She was to spend the day with her cousins who lived along the Allegheny River four and a half miles away.

The trail led through woods, but Sarah Ann, being a regular pioneer girl, had not the slightest fear. True, Indians frequently came up the river to fish, or sell their beads and baskets, but they were a friendly lot. Occasionally they even gave Sarah Ann little trinkets, and once a pair of beautiful deerskin moccasins.

The little girl met no one, but now and then she wondered at a sharp sound like that of twigs breaking. Once as her horse was drinking from a spring, she thought she heard a step on the dry leaves, but no one appeared. She decided the squirrels must be playing hide-and-seek. Finally she arrived at Aunt Polly's and was enthusiastically met by her four cousins.

Such a jolly time as the children had! When along in the late afternoon a cloud of dust appeared up the road, they ran out expecting to meet Uncle Tom, who two days before had gone to Franklin, a town some twenty miles distant. But the horseman was a stranger, a postrider. He dashed up to the door and drew his sweating horse to a quick stop.

The household gathered around to hear his errand. Terrifying news struck their ears. A band of strange Indians had that morning raided a farm down the river and driven off the cattle and horses. Mrs. McCaslin was advised to take the children to the next farm two miles north. Then the rider whirled and was off to warn others.

Aunt Polly urged Sarah Ann to go with them, but the little girl knew her parents would be worried if she did not come home. So, quickly she mounted her horse and started back along the trail.

When she entered the woods on the return trip, she kicked her heels so vigorously into the fat sides of her mount that the old mare trotted some distance in pure amazement at such treatment. Each time her horse slowed to a walk she listened intently and tried in vain to see through the fast-gathering shadows. Although she could see nothing alarming, she heard again and again faint sounds as of breaking twigs or dry leaves. At the same time she became possessed with the uneasy feeling that someone was following her.

Finally through a break in the trees she saw a light and knew it came from the kitchen window of home. Again the little heels went into action, and soon a thankful Sarah Ann was in the kitchen with the unknown terrors shut out.

As she was breathlessly telling about the Indians, the door opened noiselessly and in slipped Corn Tassel, a friendly old Indian who camped each summer along the river near them.

He moved quickly to the child's side and said softly, "Little Miss no ride. Stay home. Bad Indians," and he pointed toward the river. "Corn Tassel follow Little Miss today."

Then Sarah Ann understood the meaning of the snapping twigs. Corn Tassel had seen her set out and had stayed close to her all the way to Eagle Rock and back.

How to Tell a Story

We can learn several points about story-telling by studying "Sarah Ann's Ride."

1. This story answers at the start the questions "Who?" "When?" "Where?" and "What?" by telling us that in 1833 Sarah Ann, a girl of twelve, went on horseback along the forest trail to visit her cousins, who lived some miles distant.

2. The author arouses our interest by giving details, such as the snapping twigs, the postrider's news, Aunt Polly's alarm, and Sarah Ann's fright on her return trip.

3. The climax of the story comes at the end when Corn Tassel comes to Sarah Ann's home and tells how he protected her.

Practice 13

Does this story remind you of an exciting experience that your grandfather, aunt, or someone else in your

Courtesy Southern Pacific
AN AUTO TRIP IN THE FAR NORTH

family has told you? Do you know a true story which you can retell? The following topics may suggest one. Write it or prepare to tell it in class.

1. Early days in the West. 2. Down on the farm. 3. Digging for gold. 4. A dog's heroism. 5. An accident. 6. A runaway. 7. A haunted house. 8. Lost in the woods. 9. A surprise. 10. A painful lesson. 11. Learning to fly, skate, ski, swim, drive a car. 12. When the Indians came. 13. Moving. 14. A trip in the frozen North. 15. Unex-

pected guests. 16. A storm. 17. When the schoolhouse burned. 18. Hunting a lost cow. 19. A peddler's visit.

Practice 14

Boys and girls have good stories of their own to tell. Even though your experiences seem ordinary to you, you can interest your classmates by telling them well. Read the following stories which were written by junior high school pupils:

1. Does the pupil answer the questions "Who?" "Where?" "When?" and "Why?" in the first paragraph?
2. How does the writer arouse your interest or excite your curiosity?
3. What is the most exciting point of each story?
4. Which story do you like better? Why?

STUCK IN THE MUD

I had thought it would be fun to row around a bend behind the cottage and come out on the lake again. But I had no idea that it was so far or that a person could get so tired rowing. To make matters worse my six-year-old cousin, Jerry, sat in the other end of the boat crying that he wanted to go home. If he hadn't been so quick about wanting to go with me, he wouldn't have been wishing that he hadn't come.

As I approached a low bridge, I realized that the water was getting shallow. Halfway under, the boat stuck and I couldn't budge it an inch. At this Jerry began to cry harder than ever. Furiously I dug an oar into the water, only to get it stuck in the mud too. I tugged and tugged, getting hotter and crosser every minute.

To get out and push was the last resort. As I stepped into the muddy water, I sank down, down, over my ankles and almost up to my knees. The deeper I sank, the harder I worked, and finally with a last desperate effort, I pushed the boat loose. Covered with mud, I crawled into the boat and rowed frantically toward the cottage.

As I neared the shore, I saw my uncle on the beach anxiously looking for us. I was properly scolded for going so far, and worst of all was teased for days about getting stuck in the mud. — PUPIL

THE WRONG ROOM

I had a feeling that something unusual was going to happen as I entered the Eastman School of Music at 8:30 o'clock that Saturday morning.

I take my lesson in Room 303 on the third floor. Just around the corner is a bench. Depositing myself and my portfolio, I waited. My teacher usually comes out of his studio about 8:40 and calls me, but that morning he did not. I looked at the marble carvings on the ceilings and at the painted walls. I prayed for a good lesson, and finally resorted to twiddling my thumbs.

Presently I heard the sound of feet. Some students entered the concert hall. My watch said nine o'clock. I took out a weekly musical review and glanced at it. At last I decided to peek into the studio and see if the teacher was there. This took courage, as the small glass window is in the top of the door, and in order to see through it I had to drag the bench about a yard and stand on it. I trembled to think what a teacher would say if he caught me standing on a mahogany bench.

Just as I was ready to step on the bench, I noticed a note tacked to the door. It read: "Transferred to Room 412 on the fourth floor. All students report there."

Imagine my chagrin! — PUPIL

Practice 15

Using one of the following titles, write about an experience you have had. Make your story as entertaining as you can; lead up to the most interesting point or to a surprise. Tell the truth. Read it over carefully; then rewrite it neatly.

1. Walking home alone in the dark after the movies.
2. A leaky rowboat. 3. The evening I was alone in the house.
4. A Saturday hike. 5. Hunting the cows. 6. My first airplane ride. 7. The wrong stop. 8. My visit to an Indian reservation. 9. Coming down with the measles. 10. What happened one day in swimming. 11. The first time I went down town alone. 12. A narrow escape. 13. My first visit

Courtesy German Tourist Information Office

HIS PETS

to a circus. 14. What happened when the ice broke. 15. An exploring expedition in an attic. 16. Lost at camp. 17. When my dog came to school. 18. My first horseback ride. 19. How I almost lost my football. 20. A mountain climb. 21. Learning to ski, ride a bicycle, skate. 22. Something funny in school. 23. Locked out. 24. The day I was cook. 25. When our house caught fire. 26. Seeing an oil well shot. 27. Hunting for arbutus. 28. A thrilling ride. 29. My picture in the paper. 30. Flying at night.

Account of a Red Letter Day

Example:

THE MOST INTERESTING CHRISTMAS I EVER HAD

While all the Christmases I can remember have been most enjoyable, the one when I was five years old proved out of the ordinary.

Two days before Christmas as I was prowling around the house, the telephone rang. My mother answered and then called me, saying that Santa Claus wanted to speak to me. I came on the run, climbed on a chair, but was speechless at the thought of speaking to Santa Claus. Finally I managed to say "Hello."

A voice, deep and low, asked, "Is this Edward?"

I answered, "Yes."

The voice then said, "You have been a good boy and for Christmas I am going to bring you something very, very nice. Good-bye."

For the next two days I was all on edge wondering what it could be that Santa Claus was going to bring me. On Christmas morning I called my mother and dashed downstairs. When I reached the living room, I jumped for joy. There was my supreme desire — an electric train. I sat down and was as still as a wooden Indian as I watched the train go round and round the track. — PUPIL

Practice 16

What is the luckiest or happiest day you remember? Have you ever met a distinguished person? Have you ever had the thrilling experience of seeing and talking with the President? Does one Christmas or birthday stand out as particularly pleasant? Tell entertainingly of any outstanding day. Plan and write; then revise and copy neatly.

Practice 17

Make up a story about any one of the pictures in this unit. Imagine that the picture is to be printed as an illustration of the story.

Practice 18

Review the points which have been emphasized in this unit by answering the following questions:

1. How should you prepare a dictation?
2. What are the characteristics of an anecdote?

Telling a Story

3. Why is your voice important?
4. What is meant by clear enunciation?
5. What are three rules for good posture?
6. What part does the audience play?

Writing a Story

7. How is conversation punctuated?
8. What are the main points to remember?
9. How should you check your composition?

UNIT 4
THE PARAGRAPH

Why We Have Paragraphs

If the day were not divided into hours and minutes but were just one period from sunrise to sunset, you would find it very difficult to keep engagements, even to get to school on time. In like manner if the pages of a book had no divisions, reading would be extremely tiresome. Divisions on a page attract your attention to changes of thought and make the reading much easier to understand. If you find that they are helpful when you are reading, remember to make use of them when you are writing.

What a Paragraph Is

A group of sentences telling about one topic forms a paragraph. Its length depends on the number of sentences needed to discuss the topic. Don't make the mistake of writing paragraphs that are too long or of making every sentence a new paragraph.

Begin a new paragraph when there is a change of thought. Indent the first word of each paragraph an inch to the right of the left-hand margin.

Practice 1

Read the following paragraph and answer the questions:

1. What is the main thought?
2. What details complete the thought of the topic sentence?

The elephant's trunk is the most extraordinary part of the most extraordinary animal. It is absolutely flexible at every point. It can turn in any direction and has tremendous strength. An elephant can shoot a stream of water out of it that could put out a fire. With it he can lift a tree weighing a ton, yet it is delicate enough to pull a blade of grass. He drinks with it, feeds himself with it, smells with it, and at times fights with it. There is nothing else on earth like an elephant's trunk.[1]

Topic Sentence

If you are going on an auto ride with your father, your first question is, "Where are we going, Dad?" We all like to know what to look forward to. A topic sentence states briefly what the paragraph is about. Usually you will find it at the beginning, but it may come later in the paragraph and sometimes is the last sentence. When it is at the beginning, it is a guide for the writer or speaker. When the thought is no longer about the topic sentence, it is time to form a new paragraph.

Practice 2

Select the topic sentence of each of the following paragraphs:

1

There never was such a Christmas dinner as they had that day. The fat turkey was a sight to behold, when Hannah sent him up, stuffed, browned, and decorated; so was the plum-pudding, which quite melted in one's mouth; likewise the jellies, in which Amy reveled like a fly in a honey-pot. Everything turned out well, which was a mercy, Hannah said.

[1] From Carl Akeley's *In Brightest Africa*, by permission of the Garden City Publishing Company, Garden City, New York.

2

In a few minutes it really did seem as if kind spirits had been at work there. Hannah, who had carried wood, made a fire and stopped up the broken panes with old hats and her own cloak. Mrs. March gave the mother tea and gruel, and comforted her with promises of help, while she dressed the little baby as tenderly as if it had been her own. The girls, meantime, spread the table, set the children around the fire, and fed them like so many hungry birds.

— LOUISA M. ALCOTT

3

It was a cold December night. The wind was howling in the tree tops and the clouds looked like huge black monsters ready to pounce on their prey. The rain was dashing on the stone pavement in great torrents. Far in the distance could be seen a dim shadow of a figure slowly approaching. — PUPIL

Practice 3

A good topic sentence is a useful guide to a person writing a paragraph. In each of the following pairs of sentences which is the more helpful topic sentence?

1

(a) Orioles build peculiar nests.
(b) Orioles build nests like swinging cradles at the end of a bough.

2

(a) Swimming is an excellent sport.
(b) Swimming is an excellent sport, as it combines skill and exercise with fun.

3

(a) Jack enjoyed camping.
(b) Jack enjoyed camping, as it gave him an opportunity to hike and swim.

4

(*a*) It is easy to lose one's way in a blizzard.
(*b*) The blinding snow of a blizzard confuses a person so that he easily loses his way.

5

(*a*) Raccoons are fond of chickens.
(*b*) Robbing hen roosts is perhaps raccoons' greatest delight.

6

(*a*) Everyone in the bus smiled.
(*b*) Everyone in the bus smiled as the oranges began rolling out of a hole in the bag Mary carried.

Practice 4

Choose five of the following subjects. Then write a statement about each which you can develop into a paragraph. If your topic sentence is too broad, you cannot tell about it in one paragraph. "Many simple inventions are of great importance" is too broad a topic. In one paragraph you could not begin to name all such inventions. "The lead pencil is an invention we use constantly" is a topic sentence which can be developed in one paragraph.

1. Studying birds. 2. Keeping the streets clean. 3. The kind of book I like. 4. A busy corner. 5. Mosquitoes. 6. Oyster beds. 7. Cattle-branding. 8. A swimming lesson. 9. City traffic regulations. 10. Our football, soccer, baseball, or basketball team. 11. The park. 12. Flies. 13. My favorite subject. 14. Our camp. 15. Our library. 16. A tornado. 17. My best friend. 18. Fire protection. 19. Our dog. 20. The airport. 21. Our gymnasium. 22. My vacation. 23. My room. 24. A beautiful morning. 25. Salmon fishing.

Unity

Unity in a paragraph means that all ideas relate to one subject. If you were writing a paragraph about the tricks your dog can perform, you wouldn't tell about a circus or your father's new automobile. To give clearness and unity to the paragraph you should have every sentence say something about your dog's tricks. If you find that you have written a sentence which does not refer to the topic, cross it out. If the completed paragraph is unified, you can sum it up in one sentence.

Practice 5

Read the following paragraphs. What is the topic sentence of each? Do all the sentences in each paragraph refer to the topic? Prove your answer.

1

John fished patiently all day without even an encouraging nibble. Fishing is a most enjoyable sport. John's father teased him for being so unsuccessful. He had started out that morning with his pole and a can of fat worms. The fish, however, were not to be tempted. Several days later John urged his friend Tom to go with him. That time his luck turned. — Pupil

2

The game was exciting from start to finish. All of us from Monroe Junior High sat together. Some of the boys and girls went to the game in autos and some on the street cars. The cars were crowded that day and so they couldn't sit together. Our players were smaller than those on the opposing team. Some funny things happened on the street car I was on. — Pupil

3

After America has worn out its automobile tires, peasants in Mexico, China, Spain, and Portugal get a lot more mileage out of them. In Spain a type of shoes with soles made from the discarded automobile tires has become popular. In China the coolies cut the tires into soles for their cheap shoes. Shepherds in Portugal use inner tubes as overshoes, and pieces of casing as additional soles and heels on wooden shoes. So, you see, they shoe themselves with our old tires.

— *Scientific American*

Practice 6

Using one of the topic sentences in Practice 3, or one which you wrote in Practice 4, write a paragraph. Check to see that all sentences relate to the topic sentence.

How a Paragraph Is Built

If you are building a cabin or a playhouse, you must have boards, flooring, roofing, and nails in order to cover the framework. In a paragraph the topic sentence is the framework. After writing it, ask yourself these questions: What do I know about my topic? How do these persons or objects differ? What examples or illustrations will explain the idea clearly? In answering these three questions you will give details, comparisons, and examples or illustrations, which are some of the material out of which paragraphs are built.

Practice 7

Read the following paragraphs and answer these questions:

1. What is the topic sentence of each?
2. What are the details in 1?

3. How is the topic sentence illustrated in 2?
4. What comparison is made in 3?

1

Example of use of details:

A gift to Charlemagne by the King of Persia in 807 A.D. was a water clock which struck the hours. The dial was composed of twelve small doors, which represented the hours. Each door opened at the hour it was intended to represent, and out of it came the same number of little balls, which fell one by one at equal intervals of time on a brass drum. One could tell what time it was by looking at the number of doors that were open or by listening to the number of balls that fell. At twelve o'clock, twelve miniature horsemen appeared and closed all the doors.

2

Example of use of illustration:

Sensible people are apt to do extremely foolish things in the excitement of a fire. Last summer when I was visiting my cousin in the country, a neighbor's house caught fire. While some of the volunteer firemen were trying to extinguish the flames, others began carrying out furniture. Mr. Jackson, the sheriff, hurled pictures and vases from an upstairs window, and presently raced out of a door carrying two large pillows and a bag of clothespins. — PUPIL

3

Example of use of comparison:

Traveling was very different when my great-grandmother was a small girl from what it is now. There were no big ocean liners, no automobiles, no airplanes, not even fast trains then. The boat on which she and her family came from London took forty-nine days. Now a boat makes the trip in five or six days. In going by wagon from Kansas to what is now Portland, Oregon, they spent three months. Now my uncle covers the distance by airplane in twenty hours.

— PUPIL

THE PARAGRAPH

Practice 8

Select two of the following topic sentences and build a paragraph on each. Use details, illustrations, or comparisons. Be sure that your paragraph has unity.

1. The old house looked homelike.
2. He was popular with both pupils and teachers.
3. We were excited when our team won the skating meet.
4. A forest ranger's life is interesting but lonely.
5. The early morning is the loveliest time of the day.
6. The library is the most interesting room in our school.
7. There is no place like home.
8. I am glad that I live in the country (city, village).
9. I enjoy living by the ocean (on a ranch, in the mountains, on a lake, on a farm).
10. Last summer I learned a great deal at Scout Camp.
11. Cooking outdoors is more fun than at home.
12. Every person should be able to write a good letter.
13. There is a special trick in cooking frogs' legs.
14. I enjoy my English (art, music, science) class.
15. Many fires are caused by carelessness.
16. My dog is a real friend.
17. That was a bad half hour.
18. The Romans wrote with a stylus on wax tablets.
19. A telephone has its disadvantages.
20. I like summer better than winter.
21. Some people are very superstitious.

Beginnings and Endings

According to early legends the two most important letters in the Greek alphabet were Alpha and Omega, the first and the last. If we carry that idea into writing, we should make a special effort to have the beginnings and endings effective. To make a paragraph emphatic place the important ideas near the beginning and the end. Don't stop before you have said all that is necessary to complete the thought, and don't drag out the paragraph after the thought is completed. Close your paragraph with an important sentence.

Practice 9

Read the following paragraphs:

1. What is the topic sentence of each?
2. Does each paragraph stick to the subject? Prove your answer.
3. How is each paragraph built?
4. Are the most important ideas placed near the beginning and the end?

WHAT I LIKE TO DO

Nothing gives me more enjoyment than just reading. If I can only sit down with one of Mark Twain's, Rudyard Kipling's, or Booth Tarkington's books in my hand, I am perfectly contented. I forget everything around me. I seem to sink into that delightful fairyland where heroes and heroines really live. I loathe the villain, admire the hero, love the heroine, and sympathize with her. Whenever I find five free minutes, you may be sure I am again visiting my friends in Bookville. — PUPIL

THE TWINS

To anyone who did not know them the twins seemed much alike. Both were tall and had dark hair and beautiful complexions. Each had the same swing to her walk and the same tone of voice. They usually dressed alike. But there the similarity ended. Their dispositions certainly were different. Sarah was jolly and friendly, while Nancy was cross and critical and made few friends. It seemed hard to believe that two girls who looked so much alike could be so different.

THE AMERICAN CIRCUS

Have you ever stopped to think how typically American a big circus is? All countries have their own forms of traveling entertainment that move from town to town. In France there are small circuses of clowns and gymnasts; in Scandinavia the whole show often consists of no more than a single trapeze artist and his wife; in India the mysteries of magic are demonstrated by professional fakirs. But in this country we want more than these things. We want eye-filling spectacles that we can look forward to for weeks and remember for months afterwards. Elephants, tigers, camels, strange beasts of all kinds are brought from the corners of the earth to join the menagerie. Trapeze artists and aërialists perform hair-raising stunts, while clowns cause chuckles of amusement. All these are a part of the Great American Circus with its crowds and spielers, peanuts, popcorn, and pink lemonade.

Practice 10

Choose two of the following topics and write good paragraphs about each. In building your paragraphs remember the suggestions which have been given — a good topic sentence; unity; development by details, illustration, or comparison; and a good ending.

1. A delicious dinner. 2. A true friend. 3. My favorite work. 4. December is the most enjoyable month of the year. 5. My pets. 6. A comfortable room. 7. Good sportsmanship in school. 8. Advertising. 9. Naming our kitten. 10. Our playground. 11. Why I like general science (or another subject). 12. The first spring flowers. 13. My mother's flower garden. 14. Our next-door neighbors. 15. A church supper. 16. The desert in winter. 17. A book I enjoyed this term. 18. A kite I made. 19. Our marking system. 20. A real blizzard. 21. A hot night. 22. A messenger boy. 23. What I like best about our school. 24. Why we have assemblies. 25. A good class officer. 26. A salt mine I visited (iron, coal, gypsum). 27. Why I like my home town (city) or my country. 28. The value of learning to type. 29. What I enjoy most during vacation. 30. School spirit. 31. My party dress and one my mother had. 32. The value of horseback riding, skating, swimming.

Practice 11

Find in a magazine two good paragraphs. Show that each paragraph has (or has not): (1) a topic sentence; (2) unity; (3) a good ending. How is each paragraph developed?

Paragraphing Conversation

Paragraphs of a written conversation differ from those you have just studied, as no topic sentence is necessary and a new paragraph is begun with every change of speaker. Each speech is a paragraph. Remember that each paragraph is indented one inch.

Practice 12

Read the following conversation. Explain the reason for each new paragraph.

BIG BOY AND TAR BABY

Tar Baby, the Scottie, and Big Boy, the Boston terrier who lived next door, were fast friends. One day Tar Baby was roused from his afternoon nap by hearing his master call, "Here, Big Boy!"

"Well," thought Tar Baby, shaking himself awake, "I'd better get on the job or this young fellow will cut me out. It seems to me I saw him over here yesterday making up to the family."

He raced off the porch and into the back yard, where Big Boy was digging up one of his cherished bones. "You go home," growled Tar Baby.

Big Boy flirted his bobbed tail and went right on digging. "Hurry up! Hurry up! Get out of here!" snapped Tar Baby, at the same time nipping Big Boy in the leg.

Big Boy saw that Tar Baby meant business. After all, he didn't want the old bone. He thought to himself, "When that Scottie gets one of his domineering streaks, you can't reason with him."

"Did you hear me?" growled Tar Baby again, nipping another leg.

Big Boy left, but he didn't like such treatment and once on his own side of the fence snapped back, "Come on over! I dare you!"

Practice 13

The following paragraphs include conversation. Rewrite each, dividing it into paragraphs. Copy the punctuation and spelling accurately.

1

Alice looked round her in great surprise. "Why, I do believe we've been under this tree the whole time! Everything is just as it was!" "Of course it is," said the Queen. "What would you have it?" "Well, in our country," said Alice, still panting a little, "you'd generally get somewhere else if you ran very fast for a long time." "Now, here," said the Queen, "it takes all the running you can do to keep in the same place. If you want to get somewhere else, you must run at least twice as fast as that!" — LEWIS CARROLL

2

"How many hours a day did you do lessons?" asked Alice, in a hurry to change the subject. "Ten hours the first day," said the Mock Turtle, "nine the next, and so on." "What a curious plan!" exclaimed Alice. "That's the reason they're called lessons," the Gryphon remarked, "because they lessen from day to day." — LEWIS CARROLL

Test

Rewrite the following conversations, dividing them into paragraphs:

1

"I'm in an awful scrape, Mrs. Bhaer." "Of course; I'm always prepared for scrapes when you appear. What is it?

Run over some old lady, who is going to law about it?" asked Mrs. Jo, cheerfully. "Worse than that," groaned Tom. "Not poisoned some trusting soul, I hope?" "Worse than that." "You haven't let Demi catch any horrid thing, have you?" "Worse even than that." "I give it up. Tell me quick; I hate to wait for bad news." Having got his listener sufficiently excited, Tom launched his thunderbolt in one brief sentence, and fell back to watch the effect. "I'm engaged!" — LOUISA M. ALCOTT

2

"This is the Council Chamber, Cynthia," her father explained, "where the Governor and the Councilors discuss matters. Ah, here's the Governor now." A tall, gray-haired man had opened the door of an inner office and was coming toward them. "Well, Judge Blair," he said, "I'm glad to see you. And this must be your daughter. She looks like you." Cynthia shook hands, but words did not easily come. She was proud to find that governors were known to her father, but she had not been prepared for such cordiality. Just then a man in blue called to her father and she was left alone with Maine's Chief Executive. "Is this your first visit to Augusta, Miss Blair?" asked the Governor. "Yes, sir," said Cynthia, recovering herself, "and it's proving very delightful." "You're not the only daughter, are you?" asked the Governor. "It seems to me I remember some other girls being with your father when he came before." "There are seven of us," Cynthia explained, strangely proud of them all. "If you are ever down near Petersport, Governor Hall," she concluded, "we'd be honored to have you call, or even visit us."[1]

[1] Taken from *A Return to Constancy* by permission of the author, Mary Ellen Chase.

UNIT 5
THE FRIENDLY LETTER
Why Learn to Write Friendly Letters?

If you had lived back in '49 when boys and girls traveled with their parents in covered wagons from east of the Alleghanies to west of the Rockies, you might have wished that you could send letters to your friends. You could have told of Indian raids, of fording streams, of intense heat and bitter cold, of funny as well as of sad occurrences. Now that our postal system makes it possible for us to talk with our friends by means of letters, no matter where they are, everyone should learn how to write letters that are both correct and interesting.

A letter is a person's representative. If your letters contain careless penmanship, misspelled words, blotted pages, ungrammatical expressions, and errors in form and punctuation, they give an unfavorable impression of you. It is as though you arrived at that friend's home with a dirty face, uncombed hair, and soiled clothes.

Parts of a Friendly Letter

The five parts of a friendly letter are the heading, the salutation, the body of the letter, the complimentary close, and the signature.

Form 1

> 432 Westchester Road
> Norfolk, Virginia
> June 30, 1934
>
> Dear Jean,
> _____
> _____
> _____
>
> Sincerely yours,
> Joyce Wilbur

Form 2

> Dear Jean,
> _____
> _____
> _____
>
> Sincerely yours,
> Joyce Wilbur
>
> 432 Westchester Road
> Norfolk, Virginia
> June 30, 1934

Heading

The heading shows where the writer is and when he is writing. It includes the street number, city, state, and date, and is placed slightly to the right of the center of the page an inch or two from the top. The address is written above the date. It is better to avoid abbreviations.

Only two commas are necessary: one between the day of the month and the year, and one between the name of the city or town and the state. When streets are named by number, the numbers under ten are usually spelled out. Some correct headings are:

Moro, Arkansas	Waterford, Pennsylvania
January 14, 1934	February 14, 1934
114 Dover Road	2221 Fourth Street
Cleveland, Ohio	St. Louis, Missouri
January 10, 1934	April 2, 1934
4072 East 63d Street	R. F. D. No. 3
Chicago, Illinois	Lewiston, Montana
October 4, 1934	December 25, 1934

The address and date may be placed after the body of the letter as in Form 2, but Form 1 is preferred.

Salutation or Greeting

The customary salutations or greetings are *Dear Ethel* or *My dear Mrs. Hays*, the former being the more intimate. Capitalize the first word and all names.

A comma is used after the salutation. Some proper salutations are:

Dear John,   *My dear Mrs. Greene,*
Dearest Dad,   *Dear Elizabeth,*
Dear Aunt Edith,   *Dear Uncle John,*
My dear Miss Brown, *Dear Grandmother,*

Avoid such salutations as *Dear Friend, My dear Friend,* and *Friend Mary.*

Complimentary Close

The complimentary close, which is the same as saying good-bye, should begin about halfway across the page and should be followed by a comma. Only the first word should be capitalized.

Examples of proper complimentary closes are:

Yours sincerely,   *Your friend,*
Cordially yours,   *Affectionately yours,*
Your loving son,   *Very sincerely yours,*
Your loving sister,   *Your loving niece,*

The Signature

The signature, or the name of the writer, is placed below the complimentary close slightly to the right. No mark of punctuation follows the signature. In a friendly letter the word *Miss* or *Mrs.* never precedes the name. For example:

(Right) *Jane Smith*
(Wrong) *Miss Jane Smith*

Practice 1

1. What are the parts of a friendly letter?
2. Where is the heading placed? What is in the heading? How is it punctuated?
3. Where is the salutation placed? Give four correct salutations. How is each punctuated? How is each capitalized?
4. How is the complimentary close punctuated? How is it capitalized? Give four correct forms for the complimentary close.
5. Is any punctuation used in the signature?

Practice 2

Write the correct heading, salutation, complimentary close, and signature for the following letters:

1. Ethel Brice of 458 Huntington Avenue, Boston, Massachusetts, writes to her Aunt Mary.
2. William Drake of 7 Prescott Street, Atlanta, Georgia, writes to his chum Walter.
3. Charles Frazier of 1902 South Xanthus Street, Tulsa, Oklahoma, writes to his father.
4. Ellen Boyd of 701 Shorb Street, Canton, Ohio, writes to her grandmother.
5. Ruth Kahle of Mead's Point, Greenwich, Connecticut, writes to her Cousin Ruth.
6. Roy Miller of 6923 Wayne Avenue, Chicago, Illinois, writes to a friend of his father's, Dr. Short.
7. Frances Newlin of 231 Chase Street, Gary, Indiana, writes to Mrs. Corwin.
8. Norman Sloane of 1812 Monterey Avenue, Berkeley, California, writes to his Uncle Jack.
9. Anne Stevens of 105 Harvard Street, Seattle, Washington, writes to Martha, who is a good friend.
10. Helen White of 10 Colony Drive, West Orange, New Jersey, writes to Mrs. Murray.

The Body of the Letter

Louise was sitting at the desk writing a letter. At least she had started a letter to her best friend at home. "Dear Helen," she wrote, and stopped and chewed the end of her green fountain pen. Her pen was new and she was writing on attractive paper with a green monogram, so she should have been inspired but she wasn't.

She had so much to tell Helen about her Florida visit but she couldn't get started. Finally she wrote, "Yesterday we went to St. Petersburg and had a wonderful time."

She stopped again. The trip had been interesting but it didn't sound so. If Helen had been there, Louise would have talked at the rate of a mile a minute, telling of the fun she had had.

After mentioning a few other places she had seen, Louise gave up and ended her letter abruptly:

"I'll have so much to tell you when I get home. Your loving friend, Louise."

No one would guess from Louise's letter that she was having a good time.

Writing letters can be fun. Think what the person to whom you are writing would like to hear; then imagine that person is sitting with you and write as you would talk.

Practice 3

Read the following friendly letters which were written by pupils to former classmates; then answer these questions:

1. How are the headings punctuated?
2. Are the salutations suitable? Are they punctuated and capitalized correctly?
3. Which letter is more entertaining? Why?
4. Why does each writer divide his letter into four paragraphs? How are the paragraphs arranged?
5. Are the complimentary close and signature correctly placed and punctuated?

646 Elmwood Avenue
Buffalo, New York
January 8, 1934

Dear Mary,

You will remember that when you left last year the addition to our school was being built. It is completed now and is marvelous.

The part of the building that everyone likes best is the swimming pool. You'd be surprised at the fun that we can fit into one hour. Before we go into the pool, we all take showers. Each of us is given a clean suit and a towel. The water in the pool is so clear that it is just as though you were looking through a glass. Everything is kept clean and sanitary.

We had a lot of excitement at home last evening. Our dog caught a skunk! Father gave her a bath, but it did not do much good. Mother and I used perfume on her, but that was worse than ever. As she always sleeps in the house, we didn't know what we were going to do with her. I suggested the garage, but Father said, "Why spoil the car?" Mother thought of the tool house and there she stayed. I hope she had pleasant dreams, but did not dream of catching another skunk.

We have missed you since you went to New York, and you have missed a lot of fun. I know, however, you are having a good time and enjoying your new school. I shall be looking for a letter soon.

Your loving friend,
Ethel Baird

456 Driving Park Avenue
Rochester, New York
November 6, 1934

Dear Bill,

I hadn't heard from you for such a long time that I was afraid that you had forgotten your old pal. You may be sure I was glad when your letter arrived.

We are having an exciting time at school. The annual drive is on for the Memorial Scholarship Fund. This fund gives scholarships to boys and girls in junior *and senior high schools who have good records. The contest this year is between home rooms. The quota is ten cents per person. The home room that hands in the highest number of quotas has the privilege of putting on a Christmas play. Our class so far stands a good chance of winning.*

At Halloween we gave a play called "The Slippers of Cinderella." It is a story of a family who complained all the time. At Halloween all their wishes came true, and there was an awful mess. But of course everything turned out all right. My part was fun, as I was the noise maker and cheer leader. Since we had such a good time giving that play, we hope we'll have the chance to put on the Christmas play.

I hope you can come back to visit us soon. We miss you in our class.

Your old classmate,
Robert King

The Envelope

The address on the envelope should be written clearly. It is better not to abbreviate. If you do use abbreviations, write them so plainly that they cannot be mistaken. No punctuation is necessary unless you use abbreviations. Put a return address either in the upper left-hand corner, or on the back of the envelope.

A carelessly addressed letter is expensive. In one year in a city of 325,000 the cost of such letters was over $18,000. At this rate the total cost to our government is enormous. Do your share to avoid this expense.

ENVELOPE

```
Joyce Wilbur
   432 Westchester Road            STAMP
      Norfolk, Virginia


              Miss Jean Black
                 4500 Walnut Street
                    Philadelphia
                       Pennsylvania
```

Practice 4

Write the address as it would appear on the envelope of a letter written to the following:

1. Dr. John L. Armstrong, 420 Great Neck Road, Brooklyn, New York.
2. Miss Florence Smith, 163 Myrtle Avenue, Flushing, New York.
3. Mr. D. H. Howe, 24 College Avenue, Lawrence, Kansas.
4. Miss Marie Knight, 286 Main Street, Trinidad, Colorado.
5. Mr. Eugene M. Darrow, R. F. D. 2, The Dalles, Oregon.
6. Miss May Ames, 2325 South Street, Dallas, Texas.
7. Miss Dorothy Dotterer, 183 Lake Avenue, Newton Center, Massachusetts.
8. Dr. Frank M. Burke, Memorial Hall, Simpson College, Indianola, Iowa.

Appearance of the Letter

White or light shades of paper and black or blue ink are preferred for friendly letters. Avoid paper of peculiar size and striking color. If you use double sheets, write in order on pages 1, 2, 3, 4, and be particular about leaving margins. In a letter of two pages, write on pages 1 and 3. Leave a margin of about half an inch and indent each paragraph about the same distance.

The envelope should match the paper. Postal authorities request that tiny or huge envelopes be avoided, as they are hard to handle. When you enclose a double sheet of paper in an envelope, fold the lower half over the upper half. Place the letter in the envelope with the crease at the bottom of the envelope.

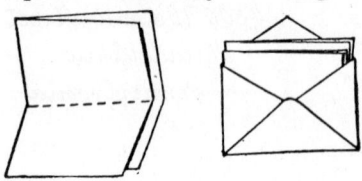

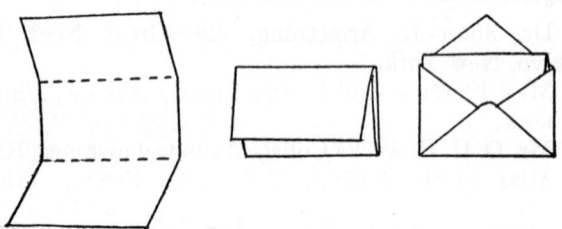

If your paper is a single sheet about seven by ten inches, fold the lower third up and the top third down.

Practice 5

Write one of the following letters. Make it lively and natural.

1. To a friend who is ill at the hospital, about your school play, a good book you have read, some new members of your class, your term tests.

2. To your mother who has gone away on a visit, about your attempts at getting dinner, the neighbors' new automobile, the party you and your sister had, the new neighbors, a stray cat you have taken in.

3. To a friend who is on a vacation, about the neighborhood baseball games, the new girl or boy on your street, a picnic, a scout hike.

4. To a friend who has moved away, about the new school building, what your class is doing, plays you have been in, a recent campaign in school, your new dog or cat, class contests in soccer, basketball, or hit-pin ball, learning to swim, skate, or ski.

5. To a friend or relative, about an auto trip you and your family are enjoying, a trip on a boat or a train, some interesting places you have seen, a zoo, a park, or a museum you have visited.

6. To a teacher who is ill or is studying at some university, about this term's honor roll, the Courtesy Campaign, the school basketball or baseball team.

7. To your father, who is on a business trip, about your joining a Saturday morning art class.

8. Write a real letter at home and bring it, or a copy, to school.

Informal Notes

An informal note differs from a friendly letter in that it discusses one topic, while a friendly letter may discuss several.

An informal invitation should be short and cordial, and should give the necessary information. It should be definite so that there can be no mistake about the time or the place. A note written in reply to an invitation should be sincere and appreciative and should be written as promptly as possible.

The form is the same as that of a friendly letter. In an informal note the address and the date are frequently placed after the signature, at the left.

Invitation

1428 Aylesboro Avenue
Pittsburgh, Pennsylvania
February 9, 1934

Dear Mary,

Unless the weather man interferes, my brother and I are having a skating party Friday evening, February 15, at the North Side Park, and hope that you can be one of the guests. We are planning to meet at the club house at 4 o'clock, skate for an hour, and have a weiner roast. We shall be disappointed if you do not come.

Cordially yours,
Jane Smith

Acceptance

Dear Jane,

I am very glad to accept your invitation to the skating party, Friday evening. I hope the weather man does not change his mind and send rain instead of snow, for nothing is more fun than skating and a weiner roast.

Sincerely yours,
Mary Neill

143 North Avenue
Bellevue, Pennsylvania
February 12, 1934

Regret

Dear Jane,

Last Friday I slipped and sprained my ankle, so it will be impossible for me to attend your skating party. I am very sorry, as I should enjoy being present. I'll be thinking of you Friday evening.

Sincerely yours,
Mary Neill

143 North Avenue
Bellevue, Pennsylvania
February 11, 1934

Note Giving Directions

428 West Avenue
Louisville, Kentucky
May 28, 1934

Dear Jack,

We are so glad your father has given his permission for you to go camping with us. We are planning to leave on Saturday, June 4, and hope you can come here Friday in order to drive out with us. If you leave home on the bus at 3 o'clock, Friday afternoon, we will meet you at the Bus Terminal at 5 o'clock. Phone me if your plans are changed.

Sincerely yours,
Bob

Practice 6

1. Invite a cousin to spend the Easter holidays with you. Suggest some entertainment which he might enjoy.

2. You and your family are driving to a near-by city. Invite a friend to accompany you and visit his or her aunt who lives there.

3. You have been invited to spend a part of the Christmas vacation at an uncle's. Accept the invitation.

4. Decline the invitation suggested in number 3. Explain clearly why you cannot go.

5. Invite a friend to go with you and your family on an auto trip which will take several days. Tell definitely when you expect to leave and to return and where you are planning to go.

6. Invite a cousin to meet you Friday afternoon and go to the movies. Give definite directions as to the time and place of meeting.

7. Invite a friend to go with you and your brother on a Saturday hike through the woods. Tell him or her definitely when and where to meet you and give any other necessary directions.

8. Accept the invitation given in number 5. State clearly when you expect to reach your friend's home.

Notes of Thanks

A letter of thanks is the courteous reply to a Christmas or a birthday gift. A letter which you write to someone you have just visited is often spoken of as a "bread-and-butter" letter. This should be written promptly and give some pleasant comment about your visit. It may tell what happened on the trip home and how you found your family.

Dear Betty,

Thank you so much for the interesting book, *Calico Bush*, you sent me for my birthday. It was lovely of you to remember the date. The book is one I have heard about and wanted for some time, and now I certainly enjoy owning it.

Your loving cousin,
Marie

4343 West Tenth Street
Los Angeles, California
June 4, 1934

"Bread-and-Butter" Letter

Avon, Illinois
April 5, 1934

My dear Mrs. Clarke,

I arrived home safe at six o'clock yesterday afternoon and spent the evening telling the family about the wonderful time I had at your house. Mother says that she may allow me to go on with the riding lessons. I certainly hope so.

I had a good time coming home, as two boys I know got on the bus at Galesburg and came the rest of the way with me.

Mother says she knows that I must have enjoyed myself, as I have gained three pounds! I never had a pleasanter Easter vacation and thank you and Jim very much for inviting me.

Sincerely yours,
Arthur Hatch

SEEING HERSELF

Courtesy Canadian Pacific

Travel experiences offer good material for talks and letters.

Practice 7

1. Thank Mrs. Stilling, the mother of a friend, for a delightful week-end you spent with the Stillings at the lake.

2. Thank a friend or a relative for a Christmas gift.

3. You have been ill for several weeks. Thank a friend for a book he or she sent you.

4. Thank your class for a jig-saw puzzle which they sent you while you were ill.

5. When you returned home from visiting your aunt, you forgot your bathing suit. Thank your aunt for mailing it.

Practice 8

Be able to write from dictation any of the informal notes given in this unit. Refer to the directions for preparing a dictation given on page 43.

Practice 9

1. Invite your cousin from out of town to spend the week-end with you and go to a movie.
2. Invite a friend from a near-by town to your birthday party. Give definite directions for reaching your home.
3. Thank a friend for asking you to a Valentine party.
4. Thank an aunt for including you in a camping party at the shore or in the mountains.
5. Thank your aunt for a Christmas gift which she sent you.
6. Your class is preparing a special Armistice Day program. Invite your principal to be present.
7. Invite a friend to visit you Friday and Saturday and go Christmas shopping with you.
8. Decline an invitation to go with a friend on a scout hike on Saturday.

Postcards and Postal Cards

On a souvenir postcard there is a small space for a message on the left side of the front. Because the space is small, it is permissible to omit the salutation and the complimentary close. Three points to keep in mind in writing a postcard are —

1. Inform.
2. Entertain.
3. Don't waste a word.

The card which is printed by the United States Post Office Department is called a "postal card." It is used most frequently for sending notices and for brief business messages.

```
┌─────────────────────────────────────────────────────────┐
│  THIS SPACE FOR WRITING  │     POSTCARD      │          │
│                          │                   │  STAMP   │
│   La Fonda Hotel         │ THIS SIDE IS FOR  │          │
│   Santa Fe, New Mexico   │   THE ADDRESS     │          │
│   February 19, 1934      │                   │          │
│                          │                              │
│  Dear Aunt Martha,     M │                              │
│    This doesn't seem   A │                              │
│  like an ordinary      D │   Mrs. H. H. Noyes           │
│  city, as there are    E │                              │
│  lots of cowboys and   I │   27 Rockland Avenue         │
│  Indians in cos-       N │                              │
│  tume. Most of the     U │   Woonsocket                 │
│  men wear sombreros.   S │                              │
│    Expect to leave     A │   Rhode Island               │
│  Saturday,               │                              │
│  February 21.            │                              │
│           Lovingly,      │                              │
│             Esther       │                              │
└─────────────────────────────────────────────────────────┘
```

Travel Letters

Stories of trips make interesting material for letters. No matter whether you are traveling for days in a new country or are just going on a short auto trip, you can usually find incidents about which your friends will enjoy hearing.

London, Kentucky
June 12, 1934

Dear Betty,

I'm tired and sleepy tonight but I like to keep you posted about our trip. How I wish you were with us! Wouldn't we have a good time together!

We didn't have any idea that eastern Kentucky was so lovely. Almost as soon as we left Cincinnati, we got into mountains. We stopped several times and took pictures, but no ordinary snapshots could show the marvelous views.

It seemed so queer to see cabins perched on the mountain side. Sometimes the mountains were so steep that you would think the cabins couldn't stick on. You ought to see the men plowing on those mountains. Mules are used for plowing and other farm work, maybe because they can hang on better than horses.

I never saw so many people riding horseback. Often we would see two people on one horse, one holding on to the one ahead. It's hard enough for me to ride horseback alone. I don't know what would happen if I tried that way. But wouldn't it be fun to have a horse of your own!

I wish we could stay here awhile, but Dad says he must be in Lexington by Friday noon. That means that we leave here tomorrow morning.

Your letter didn't tell how my dog is behaving. I hope he's getting over the habit of running after cars and doesn't bother your mother too much.

Lovingly yours,
Rachel

Practice 10

Read each of the following letters and answer these questions:

1. Is it entertaining? Why?
2. What facts does it mention?
3. What information does it give you about the writer?
4. What salutation is used? What complimentary close?

Abraham Lincoln writes to a little girl living in Chautauqua County, New York: [1]

Springfield, Ill., Oct. 19, 1860

Miss Grace Bedell,

My dear little Miss: Your very agreeable letter of the fifteenth is received. I regret the necessity of saying I have no daughter. I have three sons, one seventeen, one nine, and one seven years of age. They, with their mother, constitute my whole family. As to the whiskers, never having worn any, do you not think people would call it a piece of silly affectation if I were to begin now?

Your very sincere well-wisher,
A. Lincoln

[1] Reprinted by permission from *The Boys' Life of Abraham Lincoln* by Helen Nicolay, published by The Century Company.

J. W. Barker

FISHING SMACKS AT NANTUCKET
Such scenes offer good material for travel letters.

Henry W. Longfellow writes to Emily: [1]

Nahant, August 18, 1859

Dear Miss Emily,

Your letter followed me down here by the seaside, where I am passing the summer with my three little girls. The oldest is about your age; but as little girls' ages keep changing every year, I can never remember exactly how old she is, and have to ask her mamma, who has a better memory than I have. Her name is Alice; I never forget that. She is a nice girl, and loves poetry almost as much as you do.

The second is Edith, with blue eyes and beautiful golden locks, which I sometimes call her "nankeen hair," to make her laugh. She is a very busy little woman, and wears gray boots.

The youngest is Allegra, which, you know, means merry; and she is the merriest little thing you ever saw — always singing and laughing all over the house.

These are my three little girls, and Mr. Read has painted them all in one picture, which I hope you will see some day. They bathe in the sea, and dig in the sand, and patter about the piazza all day long, and sometimes go to see the Indians encamped on the shore, and buy baskets and bows and arrows.

I do not say anything about the two boys. They are such noisy fellows it is of no use to talk about them.

And now, dear Miss Emily, give my love to your papa, and good night, with a kiss, from his friend and yours.

Henry W. Longfellow

Practice 11

1. Write a postcard to a friend. Show it to your English teacher and read it to your class before sending it.

2. Write to a cousin or friend about a trip you have taken.

3. A boy (girl) you met at camp has written you about the members of his (her) family and their activities. Write to him (her) about your family.

[1] Taken with permission from *A Book of Letters* published by Houghton Mifflin Company.

UNIT 6

EXPLAINING

Why Learn to Explain?

If a record were made of your conversation for one day, you would find that again and again you had had to explain how to do something, or had asked someone else how to do something. Perhaps a classmate asked you how to do a problem, arrange a notebook, or draw a map of Europe or Australia; a friend asked you how to make fudge, pancakes, or biscuits; a stranger asked you how to reach the post office, the city hall, or a certain street.

Was your answer definite? Could your directions be followed easily? To be of any value an explanation must be clear, accurate, and complete. If you have only a hazy idea, you cannot explain clearly.

Practice 1

Perhaps one of your faults is that you have a general idea about many subjects but are not particular about getting accurate information. Would you actually know what to do if you were lost in the woods? Read the rules sent out by the Pennsylvania Forestry Service. How accurately could you give them to someone else?

IF YOU ARE LOST IN THE WOODS

1. Sit down and rest. Study the lay of the land; try to find out where you are.
2. Don't yell for help, and don't wear yourself out trying

to run through undergrowth or pushing through drifted snow.

3. Don't walk aimlessly. Travel only downhill. Follow a stream downwards, if possible. It usually leads to a habitation.

4. Don't try to find a way out during the night or in a storm or fog. Find a sheltered place and make camp. Gather plenty of dry wood and build a fire in a safe place. Be careful not to set the woods on fire and to extinguish your camp fire before leaving.

5. If you are injured, build a smoke signal fire, if possible, in an open spot on a knob or ridge top.

6. Don't lose your head and don't give up.

Practice 2

How many of the following do you know enough about to explain? Make a list of those about which you have accurate information. Be ready to give an oral explanation of one in class.

1. What makes thunder? 2. How to set up a Christmas tree. 3. How to tie a slip knot, a square knot, a granny knot. 4. How to kindle a fire without matches. 5. The purpose of the Junior Red Cross organization. 6. Why the days are shortest in winter. 7. How to salute the flag. 8. How to display the flag. 9. How to study a history lesson. 10. How to learn a poem. 11. How to stop bleeding from a cut. 12. What makes water hard? 13. How to tell the difference between mushrooms and toadstools. 14. How to get breakfast at camp. 15. What first aid to give a person who is burned. 16. How to introduce a friend to your mother. 17. How to put out a camp fire. 18. How to put up an aërial. 19. What causes winds? 20. Why we have day and night. 21. Why we have summer and winter. 22. How a foreigner may become a citizen of the United States. 23. How the President of the United States is elected. 24. How to make a snare. 25. Why the stars are not visible in the daytime. 26. Why foods keep longer in cold air than in warm.

Being Clear

To be able to explain clearly you must know what you are talking about. You should thoroughly understand, for example, how to make a kite before you attempt to tell someone else how to do it. Then explain in such a clear, definite manner that your listeners will be able to follow your directions.

Pictures and Diagrams

Pictures or diagrams are often helpful in making an explanation clear. If you are telling how to make a sailboat or how to go from your home to school, you will be apt to use gestures or a diagram. Be sure that your drawings accurately illustrate what you are explaining.

Practice 3

Read the directions given in the following paragraph and study the diagram illustrating them:

To reach the Art Gallery from the Wilson Junior High School turn to the left as you come from the main entrance; walk down Central Avenue to Brown Street; turn right and

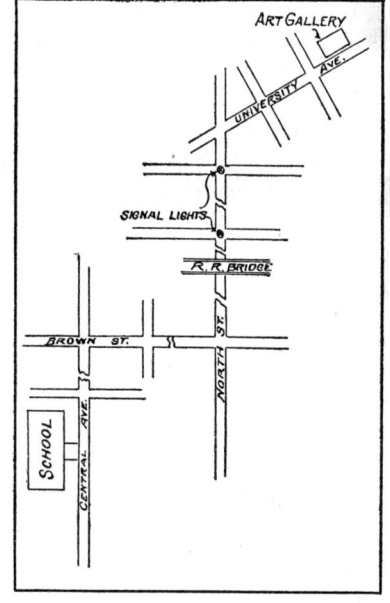

A Diagram of Directions for Going from the School to the Art Gallery

walk to North Street; then turn left, go under the elevated tracks, pass two signal lights, and continue to University Avenue. Turn right on University Avenue and walk two blocks. The large stone building on your left is the Art Gallery. — PUPIL

Practice 4

The class had been discussing how to give directions clearly. When Stan's turn came, he told an incident which had happened during his vacation. After you have read his directions, draw a diagram to illustrate them. Then answer the following questions:

1. Are the directions clear?
2. What landmarks are mentioned?
3. How are distances indicated?
4. How do landmarks help?

One day last summer when I was visiting at my uncle's farm in Iowa, a big car drew up in front of the house and a man called, "Is this the road to Ames?"

Fortunately, only a few days before I had gone with my uncle to Ames and knew that the stranger was on the wrong road.

"No," I answered, "you are several miles out of your way, but I'll tell you a short cut that will bring you to the concrete road which goes to Ames. Turn around and go back about two miles to the gas station. Turn to your right at the gas station and follow that road until you cross a one-way bridge. Turn right at the schoolhouse just beyond the bridge and keep that road until you come to the concrete. There you will find a signboard that will direct you to Ames. — PUPIL

Practice 5

Your cousin is coming to visit you and has asked whether you think it best for him to drive or come by train or by bus. Choose any one of the three ways and give directions for reaching your home. Draw a diagram for the route which you give him.

Accuracy

Directions which are inaccurate are useless. Suppose that a stranger asks you how to go to Mr. Sutton's home. If you tell him to turn left at the next corner and go to 458 Chestnut Street when you should have told him to turn right and go to 658 Chestnut Street, your directions are not only worthless but cause annoyance and loss of time.

Practice 6

Prepare to explain accurately to the class how to go from your school to one of the following: the post office, a railroad station, a church, your home, a theater, the zoo, a park, the baseball field, a skating pond, a swimming pool, a picnic ground, a store, a bank, a bus terminal, a gymnasium, an airport, a library, a factory, a playground, another school, a hospital, the dental dispensary, the telegraph office, a garage, a doctor's office, Scout Camp.

First explain the route without a diagram. Then explain it with a map or diagram. Tell whether you will walk, drive, or go by bus or by trolley.

Practice 7

The first day of school is confusing to new pupils. Prepare to explain one of the following. Draw a diagram if you need to.

1. How to go from your room to the lunch room, the library, the auditorium, the office, the cooking room. 2. How to go from the front door to the gymnasium, the art room,

the lost and found department. 3. How to go from the office to the science room, the music room, the art craft shop, the machine shop, or the cabinet shop.

Practice 8

Imagine that your class has been chosen to tell the entering classes about the various school organizations. Select a topic and prepare to explain it clearly and accurately.

1. How our home-room group is organized. 2. What the duties of class officers are. 3. How class officers are elected. 4. What the duties are of the guardians of the park or grounds, the Locker Committee, the Corridor Committee, the Lunch Room Committee. 5. How school banking is carried on. 6. How our home room is represented in the Student Forum or Student Council. 7. Who is eligible to be an officer of the Student Forum. 8. How these officers are elected. 9. What our school creed means. 10. What the requirements are for the citizenship honor roll, the scholarship honor roll. 11. How we may use the library. 12. Why we have assembly periods. 13. How one may become a member of the band, orchestra, or glee club. 14. How the home-room athletic teams are organized. 15. How one may become a member of the school athletic teams. 16. What it means to be a citizen of our junior high school.

Outlining

An outline is a written plan of a composition or a talk. It gives the points the writer considers important. There are two kinds of outlines, topical and sentence. A topical outline is briefer and easier to write than a sentence outline, which, as the name implies, is written in complete sentences. The danger in the use of the topical outline is that it may be so vague and brief as to give little or no information about the subject. Such an outline is neither interesting nor valuable.

Directions for Outlining

1. The main topics are numbered I, II, III, with the subtopics under each in capital letters, *A, B, C.*

2. Subtopics are begun farther to the right than the main topic. The second line of a topic is indented farther than the first line.

3. The numbers for the main topics must be kept directly under each other, and in like manner the letters for the subtopics must be kept in a vertical line.

4. Capitalize the first word of each topic and other words that would be capitalized in a sentence.

5. Place a period after each topic number or letter and at the end of each sentence.

Example of sentence outline:

MY DAILY TRIP TO SCHOOL

   I. I enjoy my walk to school.
     A. I cross a railroad track and a long bridge.
     B. I pass three signal lights.
     C. I go through a park which I love.

  II. I meet the same people almost every morning.
     A. A pleasant woman with red hair and a nice smile always speaks to me.
     B. A small boy grins from ear to ear as we pass.
     C. A cross-looking girl accompanies the little boy.

 III. One house interests me particularly.
     A. It is attractive in winter or summer.
     B. It has a lovely garden.
     C. I wish that I might some day live in such a house.

I enjoy my walk to school. I cross a railroad track, a long bridge, and pass three signal lights. Then I go through a park which I love. There I count the squirrels and birds and watch for the new flowers in the spring.

I meet some of the same people every morning. One of these is a woman who looks very good-natured and always speaks to me. In the next block I often pass a boy about five years old with a girl about thirteen, who looks enough like him to be his sister. He has light hair, brown eyes, and wears a funny little hat perched on the top of his head. He is always smiling from ear to ear. But the girl doesn't smile. She has hair and eyes like the little boy's, but she has a sharp pointed nose and looks so cross that I'm afraid to speak to her. Probably she is angry because she has to take her brother to kindergarten before she goes to school.

One house which I admire very much is cream-colored and has a green roof. In the winter it looks warm and comfortable. In the summer the garden is beautiful, and the grass looks like a green velvet carpet. I love to imagine that some day I'll live in a house just like that one. — PUPIL

Example of topical outline:

POISON IVY [1]

I. Why dreaded
    A. Causes painful irritation
    B. Is highly infectious

II. How recognized
    A. Three-leaved foliage
    B. Greenish-white flowers
    C. Waxy-white berries
    D. Shrub or vine

III. What parts most dangerous
    A. Broken leaves
    B. Broken stems

One of the most dreaded plant pests is poison ivy. The slightest contact with this plant brings about an extremely

[1] Adapted from an article by J. B. McNair in *Safety Education*, June, 1932.

painful irritation, swelling, and itching. Some people are so easily poisoned that they are affected even by handling garden tools or clothing of others who have walked on this plant.

Poison ivy is known by its compound leaf which is made up of three leaflets. Its flowers are greenish white and the berries are waxy and white. It grows either as a shrub or as a climbing vine, and may be found in almost every state in the Union.

The parts of the plant which one should avoid touching are the broken leaves and stems from which the sap comes, as it has been proved that the sap contains the poison. Consequently the springtime, when the plants are just budding, is the time of the year when cases of poisoning are most frequent.

Practice 9

Write an outline of each of the two articles that follow. Write either sentences or topics, not both.

HUNTING IN THE DAYS OF DANIEL BOONE

In the days of Daniel Boone hunting was not only a sport but a serious occupation, as the entire meat supply came from the wild game. A man needed to be not only a hunter but a good one. Abundance of game did not always mean easy hunting. Even though animals were numerous, they were just as wary then as now.

Besides securing a supply of fresh meat, a pioneer laid aside dried meat in strips, called "jerky." Sometimes the settlers of those days would make hunting trips at a distance for the purpose of laying in as much meat as they could to last over the winter.

CAUSES OF FOREST FIRES

Certain causes of forest fires have been known for years. The most common are the throwing down of lighted cigars, cigarettes, or matches, or leaving a camp fire that has not been completely extinguished. Lightning causes many such fires every year.

Recently a scientist who has spent many years examining the origin of fires warns us of something new to guard against. He maintains that twenty per cent of forest fires of unknown origin are due to pieces of curved glass from broken bottles thrown away by picnickers or hunters. Any one of these broken pieces may act as a magnifying glass and concentrate the sun's rays in such a way that it may start a fire even more easily than would a cigarette.

It is the duty of everyone to exercise the utmost care in the use of any materials that might cause fires.

Practice 10

Read carefully the notes which were taken by a seventh-grade pupil on a lesson in social studies. From the outline write an explanation of "Some Ways a Community Protects Its Citizens."

Example of note-taking while studying a lesson:

Some ways a community protects its citizens
  I. Lighted streets
      A. Less danger from burglars and rowdies
      B. Greater safety for vehicles and pedestrians
  II. Fire protection
      A. Fire department
          1. Salaried members in cities
          2. Volunteer members in towns and villages
      B. Sufficient water supply
      C. Apparatus for fighting fire
      D. Instruction in causes of fires
          1. Hot ashes placed in wooden containers
          2. Rubbish on stairways, in attic, or in cellar
          3. Curtains near lighted gas jet
          4. Danger from lanterns
          5. Carelessness of campers and autoists

EXPLAINING

III. Police protection
    A. Guards property
    B. Regulates traffic and crowds
    C. Lessens crime and disobedience to law

GOOD ENOUGH TO EAT

How to Do Something

Practice 11

Prepare to explain in class how to do one of the following. Write an outline; then give your explanation so clearly and accurately that everyone in the class will understand. Include necessary details but guard against a long, uninteresting talk.

Ewing Galloway
BUILDING A MODEL SIGNAL TOWER

1. Give a fire alarm. 2. Use a fire extinguisher. 3. Get a summer work permit. 4. Get a library card. 5. Plant sweet peas. 6. Open a new book. 7. Trim hedges, rosebushes. 8. Irrigate an orange grove. 9. Load a camera. 10. Alight from a street car. 11. Decorate a Christmas tree. 12. Set the dinner table for company. 13. Become a Boy Scout, a Girl Scout, a Camp Fire Girl. 14. Give your dog a bath.

15. Put out a grass fire. 16. Train a dog. 17. Care for a canary. 18. Toast marshmallows. 19. Fish for trout. 20. Select a camp site. 21. Keep a diary. 22. Get dinner at camp. 23. Transplant a seedling. 24. Mount a horse. 25. Saddle a horse. 26. Get ready for camp. 27. Make a camp fire in wet weather. 28. Dust a room. 29. Tap a maple tree. 30. "Sugar-off." 31. Become a good caddy. 32. Prepare a vegetable bed or a flower bed.

How to Make or Build Something

Explanation is a shorthand language. No words should be wasted. If the directions are not accurate and clear, they cannot be followed and are of no value. The arrangement or the order in which things are done is often shown by such words as *first, next, then, now, after this,* and *finally*.

Practice 12

Read the two explanations. Answer the questions after the first one.

HOW TO MAKE BAKING-POWDER BISCUITS

2 cups flour 2 tablespoons shortening
5 teaspoons baking powder 1 cup milk
1 teaspoon salt

First mix together the flour, salt, and baking powder, and sift the mixture twice. Then work in shortening with a knife or your fingers. Add the milk slowly. After this is completely mixed, put it on a floured board — or a floured paper if you are at camp. Pat it down until it is about one-half inch thick. Cut with a biscuit cutter and bake about 15 minutes in a hot oven.

The trick of making good biscuits is to have them not too stiff, and to bake them quickly in a hot oven. — PUPIL

1. How does this explanation differ from the following one?
2. How many steps are there in this process?
3. What connecting words are used?

HOW TO PACK A BLANKET ROLL

When you are packing a blanket roll, remember that you should not have any hard articles pressing against your shoulder, back, or chest, and that the articles should be so arranged that they will not fall out while you are walking.

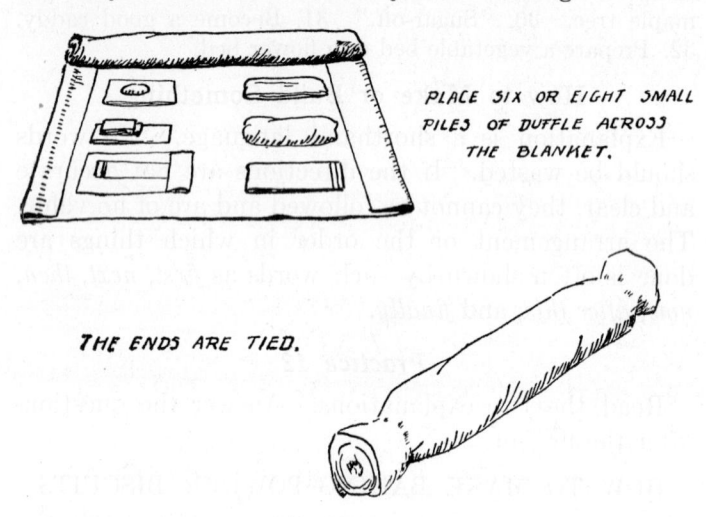

PLACE SIX OR EIGHT SMALL PILES OF DUFFLE ACROSS THE BLANKET.

THE ENDS ARE TIED.

To make the roll tight and comfortable to carry, distribute the equipment in six or eight small piles across the width of the blanket, half on one side of the center and half on the other. Fold over the two edges about eight inches. No equipment should be placed under these folds. Roll the pack tightly away from you. Then tie or strap each end to be sure nothing will fall out. — PUPIL

Practice 13

Prepare to explain clearly how you would make one of the articles in the following list or one of your own choice. Be accurate. Use a diagram if you wish.

1. A bird house. 2. A cabin in the woods. 3. A valentine box. 4. A sailboat. 5. A leather pocketbook. 6. A

silver ring or bracelet. 7. A rag doll. 8. A Japanese garden. 9. A bow and arrow. 10. Cocoa. 11. A wood or a coal fire. 12. Fudge, taffy, butterscotch, or stuffed dates. 13. A model airplane. 14. A raft. 15. A scrapbook. 16. A kite. 17. A snow man. 18. Pancakes. 19. Angel cake. 20. A wooden toy. 21. A sled. 22. Carved soap figures. 23. A rat trap. 24. A jig-saw puzzle. 25. Pop corn balls. 26. A pin-

Courtesy Memorial Art Gallery

CHILDREN CASTING THEIR WORK IN PLASTER

hole camera. 27. A dress. 28. A bookcase. 29. A lamp shade. 30. A chicken coop. 31. A dog kennel. 32. Apple or chocolate pie. 33. Ice cream. 34. A boudoir pillow. 35. A rock garden. 36. Any article you have made at home or in school.

How to Play Games

Have you ever explained a new game to some friends and then discovered to your amazement that they didn't understand it? If so, you realized that your explanation was a failure. Perhaps you were trying to explain too difficult a game. Such games as baseball and football require elaborate directions. Whole books have been written about them. Only simple games can be described in a short composition.

Practice 14

Read the explanations of the three games. Which is the clearest? Which explanation is not clear? What necessary information is omitted? Be ready to explain one of the games.

KICK-THE-STICK

This is how to play kick-the-stick. It is played in an open space out of doors with a stick about six inches long and one inch in diameter. There are from four to eight players and four bases, first, second, third, and home. A player is chosen to be "it," and the others line up at "home."

The stick is kicked by the first one in line at "home." The one who is "it" must chase the stick and bring it back to "home"; and if the runner is off base, "it" may touch "home" and call the person's name. The one caught then becomes "it." The one on base may not run until the stick is kicked. — PUPIL

WEATHERCOCKS[1]

The players are divided into four equal groups, each one representing a direction of the compass — north, south, east, and west. One player is the Wind and stands at the center of the groups. The players of each group stand in straight lines radiating out, like the lines of a compass, from the center of the field, where the Wind stands.

[1] From Elliot and Forbush's *Games for Every Day*, by permission of The Macmillan Company.

```
      x
      x
      x
x x x W x x x
      x
      x
      x
```

The Wind points in one direction and calls out the name — "North!" for instance. As those representing North are naturally facing that way, they do not move, but those who are South must turn the other way. East and West do not move. Thus three directions keep still and the fourth faces the direction called by the Wind.

When the Wind shouts "Tempest!" all must turn rapidly around three times, returning to their former positions. At "Variable!" all must teeter back and forth until the Wind cries some other point.

Those who move when they should not, or fail to move when they should, drop out and later pay forfeits.

MAKING A WILL

Pass to each person present a piece of paper and a pencil. Have each one write his or her name at the top, and after the name write the word *wills*. Divide the paper into four columns. List the number from one to five down the second, third, and fourth columns, leaving the first one blank. The paper should look like this:

JOHN CARTER WILLS

I	II	III	IV
	1	1	1
	2	2	2
	3	3	3
	4	4	4
	5	5	5

In the second column write the names of five persons present to whom you would like to will something.

Next, fold column I over column II so that no one can see what you have written. Each person then passes his paper on to his neighbor at the right.

On the paper you receive, write in column III the names of five articles you own, the funnier the better. Fold the paper again and pass it on as before.

In column IV of the paper you just received, write five ways to use different articles. Fold the paper again and pass it on.

Now comes the fun. Each one opens the will he holds and reads it aloud. For example:

John Carter wills June Harris a fountain pen for washing dishes. — PUPIL

Practice 15

Select one of the following games or any other with simple rules, and explain it so that any member of the class will be able to play it. If you know a game which nobody in the class has ever played, explain it. You may draw a diagram if it will help your explanation.

1. Going to Jerusalem. 2. Authors. 3. Lotto. 4. Old Maid. 5. Leapfrog. 6. Cross questions. 7. Up, Jenkins. 8. Ping-pong. 9. Croquet. 10. Thread the needle. 11. Forfeits. 12. Treasure hunt. 13. Three deep. 14. Tug of war. 15. Fox and geese. 16. Pachisi. 17. Poison. 18. Tenpins. 19. Duck on the rock. 20. Charades. 21. Odd man's cap. 22. Hare and hounds. 23. Blindman's buff. 24. Centipede. 25. Drop the handkerchief. 26. Black and white. 27. Tag. 28. Jacob and Rachel. 29. Pom-pom pullaway. 30. Prisoner's base. 31. Spin the platter. 32. Still water; no moving. 33. London Bridge. 34. The King of France. 35. Slipper slap. 36. Game of nations. 37. Musical guessing contest. 38. Geographical game. 39. Girls' names contest.

Complete Definitions

You will be greatly helped in explaining the meaning of a noun if you get the habit of telling to what class of things it belongs, and how it differs from others in its class. The following table is an excellent device for working out definitions. Study the examples given.

Name	Class	Particular Qualities or Description
1. Great Stone Face is	a rock formation	on a mountain side in Vermont, resembling a man's face.
2. A barometer is	an instrument	for predicting changes of weather.
3. A reservoir is	a place	where water is collected and kept for use.
4. A tourniquet is	a device	for stopping bleeding.
5. A fable is	a story	which teaches a lesson.
6. Sod is	soil	filled with roots of grass.

Practice 16

Using the form of the table given above, write definitions of ten of the following:

1. Asbestos. 2. A rainbow. 3. A shark. 4. A hotbed. 5. Fog. 6. Cicada. 7. Sap. 8. A rectangle. 9. A cartoon. 10. A president. 11. A lariat. 12. A microphone. 13. A motto. 14. A monoplane. 15. A moccasin. 16. A hangar. 17. A treaty. 18. A penguin. 19. An isthmus. 20. A tepee. 21. A compass. 22. A pianoforte. 23. A theater. 24. A telegram. 25. A tenderfoot.

Mistakes in Definitions

When you are defining a noun, use after it another noun, not *when* or *where*.

(Right) A church is a building for public worship.
(Wrong) A church is where people worship.

(Right) A pronoun is a word used in place of a noun.
(Wrong) A pronoun is when a word is used in place of a noun.

Practice 17

Correct these faulty definitions:

1. A library is where books are kept.
2. A hymn is when people sing in praise of God.
3. Summer is when the rays of the sun are most direct.
4. A triangle is when a figure has three sides.
5. A patriot is when one loves his country.
6. A bank is where you save your money.
7. A hero is when you risk your life to save someone.

Intelligent Answers to Questions

Many times when a pupil is asked a question, his answer is so incomplete that additional questions are needed to get the required information. It should not be necessary for one's hearer to have to stop him every few seconds to ask "What?" "Why?" "What for?" or "How?" Answers should ordinarily be complete sentences and should give all the required information.

Example:

What are some of the changes Rip Van Winkle found when he returned home?

Rip found the village so changed in appearance that he scarcely recognized it. His own home was in ruins. He was told that his wife was dead and his daughter married. Instead of the old inn where he had been accustomed to loaf, stood a rickety wooden building called a hotel. The Union Jack too was gone, and on a pole in front of the hotel waved a peculiar flag of stars and stripes.

Practice 18

Choose five of the following questions referring to a book you have read or to a topic you have studied in history. Prepare careful, complete answers.

1. How did Rip Van Winkle spend his time after he returned home?
2. How did Little John and Robin Hood become friends?
3. Who was Rikki-Tikki-Tavi?
4. How did Ulysses happen to enter Circe's palace?
5. Why did Priscilla say to John Alden, "Why don't you speak for yourself, John?"
6. How do you account for Ichabod's Crane's disappearance from Sleepy Hollow?
7. Why was Proserpina forced to spend half of each year in Pluto's kingdom?
8. Why was Ernest constantly looking for the man who would resemble the Great Stone Face?
9. Why was it so difficult for Tom Canty to take the place of the prince?
10. Why did Paul Revere wait to see the lantern in the Old North Church?
11. What were some of the contributions of the ancient Greeks to civilization?
12. How did the Romans spread civilization?
13. Where were the Dutch explorations in the New World? What were the results of these explorations?
14. What is the meaning of the name San Francisco? Why is San Francisco an important city?
15. Where is New Orleans located? By whom was it first settled and how did these settlers affect the history of the city?
16. Why were the original thirteen colonies located along the Atlantic coast?
17. Who were some of the early American scouts? How did they help to make American history?
18. How did the Boy Scout movement originate?

Explanation and Illustration of Proverbs

A proverb is a brief saying which has a hidden meaning. Many proverbs you know well, but can you explain them to someone who does not understand them?

Example:

He who has begun has his work half done.

This proverb means that the hardest part of doing work is getting at it. Instead of putting off a task and worrying about it, much time and energy may be saved by starting it at once. Attack the work that is to be done and you are through before you know it.

Practice 19

Choose one of the following proverbs and explain its meaning. A check-up will determine which have not been chosen. The teacher may assign these to volunteers.

1. A stitch in time saves nine.
2. All that glitters is not gold.
3. The worst wheel always creaks most.
4. A penny saved is a penny earned.
5. Pride goeth before a fall.
6. Don't cry over spilt milk.
7. A bird in the hand is worth two in the bush.
8. His bark is worse than his bite.
9. It never rains but it pours.
10. A short time is long for the unprepared.
11. A small leak sinks a great ship.
12. A chain is as strong as its weakest link.
13. Speech is silver; silence is golden.
14. Whatever is worth doing at all is worth doing well.
15. A carpenter is known by his chips.

16. Too many cooks spoil the broth.
17. He laughs best who laughs last.
18. Birds of a feather flock together.
19. Haste makes waste.
20. A word to the wise is sufficient.

Practice 20

Explain one of the following subjects. Be clear, accurate, and entertaining.

1. Why I like junior high school. 2. Why I am glad that I live in the United States. 3. Why I am glad I live in Colorado, Kentucky (or any other state). 4. How I earn money after school, in the summer. 5. How I learn a poem. 6. Why I would like to go to college. 7. Why I enjoy the school or city library. 8. How to measure distance by pacing. 9. Why I want to take the Latin, commercial, or practical arts course in junior high school. 10. How I have kept a perfect attendance record at school. 11. Why I do not like to miss school. 12. Why I think a dog is the best pet. 13. Why I enjoy playing in the band or orchestra. 14. What shop work I like and why. 15. Safety rules we should follow. 16. How one feels while going up in an airplane.

UNIT 7

THE BUSINESS LETTER

Form 1 — Slant Style

1260 Emory Street
San Jose, California
November 23, 1934

The Boys' Magazine
Frick Building
Pittsburgh, Pennsylvania

Gentlemen:

I am enclosing a money order for $2.50 in payment of one year's subscription to the Boys' Magazine.

Yours truly,
Thomas McNary

Study the forms of the letters on this page and page 115. The first, known as the slant style, is used when one writes with pen and ink. In a typewritten letter either the slant or the block style may be used. Never combine the two styles in the same letter.

The parts of a business letter are the heading, the inside address, the salutation, the body, the complimentary close, and the signature.

FORM 2 — BLOCK STYLE

```
                        1260 Emory Street
                        San Jose, California
                        November 23, 1934

The Boys' Magazine
Frick Building
Pittsburgh, Pennsylvania

Gentlemen:

   I am enclosing a money order for
$2.50 in payment of one year's sub-
scription to the Boys' Magazine.

                        Yours truly,
                        Thomas McNary
```

Heading

The heading of a letter should begin a little to the right of the middle of the page, and from one and one-half to two inches from the top of the page.

When the paper used has a printed letterhead, only the date need be written. This should be placed below the letterhead either at the right or in the center.

The only punctuation needed is two commas — one after the city or town, and one after the day of the month. It is better not to use abbreviations in the heading. Whether two or three lines are used, the date stands alone on the last line. Study the following headings:

SLANT STYLE

STREET NUMBER NOT NEEDED	STREET NUMBER NEEDED
Pleasantville, Pennsylvania	1518 Palmetto Street
February 3, 1934	New Orleans, Louisiana
	February 3, 1934

BLOCK STYLE

Robinson, Illinois   759 Michigan Avenue
August 27, 1934   Jackson, Michigan
                            December 12, 1934

E. SHANNON ROBERTS

GENERAL AGENT   OLD COLONY BANK BUILDING
AMERICAN LIFE INSURANCE COMPANY   ROCHESTER

April 6, 1934

H. H. Macy

4th STREET & BROADWAY, NEW YORK

September 12, 1934

Letterheads

Business firms and many individuals have their own letterheads. When these are used, the date may be written at the right or in the center.

Address

The inside address, which consists of the name and address of the person or firm to whom the letter is written, begins at the left margin. A study of Form 1 on page 114 shows that in a pen-written letter the inside address has the same slant as the heading.

When a letter is to an individual, the proper title should always precede the name — for example:

SLANT STYLE

Miss Dorothy Trent
  542 Abbott Avenue
    Boise, Idaho

Dr. L. J. Walker
  1700 Harvard Avenue
    Seattle, Washington

BLOCK STYLE

Mr. F. B. Jackson
1405 Cross Road
Louisville, Kentucky

Reverend James Scott
138 West Seneca Street
Syracuse, New York

Only necessary marks of punctuation are used. Always place a comma between the name of the city and of the state. The following are examples of correct addresses of letters to firms:

SLANT STYLE

Brown and Kerr Company
  228 Main Street East
    Rochester, New York

Miami Stamp Company
  Fostoria, Ohio

BLOCK STYLE

The Star-News
Colorado Street
Pasadena, California

Anchor Fence Company
Eastern Avenue
Baltimore, Maryland

Practice 1

Using your home address, write the heading and inside address of a letter to each of the following. Use the slant style.

1. R. H. Stark Company on 462 Stuart Street, Boston, Massachusetts.
2. Fielding School for Girls on 2500 Jefferson Avenue, Indianapolis, Indiana.
3. Lake Camp for Boys at Deland, Minnesota.
4. The Bar-O Dude Ranch at Sheridan, Wyoming.
5. Wilson Brothers Nursery at 10 North Maple Street, Uniontown, Pennsylvania.
6. The National Sporting Goods Company at 609 Placer Street, Milwaukee, Wisconsin.
7. Dr. J. W. Milliken, who lives on 100 Pocono Street in Hamilton, Ohio.
8. Miss Margaret Forester, Principal of Laurel Mountain School, at Manchester, Kentucky.

Salutation

The salutation should begin at the margin below the address and be followed by a colon. Capitalize the first word and all nouns. Correct salutations for a business letter are:

To an Individual
Dear Madam:
Dear Sir:
My dear Mrs. Chamberlin:
Dear Mr. French:
My dear Sir:
My dear Madam:

To a Company or Group
Gentlemen:
Ladies:

Examples of correct address and salutation:

Slant Style

Major Edward M. Iland
   1213 State Street
      Coraopolis, Pennsylvania

My dear Major Iland:
   You will ——————————————————

Block Style

The Canadian Forestry Association
51 Sparks Street
Ottawa, Ontario

Gentlemen:

    Will you please————————————————————— ———

Body of the Letter

The first word in the body of a letter should be indented about one inch from the margin. The first word in each successive paragraph should be indented the same distance.

The body of the letter should state the purpose of writing. It should be courteous, clear, and to the point. Omit unnecessary information. If you are sending in your subscription for the *American Boy*, do not tell the company you enjoy the magazine. Your subscription proves that.

A good business letter is written in good English. Neither omit words nor use unnecessary ones. Do not, as a rule, begin the last sentence with a word ending in *ing*.

  (Right) We have received your letter of June 5, and shall take care of your request immediately.
  (Bad) Yours of the fifth received and contents noted.

  (Right) I am enclosing a check for $5.00.
  (Bad) Enclosed please find check for $5.00. [Meaningless *please*.]

  (Right) I thank you for your attention to my order.
                             Yours truly,
  (Bad) Thanking you for your kindness, I am
                             Yours truly,

Complimentary Close

Begin the complimentary close a little to the right of the middle of the page. Capitalize the first word only, and place a comma after the last word.

Correct forms of the complimentary close are:

Yours truly,   *Truly yours,*
Yours very truly,   *Very truly yours,*

Signature

The signature of the writer should be placed below the complimentary close and a little to the right in the slant style, and directly underneath the first letter of the complimentary close in the block style. No mark of punctuation follows the signature.

An unmarried woman writing to a stranger should place *Miss* in parenthesis before her signature. This gives the title to be used in reply.

(Right)   *(Miss) Mary Newkirk*
(Bad)   *Mary Newkirk*

Examples of correct placing of the signature:

SLANT STYLE	BLOCK STYLE
Yours truly,	Yours truly,
Preston Cooley	*Preston Cooley*
Very truly yours,	Very truly yours,
(Miss) Barbara Lytle	*(Miss) Barbara Lytle*

Practice 2

Answer the questions on the next page concerning the form of business letters.

1. When writing with pen and ink, which style of letter is used — the slant or the block?
2. What does the heading of a business letter include? How is it punctuated?
3. Where is the inside address placed? What does it include? How is it punctuated?
4. Where is the salutation placed? How is it punctuated and capitalized?
5. Where does the first word of the body of the letter begin?
6. How is the complimentary close capitalized? What punctuation is used?
7. Where is the signature placed? How is it punctuated?
8. How does the block style differ from the slant style?

Practice 3

Using your home address, write the heading, address, complimentary close, and signature of a letter to each of the following:

1. Proctor and Gamble, Cincinnati, Ohio.
2. The Saturday Evening Post, 785 Independence Square, Philadelphia, Pennsylvania.
3. Corona Typewriters Inc., 51 Madison Avenue, New York City.
4. The Elgin Watch Company, Elgin, Illinois.
5. Baltimore and Ohio Railroad, 640 East Fifth Street, Philadelphia, Pennsylvania.
6. Mid-Week Pictorial, New York Times Company, Times Square, New York City.
7. The Registrar, Blair Academy, Blairstown, New Jersey.
8. D. C. Heath and Company, 1815 Prairie Avenue, Chicago, Illinois.
9. Beldts' Aquarium, 2141 Crescent Avenue, St. Louis, Missouri.
10. Joseph H. Dodson Company, 55 Harrison Street, Kaukahu, Illinois.

Envelope Address

Millions of letters each year are sent to the Dead Letter Office because they are misdirected or have no return address. Always write legibly the name and complete address of the person to whom you are sending the letter. Place your own address in the upper left-hand corner of the envelope.

SLANT STYLE

```
M. Q. Wilson
1157 North Lewis Avenue
Tulsa, Oklahoma                              STAMP


                Miss Harriet Lowen
                   120 West Spruce Street
                      Fort Wayne
                         Indiana
```

BLOCK STYLE

```
After 5 days return to
E. C. Palmer                                 STAMP
2902 Jackson Street
Sioux City, Iowa


                Mr. John H. MacMillan
                1500 Queen Anne Heights
                Seattle
                Washington
```

Paper and Folding

White unruled paper of good quality is preferred for all letters. The full-size sheet which is commonly used for business letters is $8\frac{1}{2}$ inches by 11 inches. The letter should be written on one side of the page only.

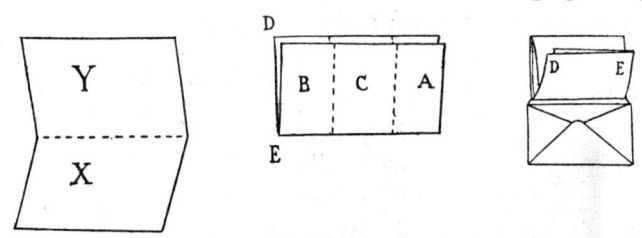

Fold the lower half of the sheet X over the top half Y to within a quarter of an inch of the top. Then fold A over C from the right and B over C from the left, each fold being less than one-third the width of the paper. Place the letter in the envelope with the open edges DE up.

Practice 4

Copy and punctuate the following letter:

Garfield Junior High School
Berkeley California
November 24 1934

The Western Publishing Company
   354 South Whitney Street
      Salt Lake City Utah

Gentlemen

On September 29 I ordered from your company a *New Atlas of the World* and enclosed a money order for $3.50. On October 8 I received notice that the book had been mailed. It has not yet arrived. Kindly check this order.

Yours truly
Preston Durley

100 Per Cent Test — *Letter Form*

The punctuation, capitalization, and arrangement of ten of the following headings, inside addresses, salutations, complimentary closes, and envelope addresses are correct for pen-and-ink letters. Write the numbers of the correct ones on a sheet of paper.

Headings:

1. July 1, 1934
   23 Stevens Street
   Claremont, N. H.

2. 414 Wazee Street
       Denver, Colorado
         July 10, 1934

3. 118 Elm Street
   Portland, Maine, May 18, 1934

4. 1450 Clay Avenue,
     San Francisco, California
       August 15, 1934

5. 875 State Street
     September 4, 1934
       Madison, Wisconsin

Addresses:

6. Miss Evelyn Jones
     400 South Lang Avenue
       Pittsburgh, Pennsylvania

7. Dr. F. S. Magill, Headmaster
     Penn Hall
       Chambersburg, Pennsylvania

8. Albuquerque Civic Council
     1345 Sunshine Building
       Albuquerque, New Mexico

9. Dr. T. W. Thoburn
    3020 Corydon Avenue, Cleveland, Ohio

Salutations:

10. My dear Dr. Brown:
11. Dear Sir:
12. Dear gentlemen:
13. My Dear Miss Weston:
14. Dear Madam:

Complimentary Closes:

15.   Yours Very Truly,
16.   Very truly yours,
17.   Yours Truly,

Envelope Addresses:

18.   Howard Boat Company
                            440 Harrison Street
                            Kalamazoo
                            Michigan

19.   Mr. Frederick J. Tanner, Agent
                            80 West Broad Street
                            Richmond
                            Virginia

20.   Burlingame Travel Bureau
                            547 W. Jackson Blvd.
                            Chicago.
                            Ill.

KINDS OF BUSINESS LETTERS

Change of Address

You will doubtless need at some time to have your mail sent to a different address. When, for example, you move to another town or city or have a long vacation, you will wish to notify the postmaster or the publisher of some magazine of the change of address.

> 545 Second Street
> Oil City, Pennsylvania
> March 20, 1934
>
> Popular Mechanics Magazine
> 200 East Ontario Street
> Chicago, Illinois
>
> Gentlemen:
>
> In the future please mail copies of *Popular Mechanics* to me at the above address. My former address was 175 Hone Avenue.
>
> Yours truly,
>
> David Haskell

Practice 5

1. You have moved to another street in the same city. Write to *Radio News*, 222 West 39th Street, New York City, to notify the company of your change of address.

2. Your family is spending the summer at the lake or the shore or in the mountains. Ask your postmaster to forward your mail.

3. You are planning to spend the summer vacation with an uncle in the country. Write to the *Girls' World*, American Building, Detroit, Michigan, asking them to send the magazine to your uncle's address until further notice.

4. You and your sister are spending the Christmas vacation at your grandmother's. Ask the postmaster to forward mail for both of you.

5. Your family has moved to another street in the same

city. Write to the postmaster and notify him of your change of address.

6. Write to the La Pasada Hotel, Winslow, Arizona, and ask that your mail be forwarded to 4761 West 12th Street, Los Angeles, California.

Request for Catalog

Almost everyone enjoys looking through catalogs and wishes that he or she had the camping outfit, the lovely garden, the aquarium, or the good-looking clothes shown in the pictures.

---

                          305 Fifth Street
                          Warren, Pennsylvania
                          April 15, 1934

Girl Scouts, Incorporated
   570 Lexington Avenue
   New York City

Ladies:

   Please send me the 1934 catalog which gives the prices of blankets, camping utensils, and other scout equipment. I should also like to have the latest bulletins giving the location of camps in western Pennsylvania.

                          Yours truly,
                              (**Miss**) **Ruth Dravo**

Practice 6

1. Write to Scrantoms, Incorporated, Main Street East, Rochester, New York, or to any sporting goods store, and ask for their most recent catalog of athletic goods.
2. Write to Smith and Frank Company, Fifth Avenue and 34th Street, New York City, or to any other dealer in wearing apparel, asking for their spring catalog.
3. Write to the Chase Brothers Seed Company, Dayton, Ohio, asking for a seed catalog.
4. Write the Scott Stamp Company, 33 West 44th Street, New York City, for their recent stamp catalog.

Order

In ordering articles, explain what you want so clearly, accurately, and completely that the company cannot possibly make a mistake in filling your order. Because your address is in the heading, it is not necessary to tell in the body of the letter where the goods are to be sent.

Explain how payment is being made — that is, whether you are sending stamps, a money order, or a check. If you are ordering more than one article, use at least one line for each.

If you are ordering from a catalog, give the number of each article.

Do not begin the last sentence with an *ing* word, like *hoping, thanking*.

Practice 7

1. Write to Harper and Brothers, 49 East 33d Street, New York City, ordering a copy of *Adventures of Sherlock Holmes* by Conan Doyle to be sent to your cousin.
2. Order a copy of *Little Women* by Louisa M. Alcott from Little, Brown and Company, 34 Beacon Street, Boston.
3. Order a copy of *Modern Pioneers* by Cohen and Scarlet

>
> 3710 Washington Boulevard
> Indianapolis, Indiana
> June 15, 1934
>
> Sellers, Reed and Company
> 45 Wabash Avenue
> Chicago, Illinois
>
> Gentlemen:
>
> Please send me by parcel post the following articles which are listed in your catalog of April, 1934:
>
> $\frac{1}{2}$ doz. Wright and Ditson tennis balls,
>   No. 21, @ $.45 $2.70
> 1 tennis net, No. 3   4.50
> 1 pair of white tennis shoes, size 9,
>   No. 5   2.00
>   ―――
> $9.20
>
> I am enclosing a money order for $9.20.
>
> > Yours truly,
> >
> > Fred Allison

from Allyn and Bacon, 11 East 36th Street, New York City.

4. Write to a department store in a neighboring city, enclosing a sample, and asking for two spools of silk thread, at 10 cents a spool, which would match the sample.

5. Write to the Curtis Publishing Company, Independence Square, Philadelphia, Pennsylvania, subscribing for the *Saturday Evening Post*, at $2.00 a year.

6. Write to A. G. Spalding, 105 Nassau Street, New York City, ordering a catcher's mitt, No. 31, at $1.75, and a baseball, No. 6, at $1.25.

7. Write to J. Fischer and Brothers, 119 West 40th Street, New York City, ordering 24 copies of the song *Maria-Mari* by DiCapua, No. 5666, at $.12 a copy.

8. Write to Beckley-Cardy Company, 17 East 23d Street, Chicago, ordering a Chicago pencil sharpener, No. 20B, at $.77; a Peerless card and paper cutter, No. 3B, at $2.70; and 2 dozen velvet pencils, No. 2, at $.35 a dozen.

9. Write to Stranway and Rouss, 417 Wabash Avenue, Chicago, Illinois, ordering a dark red bathing suit, size 6, No. 15C, at $3.50; a pair of bathing shoes, size 7, No. 31B, at $.60; and a surf ball, green, No. 106B, at $.75.

10. You want to give your mother some special bulbs for her birthday. Write to Henry A. Dreer, 1306 Spring Garden Street, Philadelphia, Pennsylvania, ordering 6 black Darwin tulip bulbs, No. 14, at $1.50 a dozen; 3 white hyacinths, No. 8, at $.10 apiece; and 6 Royal lilies at $2.00 a dozen.

11. Write to Bullock's, 810 Wilshire Boulevard, Los Angeles, California, ordering the following articles which were advertised in yesterday's *Daily News:* 3 green bath towels, No. 6, at $.35 apiece; a camp stove, No. 2A, at $13.75; and a one-gallon thermos jug, No. 12, at $1.98.

12. Write to Mally and Company, Broadway and 37th Street, New York City, and order from a special sale catalog 3 pounds of Princess coffee at $.31 a pound; 6 cans of Gold Seal salmon at $.19 a can; 2 jars of peanut butter, No. 4, at $.28 a jar; and 4 cans of Orton's cocoa at $.29 a can.

Practice 8

Answer these questions concerning the faulty order letter on page 131:

1. Why is *please* in the first sentence unnecessary?
2. Why couldn't Wells and Hunt fill this order?
3. What more should Mary Ellis have told about the stockings? About the gloves? About the necktie? About the blanket?
4. Why are the last two sentences useless?
5. Rewrite the letter.

Faulty Order Letter

---

121 East Fourth Street
Cincinnati, Ohio
April 27, 1934

Wells and Hunt
 333 North Michigan Avenue
 Chicago, Illinois

Gentlemen:

Enclosed please find a check for $9.25 for the following articles:

3 pairs of brown silk stockings @ $1.25	$3.75
1 pair of gloves	1.75
1 necktie	1.00
1 blanket	2.75
	$9.25

Send the articles as quickly as possible. Send them to 121 East Fourth Street, Cincinnati, Ohio.

Yours truly,

Mary Ellis

Correction of an Error

When you are writing a letter asking that an error be corrected, you should be courteous and tactful. Don't growl and grumble. Merely state the mistake and ask that it be corrected.

> 1488 South Second Street
> Evansville, Indiana
> June 15, 1934
>
> Charles Wilson's Sons
> 147 Fifth Avenue
> New York City
>
> Gentlemen:
>
> On June 1, 1934, I ordered from you an illustrated copy of *Smoky, the Cow Horse* by Will James.
>
> The book arrived this morning, but when I examined it, I found that pages 77 to 85 were missing. I am returning the book to you and ask that you mail me a perfect copy in its place.
>
> Yours truly,
>
> (Miss) Margaret Chapin

Practice 9

1. Write to the Winchester Sporting Goods Company, 1172 President Street, Cleveland, Ohio, informing them that the tennis racket which you received is heavier than the one you ordered and asking them to change it for one weighing thirteen ounces.

2. You ordered a No. 3 Howard fountain pen in green from a department store in a neighboring city. A black pen was sent to you. Write to the store asking that the error be corrected.

3. Write to the Crowell Publishing Company, Springfield, Ohio, telling them that your father has not received the *American Magazine*, which you ordered for him a month ago.

4. A fishing rod ordered from the Rochester Sporting Goods Company, 428 State Street, Rochester, New York, was broken when it arrived. Write to the company telling them that you are returning the rod and asking that another be sent in its place.

5. Write to the Sutcliffe Company, Louisville, Kentucky, telling them that a basketball, No. X12, was ripped when you received it. Ask that they exchange it as soon as possible.

Notebook Work

Make a collection of various kinds of letterheads and different types of signatures and paste them in your notebook.

Practice 10

1. You have moved to another street, city, or town. Ask that a magazine which you are taking be sent to the new address.

2. Your class has decided to study the *Literary Digest*. The subscription rate for fifteen weeks is ninety cents per pupil. For the class, order the papers from Funk and Wagnalls, 354 Fourth Avenue, New York City. Have all the papers sent to your English teacher.

3. Order for your class copies of the *Scholastic*, from the Scholastic Publishing Company, Wabash Building, Pittsburgh, Pennsylvania. The subscription price is seventy-five cents for six months.

4. Subscribe for a magazine as a gift to your mother, an aunt, or an uncle.

5. Write for a catalog of prints of famous pictures from F. A. Cobb, 205 Delaware Avenue, Buffalo, New York.

6. Write to your newspaper asking that your address be changed for the summer vacation. Give definite information.

7. Write to Joseph Horne and Company, Pittsburgh, Pennsylvania, ordering a sweater, a pair of pigskin gloves, and a scarf. Be accurate, give catalog numbers, tell how you are paying for the articles.

UNIT 8
READING AND MEMORIZING

A reader stores up facts and thoughts for use in his conversation and writing.

Two Kinds of Reading

A person ordinarily reads a story just for fun but an encyclopedia article for facts. In one case the reader is enjoying himself; in the other, he is studying to master and later to use information.

Reading for Pleasure

It is easy to follow a "talkie" story because the actors, places, and happenings are shown on the screen. When, however, one reads a story or a poem, he must use his imagination. The mind of a good reader changes the printed words of the story to talking pictures. Illustrations in the book or magazine help the reader to see the people and the action of the story.

Do you like a moving picture that travels along at a snail's gait? Of course not. Everybody likes life and action. The reader partly determines how fast a story will march. For a person who reads 400 words a minute every story moves twice as fast as for one whose rate is 200 words a minute. Also the person who reads 400 words a minute can in the same time read twice as many stories as one whose rate is 200 words a minute. A slow reader cannot keep up with the times or his job.

Reading rapidly is a habit you can form. Avoid moving your lips or pointing to words with your finger.

Read with enthusiasm. Concentrate. Occasionally time yourself, figure out your speed, compare with your classmates, and see whether you are making satisfactory progress. You can estimate the number of words in a selection by counting the lines and multiplying by the average number of words in a line. Of course don't read so rapidly that you don't understand what you read. A desirable rate for seventh-grade pupils is 250 words a minute.

Practice every day reading rapidly, enthusiastically, accurately. Paderewski once said, "If I go one day without practicing at the piano, I notice it in my playing. If I go two days, my friends notice it. If I go three days, the audience notices it."

One reads more slowly when he wishes to understand everything the author says in a difficult selection and remember the main points. In that case he studies the sentence or paragraph.

How well can you read magazines, newspapers, directions, and letters?

Magazine Story

Practice 1

In the following story there are 1779 words. Time yourself while reading. Read rapidly, but be sure you understand the story. Then figure the number of words you read a minute.

FLYING STICKS [1]

By Captain John P. Ferriter, United States Army

Captain Cook, the instructor, was talking to Red, in the rear cockpit, over the phone.

[1] Reprinted by permission of the *Open Road for Boys* and Captain John P. Ferriter.

"When I lift my hands, take the controls. And don't forget what I've been telling you. Hold her steady."

A moment later — "Now take her."

The pilot's hands were lifted high in the air to show that he had relinquished control.

Red's grip on the stick tightened. The ship sailed along evenly for a minute and then began to wabble. It was cold, away up there in the air, but Red could feel the sweat trickling down inside his helmet. He gripped the stick and tried to steady the plane. But the more he tugged, the worse things seemed to get. He glanced at the pilot and marveled to see how unconscious he seemed of the imminent peril. Freezing to the stick, he spoke to the pilot over the phone:

"There's something the matter, Captain. I can't hold her."

He waited what seemed like an hour, but the captain apparently had not heard him. Could it be that the phone had become disconnected? The thought sent a chill up his spine. He looked over the side, and, to his horror, the ground seemed to be coming up to meet him. The stick seemed to be trying to get away from him. He would have stood up and reached over to the captain, but he couldn't let go of the stick. Frantically he tugged, and the plane seemed to stand on end. In his fright he screamed into the phone:

"Do something, Captain! Do something! We're going into a spin!"

"Let go of the stick," came the calm voice of the captain.

Then, sharply — "I said, let go of the stick!"

Red dropped the stick with difficulty, his hand hovering over it as if reluctant to obey his will. But, miraculously, the plane straightened out and began to climb.

"That finishes me," whispered Red, regaining his lost breath.

The plane spiraled upward and Red reviewed bitterly his short experience as a flying cadet.

He had arrived at Brooks Field two months ago, full of enthusiasm and ready to learn everything the army had to teach him about flying. Two months ago — but it seemed that ages and æons had passed; ages of setting-up exercises, close order drill, lectures on discipline, together with painfully meticulous practical demonstrations of the same, calculated to take the heart out of any young man of spirit — and Red rather fancied himself as a man of spirit. And Captain Cook had been his nemesis from the beginning.

He seemed to pay particular and unflattering attention to Red. At first, Red had been eager to have the ace like him. He had thrilled at the stories of his courage in many an air battle in France and at the skill and resourcefulness which had enabled him to land a burning plane at the cost of numerous fiery scars on his face and body.

But Red's hero worship was too tender a plant long to survive the cold efficiency with which Captain Cook administered discipline, and his entire lack of response to Red's attempts to attract his favorable attention.

So, as thwarted hero worship often has a way of doing, Red's had turned, if not exactly to hate, at least to a sort of helpless antagonism. In other words, the captain had his goat.

Red glowered at the instructor's back and fumed at the idiotic failure of his first attempt to perform a perfectly simple task and at his resultant panic when the ship went out of control. He got hot and then cold. He despised himself, and quite unreasonably blamed the captain for all his troubles.

"If I had been with anybody else, I could have done it with my eyes shut. Old Cook has me jinxed. I might as well quit right now — if they will let me. Fell all to pieces the first chance I got. I'll leave before mess tonight and let them run this man's army without me."

With this all settled, he was startled to hear Captain Cook's voice:

"Try it again. And don't forget that the ground is three thousand feet away. You won't hit it every time her nose goes down. And don't freeze to the stick!"

His hands went up. Red had the stick.

For a moment the plane traveled smoothly on an even keel and Red began to feel confident. Then they hit a bump and her nose went down.

Red's first reaction was to pull sharply on the stick, but

his decision to quit the school cold had calmed his nerves somewhat and enabled him to recover his poise. He let her ride and, as usual, the ship leveled out and roared along as if nothing had happened.

It became intensely interesting. Soon he had the knack. Nothing to it. His heart sang. Quit the school? Hardly. Red felt, all at once, that he could handle a plane with any of them. Why all this mystery about piloting? Nothing to it. Nothing —

The captain's voice reached him, cold and unenthusiastic:

"Go up to thirty-five hundred. Be careful and don't go into a stall."

"The old scoundrel!" thought Red joyously. For a moment he almost loved the captain.

He gave her the gun and banked gently, at the same time dropping her tail. And, right there, Red had his first lesson in the difference between theoretical knowledge and practical application. He was immediately brought to a painful realization of the need for much practice in the coördination of movements before the simplest evolution could be performed.

Courtesy Southern Pacific
AWAY UP THERE

The ship responded only too well and faithfully assumed a vertical position.

Red's automatic response leveled her off — but his horror had returned.

"Not straight up," came the captain's chill tones. "Spiral."

Red swallowed something that was trying to escape through his mouth and tried again cautiously.

A little less tail depression and the thing was done. Around and around she roared in great spirals, up and up until the gauge showed thirty-five hundred feet.

"O.K.," said the captain. "Now, fly around a bit and I'll let you take her home and land her."

Red flew around, as directed, but he couldn't keep his mind on his work. What did the captain mean by saying he could land the plane? That simply was not done. No student was allowed to make a landing so early in the game. Red shook his head. The captain must be kidding.

"Well," Red decided, "if that's his game, I'll play with him."

"Take her in," said the captain, interrupting Red's thoughts. "Let's see you make it on three points."

He turned his head and grinned.

"Just to give you confidence," said he, removing his stick and holding it up to Red's view, "I'm throwing this away."

He threw the stick far out into space and settled himself comfortably in his seat.

Red watched the stick darting to the earth. He could hardly believe what he saw. This seemed some sort of crazy dream! His eyes turned to the captain lolling nonchalantly in the front seat, and slowly realization of the true situation came to him. Surely none but a madman would have pulled this crazy trick! The captain must be insane!

The plane was hurtling through space, apparently of her own volition, seeming to handle herself better without than with Red's attention.

What was to be done?

He looked over the side, trying to get his bearings. The earth looked unfamiliar to him. He had no idea how far they had flown or where they were.

Carefully he raised himself in his seat and looked over into the front cockpit. The captain seemed quiet enough.

Gently, he banked, so as to fly in a great circle. A risky thing, at the best, landing a plane the first time. But — with a crazy man aboard! Red licked his dry lips and shook his head doubtfully.

His attention was suddenly attracted to the captain, who was bent over, apparently tinkering with the controls. Red gave a sigh of relief when the captain sat back again, quiet enough to all appearances.

"I'll have to watch him," muttered Red. "If he starts anything, one good crack on the head will keep him quiet for a while."

Then something happened to Red that happens to many young soldiers when they go into their first battle. He knew it was up to him to land the plane and there was no one to advise or help him. A feeling of peace and confidence came to him. He wondered at his former lack of nerve. Here was a thing to do. He must do it!

Gradually he straightened the plane out, so as to approach the field from the north. He looked for the sock, to check the wind direction. Yes. There it was, bellying out from the top of the pole. Now for the grand finale!

Red had rehearsed this landing a hundred times in his mind. He ought to know exactly what to do. But now, when put to the test, how awkward he felt!

He pushed the stick forward and shut off the gas — and they started down, the wind shrieking through the wires. He noticed that the captain had his head over the side and seemed to be taking considerable interest in the maneuver.

"Hope he doesn't take it into his crazy head to start anything now," prayed Red fervently.

But he had other things to engage his attention. The ground was rising rapidly. He straightened out and started the motor. They were rapidly approaching the field. They were over the fence — And now he must land!

Carefully, he shoved her nose down and then, with a silent prayer, he cut the motor and straightened her out.

"And that's that!" said Red, a minute later, unsnapping his belt.

"And not so bad, either," remarked the captain smiling from the front seat.

Red gasped. He had forgotten the captain in his concentration on a safe landing. Something in the front cockpit caught his attention.

READING AND MEMORIZING 141

"I thought you threw that joy stick away!" he blurted out, astonished.

"This one? Oh, no, indeed. This is a spare stick I carry for emergencies."

He grinned.

"It has cured more than one case of nerves in its time."

"And you could have taken control at any time!" exclaimed Red, in sudden realization of his own idiocy. He felt dejected.

Then he was conscious of the captain's arm across his shoulders, and his crooked grin warmed Red's heart.

"But I didn't have to take control," said he.

And Red wondered how he could ever have thought he hated the little ace.

Test

How accurately do you read? Can you answer the questions below without turning back to the story?

1. What is the title of the preceding story?
2. Who wrote the story?
3. What was the nickname of the student?
4. How long had the cadet been at Brooks Field?
5. In what country had the instructor shown his courage in air battle? What was his name?
6. When the captain threw away his stick, what did the student think of him?

Supply the missing word in each of the following:

7. "Go up to —— hundred."
8. "Not straight up," came the captain's chill tones. "——."
9. "This one? Oh, no, indeed. This is a —— stick I carry for emergencies."

Newspaper

Nobody reads his morning newspaper like a story book, from first page to last, advertisements included.

If a busy person spends hours every day on the newspaper, he has little or no reading time left for magazines and books. Hence one should learn to get the important news from a paper quickly.

Fortunately news stories are written and arranged for busy people. In an ordinary story — "Flying Sticks," for example — the point or climax is kept till the end; in a news story the point or exciting part comes at the beginning. The headlines give the most important facts; the first paragraph tells the story briefly; the remaining paragraphs give details. For this reason, by reading headlines, a number of first paragraphs, and a few complete stories of special interest, one can get a good idea of the happenings of the day. Also the latest or most important news is on the front page.

Practice 2

1. What facts are told in the headlines about the tiger? About snoring?
2. What facts are added in the first paragraph about the tiger? About snoring?
3. Can you guess what details the reporter put into the second and third paragraphs of each news story?

TIGER OPERATED ON

Remains Calm While Ingrown Nails Are Treated

With stoic calm Old Dick, the eighteen-year-old Bengal tiger in the Central Park Zoo, yesterday underwent his third operation for the treatment of ingrowing claws. The operation was performed by Dr. Henry Nimphius, park veterinarian.

PUTS END TO SNORING

Electrical Device Sticks Pin into Noisy Sleeper

LONDON (U. P.). — An anti-snoring device that sticks a pin into a sleeper, or gives an electric shock every time the sleeper snores, has been registered with the British Patent Office.

Practice 3

1. Prepare to tell in three ways the following story:
    (1) in not more than twenty words, as it is told in the headlines;
    (2) briefly, as it is told in the first paragraph;
    (3) fully, as it is told in the whole news story.

Dog on Railroad Track "Flags" Iowa Train And Saves Master Overcome by Heart Attack

CEDAR RAPIDS, Iowa, Jan. 31. — G. C. Clark, a farmer living near Wadena, has been kind to dogs all his life, and one may be sure that he will continue to be after what happened yesterday.

Mr. Clark was returning to his home accompanied by Treve, a white collie, and Freckles, a coach dog. He was overcome by a heart attack and fell unconscious between the rails of the Milwaukee Railroad.

Treve immediately squatted down by his prostrate master and began howling. Not so Freckles. He started up the track on a run and yelping as loud as his lungs would permit. A quarter of a mile away a passenger train was approaching. George Craft, the fireman, first saw the dog and, sensing something was wrong, advised the engineer, William Luther, to slow down.

Luther put on the brakes and brought his train to a stop within a few feet of the unconscious man between the rails. Then the engineer looked around to see what had become of the coach dog. He saw him perched on the pilot of the locomotive, still barking. This time he was wagging his tail, and Luther says that if ever a dog smiled, Freckles did when he saw his master was out of danger.

Mr. Clark was placed aboard the train, and the two dogs perched themselves on either side of him in the seat and guarded the unconscious man until the train stopped at Wadena. There Clark was placed in an ambulance and sent to his farm home with the dogs riding behind him. The dogs remained with him until they saw him safely in the house.

Clark raised the dogs from puppies. They are his constant companions, and he says he has never given either a cross word. They are about five years old. — *New York Times*

Directions

The Boy Scouts' *Handbook for Boys*, Johnson's *First Aid Manual*, a cookbook, or an automobile instruction book is of no value to a person who can't read it, understand it, and carry out the directions.

How to Read Directions

1. Read each sentence thoroughly. Study a hard sentence until you know what it means.
2. Look up new words.
3. As you read, picture yourself carrying out the directions.
4. Think why each act explained is important.

Practice 4

Read the following directions and answer the questions at the end:

FAINTING [1]

Fainting and shock resemble each other closely and are often confused. Shock usually follows severe injuries, is lasting and serious. Fainting is transitory. Shock is seldom accompanied by complete unconsciousness.

Fainting usually requires little treatment, unless the heart is diseased or very weak. Lay the fainting person out flat at once, with the head lower than the body. See that he has plenty of fresh air to breathe. Keep bystanders away.

Remove or loosen heavy wraps, tight collars, corsets, and waistbands. Gently dab water upon the face, and hold smelling salts, spirits of camphor or ammonia under the nostrils, without touching them. Do not scald the nose of the patient by holding these applications too close or using them too long. Elevate and rub the limbs of the patient toward the body to quicken the circulation. If the person is slow in reviving, apply gentle heat to the pit of the stomach. After recovery, give a cup of hot tea or coffee, or a teaspoonful of aromatic spirits of ammonia in half a cup of water. Do not let the patient assume an erect position for some time after fainting. To prevent fainting bend the head between the knees, but do not resort to this after fainting has taken place. Have the patient see a physician.

[1] From Johnson's *First Aid Manual*, tenth revised edition, copyrighted by Johnson and Johnson, New Brunswick, New Jersey.

Thought Questions

1. How do fainting and shock differ?
2. Why should the head of a fainting person be lower than the body?
3. Why should tight clothes be removed or loosened?
4. Of what use is hot tea or coffee or aromatic spirits of ammonia after recovery?
5. Why should one bend the head between the knees to prevent fainting?
6. Why should the patient see a physician?
7. Explain the meaning of *confused, transitory, accompanied, unconsciousness, reviving,* and *elevate.*
8. Explain fully how to treat a person who has fainted.

Practice 5

Explain clearly and completely the directions on pages 44, 97, and 104.

Letters

Failure to read a letter carefully and to understand it may lead to the losing of dollars or a friend.

Practice 6

Read the following letter and answer these two questions about it:

1. What mistakes did the store make?
2. How is it correcting the mistakes?

Dear Madam:

We apologize for the unsatisfactory handling we gave your order for a set of glass bowls.

Instructions were issued to call for the cheese dish we sent to you by mistake, and a credit of $.57 for it will be applied to your account.

Since the bowl set at $.69 was also charged against your

account, and you are not interested in having it delivered now, we are applying credit to offset this charge.

Please let us have another opportunity to serve you in a more satisfactory manner.

Yours very truly,

Memorizing

You admire a person who frequently quotes gems of poetry and prose to illustrate his points. Because young minds remember better than old ones, you should in junior and senior high school store away in your memory poems and prose which you will always enjoy.

There are usually at least two ways to do a job — a right and a wrong. Memorizing is no exception. A boy or girl who learns to memorize the right way saves time and remembers longer.

BARTER[1]

Life has loveliness to sell —
All beautiful and splendid things,
Blue waves whitened on a cliff,
Climbing fire that sways and sings,
And children's faces looking up
Holding wonder like a cup.

Life has loveliness to sell —
Music like a curve of gold,
Scent of pine trees in the rain,
Eyes that love you, arms that hold,
And for your spirit's still delight,
Holy thoughts that star the night.

Spend all you have for loveliness,
Buy it and never count the cost;

[1] From *Love Songs*. Reprinted by permission of The Macmillan Company, publishers.

For one white singing hour of peace
Count many a year of strife well lost,
And for a breath of ecstasy
Give all you have been or could be.

— Sara Teasdale

How to Memorize a Poem

1. Understand and see before memorizing. Find out what the poem means. Use your dictionary. Think. Use your imagination. See the pictures the poet has painted.

> **barter** — trade or exchange of one article for another
> **ecstasy** — overmastering joy; rapture

a. What pictures do you see when you read the first and second stanzas?
b. What does the first line mean? The last line of the first stanza? The first line of the third stanza?
c. When do blue waves whiten?
d. Have you ever heard the singing of a fire? Have you smelled the scent of pine trees in the rain? When?
e. With what does the poet compare music? Holy thoughts?
f. What do the last two lines mean?
g. What is the central thought of the poem? [Enjoy the beauties around you, and spend your time, energy, and money in finding other lovely things.]
h. What places that you know does the poem suggest to you?
i. What other bits of loveliness have you bought from life?

2. Read the poem aloud, getting and giving the thought, the pictures, and the feeling.

3. Make a simple outline of the poem. Memorize this outline.

Loveliness for sale
  Waves
  Fire
  Children's faces
  Music
  Pine trees
  Eyes and arms
  Holy thoughts
Spending for loveliness
  Hour of peace
  Breath of ecstasy

4. Answer these questions in the words of the poet —

a. What does the poet say about waves? Fire? Children's faces? Music? Pine trees? Eyes and arms? Holy thoughts?

b. How does Sara Teasdale say, "Be willing to fight a long time for an hour of peace"?

c. How does the poet say, "For a moment of great happiness give everything you have or hope to have"?

d. What is the first line of each stanza?

5. Notice the rhyme of each stanza: lines 2 and 4 (*things, sings*); and 5 and 6 (*up, cup*).

6. After reading the poem again, close your book and repeat as much as you can recall. Do not memorize a stanza at a time. When necessary, open your book to find what comes next. Then run through the poem in the same way a number of times until you rarely need to open your book. As you recite, think, see, and feel.

7. For three or four days recite the poem occasionally. Then at longer intervals review it.

Practice 7

Memorize a poem assigned by your teacher. Save time and remember longer by memorizing in the way just explained.

JUNIOR ENGLISH IN ACTION

Book One

Part II — The Sentence and the Word

UNIT 9

SUBJECT AND VERB

Sentence

Which of these groups of words express complete thoughts?

1. The Tigers *hit* the ball hard.
2. Archery *grows* in popularity each year.
3. New York *is* the greatest manufacturing city in America.
4. Eight hits and four runs.
5. The popularity of archery.
6. The greatest manufacturing city in America.

Numbers 1, 2, and 3 are sentences, because they express complete thoughts. In each the italicized word makes a statement (tells something) about a person, a place, or a thing. In 4, 5, and 6 we do not know what the thoughts of the writer are. These groups of words do not express complete thoughts, do not make statements, do not say anything, and are therefore not sentences.

A sentence is a group of words expressing a complete thought.

Every sentence has a subject and a predicate.

Verb or Simple Predicate

Which word in each sentence makes a statement about a person, a place, or a thing?

1. Then his face brightened.

Brightened makes a statement about his face.

2. The flames leaped higher and higher.
Leaped makes a statement about the flames.

3. The two boys fairly flew into their clothes.
Flew makes a statement about the boys.

Which word in each sentence asks a question?

4. Is that your hat?
Is asks about the hat.

5. Are the boys ready for breakfast?
Are asks about the boys.

Which word in each sentence gives a command?

6. Come here at once.
Come tells you to do something.

7. Capitalize the first word of a sentence.
Capitalize tells you to do something.

These words which make statements about persons, places, or things, ask questions, or give commands are the simple predicates, or verbs, of the sentences.

The simple predicate, or verb, makes a statement, asks a question, or gives a command.

Practice 1

What is the verb in each sentence?

1. The wind howled.
2. Coal burns.
3. Towser barks every night.
4. Arthur speaks clearly.
5. Ned studies hard.
6. Many birds fly south in the fall.

SUBJECT AND VERB

7. The airplane landed in a field of corn.
8. Few people were on the streets.
9. Is that towhead your brother?
10. Have you a knife?
11. What is your answer?
12. Watch for automobiles.
13. Speak distinctly.
14. Well, figure that out for yourself.
15. Many good deeds he did in his time.

Two-Word Verbs

What are the verbs in these sentences?

1. St. Paul and Minneapolis are called the Twin Cities.
Are called is a two-word verb.

2. One should eat fruit and greens every day.
Should eat is a two-word verb.

3. We shall spend the night in Bennington.
Shall spend is a two-word verb.

4. Jamestown, Virginia, was founded in 1607.
Was founded is a two-word verb.

The first word of a two-word verb is: *is* (*be, am, are, was, were*), *have, had, do, did, may, can, might, could, must, shall, will, should,* or *would*.

Practice 2

Find the two-word verb in each sentence:

1. Poinsettias are grown in Florida.
2. The telegraph was invented by Samuel Morse.
3. Paul Revere was born in Boston in 1735.
4. You should sleep with the windows of your bedroom open.

5. One should breathe through his nose.

6. Many cattle are pastured on the plains of Oklahoma and Texas.

7. The District of Columbia is located between Maryland and Virginia.

Courtesy Atchison, Topeka, and Santa Fe Railway
PUPILS OF PEOPLE'S VALLEY SCHOOL NEAR KIRKLAND, ARIZONA

8. From the first, Captain John Smith had been the natural leader of the Virginia colony.

9. A boy should have energy and courage.

10. Washington had brought hope to every patriot heart.

11. During Jefferson's administration Louisiana was purchased.

12. Every scout must report in front of the mess hall promptly at eight-fifteen.

13. The bus was waiting on the narrow mountain road.
14. Of course the boys will help with the work.
15. We'll have supper ready about six.

Practice 3

By adding two or more words complete each sentence. Use a two-word verb and draw a line under it.

1. The birds
2. Henry Ford
3. The grass
4. Our school
5. Lindbergh
6. An airplane
7. My father
8. The old horse
9. The kite
10. The old bear
11. Our team
12. Chicago

Separated Verbs

Sometimes one or more words separate the two parts of a verb.

What is the verb in each sentence?

1. The defeat did not discourage Andy.

Did discourage is the verb.

2. I will surely be ready at eight o'clock.

Will be is the verb.

3. Mystery stories do not always appeal to our feelings.

Do appeal is the verb.

Practice 4

Find the two-word verb in each sentence:

1. You have already said too much.
2. You can easily arrive before dark.
3. Dorothy has just started to school.
4. Mother was busily packing the lunch.
5. The house was almost hidden by the trees.
6. I have never seen the capital of the United States.

7. The Great Lakes are now used for the transportation of freight.
8. Fishing off Newfoundland is often interrupted by storms.
9. Garry Haven didn't look stupid.
10. Cuba was cruelly treated by Spain.
11. The buckwheat cakes did not last long.
12. I could easily climb Whiteface in five hours.
13. Without dogs the tribes of the North would doubtless perish.
14. Jim didn't answer.
15. Flyers have often gone to the aid of snow-bound miners.

Verbs in Questions

What is the verb in each sentence?

1. The calf has stuck its nose through the fence.
2. Has the calf stuck its nose through the fence?

In both sentences *has stuck* is the verb. In the question the two words of the verb are separated.

3. Tom is climbing Quaker Mountain today.
4. Is Tom climbing Quaker Mountain today?

In both sentences *is climbing* is the verb.

5. Uncle Joe has always spent his summers in Keene Valley.
6. Has Uncle Joe always spent his summers in Keene Valley?

In both sentences *has spent* is the verb.

In every question the two words of the verb are separated.

Practice 5

Change each statement to a question. Do not add or omit any word in the sentence. Just rearrange the words and put a question mark at the end. Then draw a line under the two-word verb in each question.

1. The hall was filled.
2. Edna has waited for an hour.
3. It was getting dark.
4. The Mississippi is called the Father of Waters.
5. Fred is enjoying his summer at camp.
6. The green turtle is used for soup.
7. Archie is going to the Cornell-Princeton game.
8. The people in Syria are noted for their hospitality.
9. California has charmed many Eastern visitors.
10. A child should drink a glass of milk at every meal.
11. Ted's voice was raised vigorously in every song.
12. The bus will be ready at eight-thirty sharp.
13. Ed Sloane has planned a four days' bicycle trip.
14. Herbert and Ben are going on a canoe trip.
15. The "Singing Tower" is considered one of the beautiful sights of Florida.

Verbs of Three Words

Some verbs are made up of three words.

1. Governor Wilson *has been living* at the Biltmore Hotel for about a year.
2. I *couldn't have wished* for a happier vacation.
3. All summer the carpenters *have been working* hard on the new schoolhouse.

Notice that *at*, *n't*, *for*, *hard*, and *on* are not parts of the verbs.

How can we know a verb when we meet it? A good way is to ask it this question: "Have you an *ing* form?" If the answer is "Yes," it is, as a rule, a verb; if "No," it is not a verb.

The *ing* forms of the verbs *has* and *been* in sentence 1 above are *having* and *being*. *Living* is the *ing* form of the verb *live*. "Atting," "n'tting," "forring," "hard-ing," and "onning" are nonsense; hence *at, n't, for, hard,* and *on* are not verbs.

Exceptions. Sometimes the first word of a two- or three-word verb does not have an *ing* form: *may, can, might, could, must, shall, will, should, would.*

Practice 6

On a piece of paper write the numbers 1 to 25. After each number write the verb in the sentence. The verb may be one word, two words, or three words.

1. Someone came in hurriedly.
2. Mosquitoes always breed in water.
3. Did Otis win the race?
4. Where does cotton grow?
5. I scrambled to my feet.
6. We may not return till next week.
7. I couldn't believe my eyes.
8. At six o'clock next morning we were on our way.
9. I could have answered that question.
10. How long have you been living in Portland?
11. How did you tear your coat, Lewis?
12. Pikes Peak is in the central part of Colorado.
13. Why didn't you start sooner?
14. Some day fog will be conquered for the aviator.
15. Static has been called radio's worst enemy.
16. At least two kinds of vegetables should be eaten every day.
17. Drink a glass of water before breakfast.
18. Ted Baxter could always be counted on in a game.
19. There was firmness about his big, good-humored mouth.
20. Some of you boys might have stirred yourselves a little more.
21. The gold medal will not be awarded this year.
22. The British were amazed at Washington's daring feat.
23. The medals will be presented on Friday.

Girl Scouts Raising Old Glory

Publishers' Photo Service

24. Ben Wheeler had been looking forward for some time to the bicycle trip.

25. The victory has been won at a heavy cost.

Simple Subject

In each sentence what word names the person, place, or thing spoken of?

1. Campers often find shelter in a hollow tree.

Find is the verb. *Campers* answers the question "Who or what *find?*" and is the subject of the sentence.

2. With this machine two hundred men can do the work of two thousand.

Can do is the verb. *Men* answers the question "Who or what *can do?*" and is the subject of the sentence.

3. Here's a new puzzle.

The verb is *'s*. *Puzzle* answers the question "Who or what *'s* (is)?" and is the subject of the sentence.

4. Until two years ago all packing in a New York food factory was done by hand.

Was done is the verb. *Packing*, the subject, answers the question "Who or what *was done?*"

One can easily find the subject in a question by writing the question as if it were a statement and then asking "Who or what?"

(Question) Are you ready? (Statement) You are ready.

Are is the verb. *You*, the subject, answers the question "Who or what *are?*"

(Question) What is the Gulf Stream? (Statement) The Gulf Stream is what.

Is is the verb. *Gulf Stream,* the subject, answers the question "Who or what *is?*"

In commands and requests the subject is commonly omitted.

"Close the door" means "(You) close the door."
"Look again over the valley" means "(You) look again over the valley."

You understood is the subject of both sentences.

The simple subject names the person, place, or thing spoken of.

Practice 7

Copy these sentences. In each sentence draw one line under the subject and two lines under the verb.

1. We certainly felt cheap.
2. Then a strange thing happened.
3. England is famous for its delicious mutton.
4. In England the country is like a garden.
5. For what goods is Paris famous?
6. Icebergs are seldom seen south of the Banks of Newfoundland.
7. How fresh the air is!
8. Behind the village lay the long dark mountain.
9. At the sound of the shot the white pig squealed.
10. Where are the elephants?
11. Some of the turns the wagon made on two wheels.
12. At that moment Bill spied the old partridge.
13. For just a minute nobody moved.
14. The chief pastures of Switzerland are high up in the mountains.
15. We fished along without much luck till about eleven o'clock.
16. For an instant Ben did not get the idea.
17. Art is important in the design of cars.
18. Here was a difficulty at the very start.

19. A ruddy glow danced on the inner wall of the room.
20. Why aren't you in school today?
21. See that man with the white smock over his clothes!
22. In Edinburgh on Sunday the streets are almost deserted.
23. What is a glacier?
24. Over on the bench sat an extremely unhappy fellow.
25. The first pitch whizzed by the outside corner of the plate.

Introductory Word *There*

What is the subject of each sentence?

1. There were four airplanes above us.

Airplanes, the subject, answers the question "Who or what *were?*"

2. There was a bulldog in the yard.

Bulldog, the subject, answers the question "Who or what *was?*"

Sentences beginning with *there* are turned around. The verb comes before the subject. *There* is never the subject. No sentence tells about *there*.

A good way to find the subject and the verb is to omit *there* and rearrange the other words.

1. Four airplanes were above us.
2. A bulldog was in the yard.

Practice 8

Copy these sentences. Draw one line under each simple subject and two lines under each verb.

1. There was no sound.
2. There was no water in the bucket.
3. There are bookcases on both sides of the hall.
4. There was much excitement around the house.
5. There floated the full moon in all her glory.

SUBJECT AND VERB 163

6. There was a report like a cannon shot.
7. There were three men in the rear seat.
8. There was a moan close beside them.
9. There are many miles of swamp land in our country.
10. At present there are but two herds of wild bison in existence.

Ewing Galloway

A Monkey with Two Adopted Kittens

Practice 9

Write six good sentences about the pictures on pages 154, 159, and 163. Have only one verb in each sentence.

In each sentence draw one line under the subject and two lines under the verb.

Mastery Test 1A — Subject and Verb

Copy these sentences. In each sentence draw a line under the subject word and two lines under the verb. The verb may be one word, two words, or three words.

1. In Berlin a dog must not bark on the streets after ten o'clock in the evening.
2. Andover won the game by a score of 6 to 3.
3. The Edgeville pitcher had been wild.
4. Against the strongest of teams Perry had won sixteen games.
5. How far is San Francisco from New York?
6. There were not many amusements in those days.
7. What four great rivers rise in the Swiss mountains?
8. Then came a stroke of good luck.
9. The potato might be called the bread food of Ireland.
10. Still Baxter looked off into space.

Mastery Test 1B — Subject and Verb

Copy these sentences. In each sentence draw a line under the subject word and two lines under the verb. The verb may be one word, two words, or three words.

1. I have just had the biggest thrill of my life.
2. In northern Norway the sun shines at midnight.
3. The smile was gone from Wally's face now.
4. This time the ball was headed straight over the plate.
5. Why is Switzerland called the playground of Europe?
6. That night there were parsnips for dinner.
7. Have you read about William Tell?
8. Then there burst forth a loud applause.
9. Barbara has been elected president of the Better English Club.
10. On Saturday Jack Coburn was out of the line-up.

UNIT 10

THE PARTS OF SPEECH

If you were building a bird house or a dog kennel, you would use a number of kinds of tools — hammer, saw, plane, square. When you write or speak, you likewise use a number of kinds of word tools. Although there are three hundred thousand words in our language, all belong in eight groups or classes called the "parts of speech."

A hammer is used for pounding; a saw, for sawing. So each kind of word has a particular work to do in the sentence. A verb, you have learned, makes a sentence by saying something, asking something, or giving a command.

Remember that words are grouped according to their use — that is, according to the work they do in sentences.

Nouns

A noun is a name. Nouns name —

Persons — *pupil, teacher, Laura, Franklin D. Roosevelt*
Animals — *rabbit, chipmunk, bear*
Places — *Lexington, Milwaukee*
Things we can see and touch — *table, dish, map*
Things we can't see or touch — *kindness, justice, depth, laughter, sickness, happiness, doubt*
Groups of persons or things — *army, flock, herd, class, school, fleet, committee*

Practice 1

1. Add two names to each group given above.
2. Name ten objects in your home.
3. Name ten kinds of games.
4. Name ten objects in your schoolroom.
5. Name ten things you saw on your way to school.

Game — Nouns

1. In class your teacher will give you three minutes in which to write nouns beginning with *a* or *b* or *c*. The pupil who writes the longest list will be declared the winner if every word is a noun. If any word on the list is not a name, that list will not be totaled at all.

You may prepare for this game by glancing through the *a*, the *b*, and the *c* of your dictionary and noticing the words with *n.* (noun) after them.

2. Try this game again with *m* or *s* or *t*.

Where did you rank in your class in each game?

Practice 2

In each sentence make a list of the nouns. The number in parenthesis shows how many nouns there are in the sentence.

1. From trees we obtain fruit, lumber, paper, and chemicals. (5)
2. Grains include wheat, barley, oats, and rye. (5)
3. My father owns a farm with horses and cattle and also a house in town. (6)
4. During the winter most of our outdoor sports are played on the ice. (3)
5. You will need a short, circular skirt of thick, smooth wool, a heavy sweater, woolen mittens, scarf, and hat. (6)
6. For several hours the group rode in a mass. (3)

7. The men wear blue smocks, brown trousers, and little misshapen caps; the women are bareheaded and wear little coats and large full skirts. (7)

8. The place for happiness, peace, rest, health, and genuine leisure is the country. (7)

9. Surprise, sorrow, and anger were mixed in Arthur's face. (5)

10. Because of his intelligence and kindness Harold was elected president of his class. (5)

Nouns and Verbs

When an apple is used for apple pie, apple sauce, apple pudding, or apple tart, it changes its name to pie, sauce, pudding, tart. In the same way words change their names if used in different ways. Many words are used as both verbs and nouns.

What is the part of speech of the italicized word in each sentence?

1. Never throw a *stone* at a bird.

Stone names an object and is a noun.

2. Never *stone* a bird.

Stone gives a command and is a verb.

3. May I have a *drink?*

Drink is a noun.

4. I *drink* milk for lunch every day.

Drink makes a statement and is a verb.

Practice 3

Tell the part of speech of each italicized word:

1. I *wish* to see your father.
2. What is your *wish?*
3. There isn't a *drop* in the bucket.

4. Don't *drop* the hammer.
5. Mr. Stilwell will *paper* my bedroom.
6. What did you see in the *paper?*
7. *Right* is stronger than might.
8. Will you *right* that wrong?
9. Will you *play* with me?
10. Let us go to see a *play.*
11. Did you *drink* the milk?
12. May I get a *drink?*
13. Why don't you kill that *fly?*
14. We shall *fly* to Chicago.

Courtesy German Tourist Information Office
GETTING READY FOR A SKI RACE

Practice 4

In sentences of your own use each of the following words (1) as a noun and (2) as a verb:

run	paint	bark	dance	dress
smoke	row	cook	stick	suit

Pronouns

Can you improve this retelling of a story?

1. *Without Pronouns*

Quentin Roosevelt called *Quentin's* gang to the rail of the White House roof and laid *Quentin's* plan before the *gang*. The *plan* was accepted, and the *gang* went to work. The *gang* first rolled a great snowball. The *gang* then placed the *snowball* on the ledge at the edge of the roof. After taking careful aim Quentin gave the snowball a push. Down the *snowball* sped, and smack, right on a guard's head the *snowball* landed. The guard did not utter a sound when the *guard* fell. The boys thought the *boys* had killed the *guard*.

Notice the constant repetition of words. Of course you don't write or speak like this. The italicized nouns are blots on the story, however interesting it may be. Let us get rid of them. This is the way a boy told the story to his class.

2. *With Pronouns*

Quentin Roosevelt called *his* gang to the rail of the White House roof and laid *his* plan before *them*. *It* was accepted, and *they* went to work. *They* first rolled a great snowball. *They* then placed *it* on the ledge of the roof. After taking careful aim Quentin gave the snowball a push. Down *it* sped, and smack, right on a guard's head *it* landed. The guard did not utter a sound when *he* fell. The boys thought *they* had killed *him*.

A pronoun is a word used in place of a noun. The italicized pronouns in number 2 are used in place of the italicized nouns in number 1. *Pronoun* means *for a noun*.

Pronouns save our time and make our sentences more pleasing.

Practice 5

Make each of these sentences more pleasing by using a pronoun in place of one of the nouns:

1. Quentin Roosevelt, like most boys of Quentin's age, was often in trouble.
2. Quentin's father often got Quentin out of trouble.
3. When the President saw the fallen guard, the President ordered the boys to come down.
4. Quentin was punished for Quentin's mischief.
5. At the age of nineteen Quentin Roosevelt was killed while Quentin was fighting in France.
6. Quentin died for Quentin's country.
7. Miss Adams told the pupils about Miss Adams's trip to England.
8. Barbara had not told anybody that Barbara had sent a telegram.
9. One day Joan and Joan's friends were sitting in the garden.
10. Joan calmly approached Mr. Doumer and began speaking to Mr. Doumer.

What are the pronouns in each sentence?

1. I said to Bill, "Did you see that?"

The pronouns are *I*, *you*, and *that*. *I* is used in place of the name of the speaker; *you*, instead of *Bill;* and *that*, in place of the name of what he saw.

2. Is this your book or mine?

This, *your*, and *mine* are pronouns. *This* is used in place of *book;* *your*, instead of the name of the person spoken to; *mine*, in place of the name of the speaker.

Practice 6

Make a list of the pronouns in the following sentences. If you don't know whether a word is used in place of a noun, turn to the lists on pages 274 and 282. The number after each sentence shows how many pronouns there are in the sentence.

1. Did you expect him? (2)
2. "I wouldn't have believed it," he said slowly. (3)
3. I did not say that, my son. (3)
4. You'll ride with us in our car. (3)
5. I don't know them by name. (2)
6. He was there to meet me. (2)
7. That's the story he told us. (3)
8. Behind him we were standing quietly. (2)
9. After this our markets were overstocked with blue pigeons; they sold for fifty or sixty cents a pair. (3)
10. He and Ted could get in there, drag a bookcase over to shield them, and from behind it ward off an attack with their bats. (4)
11. May we have our next meeting in your home? (3)
12. My brother bought three tickets for our concert. (2)

Modifiers

Compare numbers 1 and 2, also 3 and 4:

1. Tree
2. That big shaggy elm tree
3. House
4. The tiny white house beside the post office

Tree means any tree in the world; *house*, any house. The modifiers *that, big, shaggy, elm* change the meaning from any tree to a particular one. Likewise the modifiers *the, tiny, white, beside the post office* add to the meaning of *house*.

A modifier changes the meaning of the word to which it is attached.

A modifier of a noun commonly answers one of the questions under *subject;* a modifier of a verb, one of the questions under *verb*.

172 JUNIOR ENGLISH IN ACTION

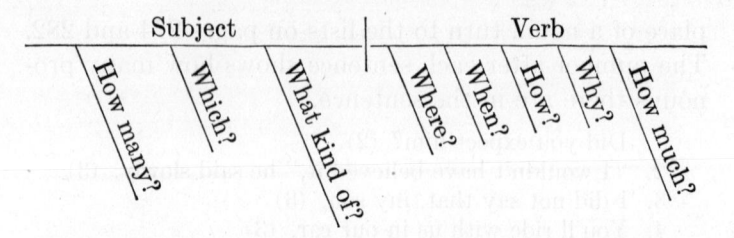

```
         Subject                    |        Verb
How many? / Which? / What kind of?  |  Where? / When? / How? / Why? / How much?
```

What are the modifiers in sentences 1 and 2?

1. That big dog can run fast.
2. My dear grandmother came yesterday.

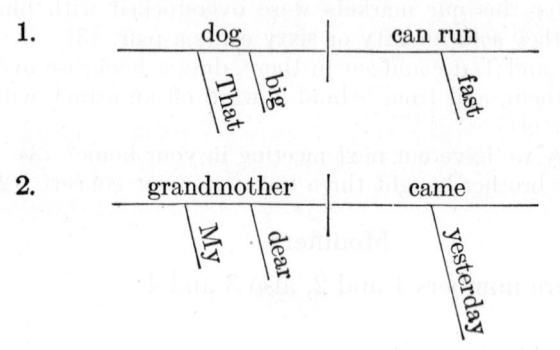

1.   dog | can run
      \That \big   \fast

2.   grandmother | came
      \My \dear   \yesterday

Adjectives

An adjective is a word that modifies a noun or a pronoun.

ADJECTIVES		ADJECTIVES	
The		the	
Two		six	
Those		many	
Several	boys picked	red	apples
Tiny		yellow	
Tall		green	
Bright		large	
Lively		small	

THE PARTS OF SPEECH

The nouns *boys* and *apples* include all the boys and apples in the world. The adjectives tell which boys and apples are meant. *The* and *those* answer the question "Which?" *Tiny, tall, bright, lively, red, yellow, green, large,* and *small* answer the question "What kind of?" *Two, several, six,* and *many* answer the question "How many?"

An adjective usually answers one of these questions: "What kind of?" "Which?" "How many?"

Practice 7

Find the adjectives and tell what each modifies. The figure in parenthesis tells how many adjectives there are in the sentence.

1. His greatest friend is an Irish wolf-hound. (3) [*The, a,* and *an* are adjectives.]
2. The cement industry has had a rapid growth. (4)
3. This plant grows in shady places in damp woods. (3)
4. For thirty long minutes we waited for our tardy friends. (3)
5. The wide, marshy brook was edged with yellow cowslips. (4)
6. A flat country near the sea may have many swamps. (4)
7. Houston has brought the Gulf of Mexico to her door by a fifty-mile channel for ships. (3)
8. The palace was a dreary old black castle on a grimy street of a dull town. (9)
9. Late that afternoon, wet, cold, and hungry, we stopped at a tiny hut in the dense woods. (8)
10. The first person in this unusual parade, a tall, skinny man, wore rusty armor. (8)

Practice 8

In a newspaper or a magazine find twenty adjectives. Copy the sentences. Underscore all adjectives.

Game — Adjectives

Two teams, the Cubs and the Tigers, stand. The first pupil of the Cubs selects one of the following nouns and gives an adjective to modify it — for example, *girl, lively*. The first pupil on the Tigers gives another adjective to modify *girl;* the second on the Cubs, still another; and so on. If a pupil repeats an adjective already given or can't give an adjective to modify *girl*, he sits down, and the next pupil on the other side has a chance. After two have failed on *girl* and sat down, the next pupil on the opposite side selects another noun and gives an adjective.

The team having the larger number standing at the end is the winner.

boy	hat	eyes	face	house
girl	suit	nose	hands	book
dog	shoes	mouth	voice	letter
horse	river	hair	tree	room

Practice 9

In two or more sentences describe the picture on page 168. Draw a line under every adjective.

In two or more sentences describe the picture on page 175. Draw a line under every adjective.

Pronouns and Adjectives

To find what part of speech a word is, notice what the word does in the sentence. Some words are used as both adjectives and pronouns.

1. May I see *that* book?

That is an adjective, because it modifies *book*.

HAPPY DAYS

Ewing Galloway

2. May I see *that?*

That is used in place of a noun and is a **pronoun**.

3. *Many* were late. [Pronoun.]
4. *Many* boys were late. [Adjective.]

Practice 10

Tell the part of speech of each italicized word:

1. I prefer *this* prize.
2. I prefer *this*.
3. *All* of us like the mountains.
4. We stayed in the mountains *all* summer.
5. *Both* are workers.
6. *Both* boys are workers.
7. *Neither* answer is correct.
8. *Neither* is correct.
9. *One* of my friends told me that story.
10. I have only *one* pencil.
11. *Some* girls aren't ready.
12. *Some* aren't ready.

Adverbs

How are the italicized adverbs used?

1. *Yesterday* I saw a woodpecker.

Yesterday adds to the verb *saw* by telling when.

2. Through the garden he walked *slowly*.

Slowly tells how he walked.

3. *Where* are you going?

Where modifies the verb *are going*.

4. The minutes passed *very rapidly*.

Rapidly modifies the verb *passed*. *Very* modifies the adverb *rapidly*.

5. That stick is *perfectly* straight.

Perfectly modifies the adjective *straight*.

An adverb is a word that modifies a verb, an adjective, or an adverb.

Many adverbs end in *ly: rapidly, perfectly, fiercely*.

Usually an adverb answers one of these questions: "How much?" "When?" "Where?" "How?"

When?	1. I can go swimming *tomorrow*.
	2. Can't you go *now?*
Where?	1. I looked *everywhere* for my book.
	2. *Here* it is.
How?	1. Ruth speaks *clearly*.
	2. Doris dances *gracefully*.
How much?	1. Father is *very* tired this evening.
	2. That hat is *too* large for me.

Practice 11

Find the adverbs and tell what word each modifies:

1. His father still slept. (1)
2. She glanced at her watch anxiously. (1)
3. When will you be ready? (1)
4. He jumped out hastily and paid the fare. (2)
5. The month dragged by very slowly. (3)
6. They were watching her closely. (1)
7. Soon the sea was breaking over us. (1)
8. I am not too tired for a game of handball. (2)
9. Topsy turned around and came back to us. (2)
10. No team ever fought more fiercely or more stubbornly. (5)

Practice 12

Fill each blank with an adverb:

1. Mr. Brandt walked —— down Main Street.
2. That statement is not —— true.

3. I looked more —— at the caterpillar.
4. Archie worked —— all forenoon.
5. A submarine must be manned by —— trained experts.
6. Wilkins described quite —— how such a ship would work.
7. Laura talks ——.
8. Jane writes ——.
9. Pinky Brown handled his small boat ——.
10. Harold studies English ——.

Practice 13

Copy the following sentences. Draw a line under an adjective and two lines under an adverb. With a line and an arrow show what word each adjective and each adverb modifies.

MODEL

Sometimes I come upon a story about real people.

If an adverb modifies a two-word verb, draw the line and arrow to the last word of the verb.

The clock will soon strike.

1. Luke played his new position well. (1 adj.; 1 adv.)
2. The two boys raced madly down the street. (3 adj.; 1 adv.)
3. Buy some good apples today. (2 adj.; 1 adv.)
4. Jimmy had never thought of such a thing. (2 adj.; 1 adv.)
5. You probably know the story of the three black bears. (4 adj.; 1 adv.)
6. That word is not spelled correctly. (1 adj.; 2 adv.)
7. Then Gerald played a piano solo. (2 adj.; 1 adv.)
8. There she was in a big chair in the corner. (3 adj.; 1 adv.)

9. Teddy picked his way very carefully between the scrubby little trees. (3 adj.; 2 adv.)

10. Yesterday the soft air was filled with robin notes and bluebird calls. (4 adj.; 1 adv.)

11. We waited patiently for the signal. (1 adj.; 1 adv.)

Prepositions

Some little words like *in, under, beside, behind, into, from,* and *around* are so important that a change of one of them changes the meaning of the whole sentence.

1. Harry is *in* the car.
2. Harry is *under* the car.
3. Harry is *behind* the car.
4. Harry is *beside* the car.

Car is a noun. *In, under, behind,* and *beside* join the noun *car* with the verb *is*. These little joining words have a big name — preposition.

A preposition is a word that shows the relation of the noun or pronoun following it to some other word.

The noun or pronoun after the preposition is the object of the preposition.

In the car, under the car, behind the car, and *beside the car* are prepositional phrases. **A prepositional phrase is made up of a preposition, its object, and sometimes modifiers.**

1. The horse ran *into* the barn.
2. The horse ran *from* the barn.
3. The horse ran *around* the barn.
4. The horse ran *behind* the barn.

Into, from, around, and *behind* are prepositions joining *barn* and *ran*. *Barn* is the object. *Into the barn, from the barn, around the barn,* and *behind the barn* are prepositional phrases.

What words in these sentences are prepositions? What is the object of each preposition? What are the prepositional phrases?

1. We are near land.

Near is the preposition. The noun *land* is its object. *Near land* is the prepositional phrase.

2. I couldn't think of a better one at the moment.

Of is a preposition. The pronoun *one* is its object. *Of a better one* is a prepositional phrase.

At is a preposition. The noun *moment* is its object. *At the moment* is a prepositional phrase.

3. You would have liked that trip into the mountains.

Into is the preposition. The noun *mountains* is its object. *Into the mountains* is the prepositional phrase.

Practice 14

The italicized words are prepositions. What is the object of each preposition?

A scientist *during* a talk *to* his class said, "Now I'll show you this frog *in* my pocket." Then he reached *into* his pocket and pulled *from* it a ham sandwich. He looked puzzled *for* a minute, thought hard, and said *to* himself, "I don't understand this; I distinctly remember eating my lunch."

Practice 15

In each sentence what is the preposition? Its object? The prepositional phrase?

1. Many alligators are killed for their skins.
2. The polar bear is found in the arctic regions.
3. Wheeling is the largest city in West Virginia.
4. The western coast of the United States has few good harbors.

THE PARTS OF SPEECH

5. Gerald lives in Louisville.
6. Tulsa is the center of a rich oil district.
7. *Robinson Crusoe* was written by Defoe.
8. How many seasons are there in the year?
9. Beside me stood Fred.
10. The tears streamed down Ted's cheeks.
11. I am a great collector of stamps.
12. Up the hill we went together.
13. Among the flock was a young gander.
14. For an instant the eagle watched the swans.
15. A submarine is not blocked by ice.
16. Keep yourself in good physical condition.
17. On Christmas Eve Washington and his men crossed the Delaware.
18. The news of Amelia Earhart's brave deed thrilled the world.
19. The Pilgrims set sail in the gallant little *Mayflower*.

Practice 16

Each of the following sentences has two or more prepositional phrases. The number in parenthesis shows how many. Find the prepositional phrases. On your paper draw one line under the preposition and two under the object.

MODEL FOR WRITTEN WORK

One of these giant bears will eat about a hundred pounds of salmon during a single night's feasting. (4)

of these giant bears

about a hundred pounds

of salmon

during a single night's feasting

1. A large part of our tea comes from Ceylon. (2)
2. The bay was filled with ships of every kind. (2)
3. Bill Jenkins dashed into the locker-room of the gymnasium. (2)

4. In the heat of the contest Luke forgot his lameness. (2)
5. The man looked at him in surprise. (2)
6. Were you born with an ear for music? (2)
7. Above the noise of the motor came a faint song through the window. (3)
8. On Saturday afternoon we went down to the beach for clams. (3)
9. In many of Stevenson's books we find his love for the ocean. (3)
10. Roots of plants often grow into the cracks of rocks in their search for water. (5)

Beginning Sentences with Prepositions

Many boys and girls begin every sentence with the subject. Chocolate cake is good, but how would you like to have chocolate cake for breakfast, lunch, and dinner three hundred sixty-five days in the year? Any kind of sameness is tiresome. We all like variety.

One way to vary our sentences is by starting some of them with prepositions. Notice these sentences beginning with prepositional phrases:

1. *About their fires* the Indian chiefs planned their wars.
2. *After some discussion* an agreement was reached.
3. *Through the long spring evening* we listened to the frogs and crickets.

Practice 17

Rewrite each sentence and place a preposition at the beginning:

MODELS

1. A blinding snowstorm blew *through the deep valley.*
Through the deep valley blew a blinding snowstorm.

2. I hurried home *with a light purse.*
With a light purse I hurried home.

1. I read *Peter and Wendy* after dinner.
2. We reached Tucson in three days.

CANOEING ON LAKE PLACID

Ewing Galloway

3. I haven't seen Betty since last Saturday.
4. I like Marjorie best of all my friends.
5. The stove is in the front of the room.
6. Babe Ruth knocked the ball into the bleachers in the sixth inning.
7. Father and the twins were at the station.
8. Monroe Junior High will play Adams Junior High on Saturday afternoon.
9. Joe Dickson considered himself a hunter at sixteen.
10. An almost perpendicular rock rose above them.
11. Joe waited for a long hour.
12. Edison found study with his mother easy and pleasant.
13. Billy replied politely to all her questions.
14. We all rested after the second set.
15. A boy waved his crutch excitedly in the grandstand.
16. A great roar came from the grandstand.
17. The football sailed into Dick's arms.
18. Dick started up the field.
19. The Washington team made a desperate stand at the ten-yard line.
20. The Wilson infield wobbled a bit in the first inning.

Practice 18

In sentences about the picture on page 183 use five or more of the following words as prepositions. Draw one line under every preposition and two lines under every object of a preposition.

about	around	between	in	through
above	at	beyond	into	to
across	before	by	near	toward
after	behind	during	of	under
against	below	for	on	upon
among	beside	from	over	with

Prepositions and Adverbs

What part of speech is *down* in sentence 1? In sentence 2?

1. Please sit *down*.
2. Don't fall *down* the hill.

A preposition always has an object. In sentence 1, *down* has no object; it is an adverb modifying the verb *sit*. In sentence 2 the preposition *down* joins its object *hill* to the verb *do fall*.

What part of speech is *before* in sentence 1? In sentence 2?

1. I have seen that man *before*. [Adverb — has no object and modifies the verb *have seen*.]
2. I saw Harry *before* the game. [Preposition — joins its object *game* to the verb *saw*.]

Practice 19

Is the italicized word in each sentence an adverb or a preposition? How do you know?

1. Come right *in*.
2. Father is *in* the garage.
3. Keep *off* the grass.
4. Keep *off*.
5. We looked *around*.
6. We walked *around* the lake.
7. We walked *up* the hill.
8. Get *up*.
9. Ralph is going *along*.
10. There are many sheep *along* the road.
11. My clothing was scattered *about*.
12. Look *about* you.

Conjunctions

What do the italicized words do in the sentences?

1. Little Rock is the capital *and* principal city of Arkansas.

And connects the nouns *capital* and *city*.

2. I caught the pig *but* could not hold it.

But connects the predicates *caught the pig* and *could not hold it*.

3. Would you rather live on a farm *or* in a city?

Or connects the prepositional phrases *on a farm* and *in a city*.

4. I've looked it all over, *and* I can't find anything wrong.

And connects *I've looked it all over* and *I can't find anything wrong*.

In these sentences *and, but*, and *or* are conjunctions. **A conjunction connects words or groups of words.** Conjunctions, unlike prepositions, do not have objects.

Learn these conjunctions that are used in pairs:

either......or   both......and
neither......nor   not only......but also

1. Enter *either* through the front door *or* by the outside staircase.
2. *Both* Elmer *and* Grant are going.
3. *Neither* boys *nor* girls should go to work young.
4. Jean is *not only* ignorant *but also* lazy.

Practice 20

Point out the conjunctions:

1. Are you going to study music or art this winter?
2. I should like to visit either the Adirondacks or Canada this summer.
3. Both California and Florida are delightful states for the motorist.
4. Corn is also known as maize and is often called Indian corn.
5. Atlantic City is both a summer and a winter resort.

6. Annapolis is the capital of Maryland and is the seat of the United States Naval Academy.

7. Already one or two bonfires gleamed through the darkness.

8. The snow rolled along the ground but was not drifting high.

9. I was not only tired but also hungry.

10. The ball struck in Andy's palm but bounced out and rolled to the fence.

Interjections

What part of speech is each italicized word?

1. *Oh*, what a shame!
2. *Wow!* Some speed to that snow!
3. *Gee-whiz!* You — you mean ski down that road?
4. *Help!* Look at what's coming!
5. *Ouch!* That hurts.

The interjections *oh, wow, gee-whiz, help,* and *ouch* are not connected grammatically with the rest of the sentences. They are words "thrown in" to express strong or sudden feeling.

An interjection is a word that expresses strong or sudden feeling.

Game — The Same Word as Different Parts of Speech

For the game Right-Down the class is divided into two teams — the Blues and the Reds, for example. The two teams stand facing each other as if for a spelling match. As in a spelling match the sides answer in turn. If a pupil answers correctly, he sits down; if he fails, he remains standing. The team that is seated first or has the smaller number standing at the end is the winner.

Let us call the first two Blues Ruth and Mary, the first two Reds Otis and Ralph. The Blues begin the

game. Ruth selects a word from the following list —
that, for example — uses *that* in a sentence, and tells the
part of speech of *that*. Then she uses *that* in a sentence
as another part of speech, and tells the part of speech.
If the entire answer is correct, Ruth sits down.

Then Otis selects *off*, uses *off* in two sentences as two
different parts of speech, and tells the parts of speech.
If he makes a mistake, he remains standing, and Mary
uses *off* in two sentences and tells the parts of speech.
Ralph's turn comes next.

all	down	lock	play	suit
along	dress	mail	right	that
around	drink	near	row	this
bark	drop	neither	run	up
bear	either	off	sail	walk
before	fast	on	since	warm
behind	fish	one	slow	watch
both	fly	paint	smoke	well
cook	in	paper	stick	wish
dance	jump	pin	stone	work

**To find what part of speech a word is, always ask
yourself the question "What does this word do in the
sentence?"**

Practice 21

Copy the following sentences, omitting a line after
each line you write. Then, using the following abbreviations, tell what part of speech each word is. Write
the abbreviation above the word.

n. — noun
pro. — pronoun
adj. — adjective
adv. — adverb
v. — verb
prep. — preposition
conj. — conjunction
int. — interjection

Model

adj. adj.   n.   v.   adv.   v.   conj.   adv.   v.
All wild geese are well led and strictly governed.

1. Are the banks of the river lined with bushes, flowers, and trees?
2. My mother had a prejudice against ducks and never cooked them.
3. The men did not return at noon but ate their cold lunch in a clump of hazel bushes.
4. The stacks of wheat were often six or eight yards in diameter.
5. The two boys carried lanterns but the road was a rough path through dense forest.
6. Edison dropped his papers and his cap and made a dash for the child.
7. Memphis is the largest cotton market in Tennessee and the most important river port between St. Louis and New Orleans.
8. During the last three generations the prevention and cure of disease have become a science.

Practice 22

Following the directions in Practice 21, tell the part of speech of each word in this anecdote:

ONLY SEVEN

James McNeill Whistler and a friend came upon a very small and very dirty newsboy in a London street. Whistler bought a paper and said, "How long have you been a newsy, my boy?" [*How* is an adverb.]

"Three years, sir," replied the boy.

"How old are you?"

"Seven."

"Oh, you must be older."

"No, sir." [*No* is an adverb.]

"I say, Charley," said Whistler to his friend, "I don't think he could get so dirty in seven years, do you?"

Mastery Test 2A — Parts of Speech

Copy the following sentences, omitting a line after each line you write. Then, using the abbreviations in Practice 21, tell what part of speech each word is. Write the abbreviation above the word. There are fifty words.

On Tuesday afternoon we had just left our history recitation and were having our class elections in our civics class. The teacher called for nominations for president, and one of the bright pupils in the class stood up and said, "I nominate George Washington." The whole class and the teacher laughed.

Mastery Test 2B — Parts of Speech

Copy the following sentences, omitting a line after each line you write. Then, using the abbreviations in Practice 21, tell what part of speech each word is. Write the abbreviation above the word. There are fifty words.

"It certainly is dark along this road. The country is different from the city in the night time," I said to myself. Then I saw strange shadows. A little chill ran up my spine. I heard a queer noise behind me and turned quickly around. There was a young rabbit.

UNIT 11

PARTS OF THE SIMPLE SENTENCE

Predicate Adjective

An adjective generally comes before the word it modifies.

The old chief had *a thin, dark* face.

Sometimes, however, an adjective completes the verb and modifies the subject.

What does each italicized word do in the sentence?

1. The day was *cold*.

The day was is incomplete. The adjective *cold* completes the verb *was* and describes the subject *day*.

2. In the spring the shad fisheries along the Delaware are very *profitable*.

Profitable completes the verb *are* and describes the subject *fisheries*.

3. Marjorie turned *pale*.

Pale completes the verb *turned* and describes the subject *Marjorie*.

4. Why are bones so *strong?*

Strong completes the verb *are* and describes the subject *bones*.

An adjective which completes the predicate and modifies the subject is called a predicate adjective.

Commonly used verbs that take predicate adjectives are: *be (am, is, are, was, were, has been, have been, had* been), become, grow, seem, appear, taste, smell, sound, look, feel.

A verb that joins an adjective, a noun, or a pronoun to the subject is called a linking verb.

The arrow shows how a linking verb joins a predicate adjective to the subject.

1. The wind grew icy.
2. Maude was happy.
3. Her salary is small.

Practice 1

Complete each sentence by adding a predicate adjective to the linking verb:

MODELS

1. The apple tastes ——.
   The apple tastes sour.
2. The baby was ——.
   The baby was healthy.

1. My dog is ——.
2. The flowers are ——.
3. Our house is ——.
4. That rose smells ——.
5. His voice sounds ——.
6. Martha seems ——.
7. Dinner tasted ——.
8. Isabel looked ——.
9. My hands are ——.
10. I am ——.

Practice 2

Find the predicate adjectives in these sentences. What does each predicate adjective do in the sentence?

1. We were hungry.
2. The sky was blue.
3. The game was close.
4. Our car is old.
5. These are not cheap.
6. The girls' new basketball uniforms are pretty.
7. Spain is hot in the summer time.
8. The children were quiet for a long time.
9. The rainfall on the Rocky Mountains is not heavy.

10. The conversation at the table should be pleasant.
11. By this time the snow was deep.
12. The next morning I felt better.
13. The two boys sat silent in the glow of the fire.
14. At fourteen Andrew Jackson was alone in the world.
15. Why is one drowsy after a heavy dinner?

Predicate Nominative

Linking verbs often join nouns and pronouns to the subject. What does each italicized word do in the sentence?

1. My dog is a *collie*.

Collie completes *is* and explains the subject *dog*.

2. Baseball is a popular summer *game*.

Game completes *is* and explains the subject *baseball*. (*A, popular,* and *summer* are modifiers of *game*.)

3. It is *he*.

He completes *is* and explains the subject *it*.

4. A visit to a turpentine grove is a very interesting *experience*.

Experience completes *is* and explains the subject *visit*.

5. Most of the people in Europe in the fifteenth century were *farmers*.

Farmers completes *is* and describes the subject *most*.

The italicized word in each sentence means the same as the subject and tells what the subject is, was, or became.

1. Dog = collie.   4. Visit = experience.
2. Baseball = game.   5. Most = farmers.
3. It = he.

A noun that completes the predicate and explains or describes the subject is called a predicate nominative.

Each picture shows that the predicate nominative refers to the same person or thing as the subject.

1. Johnny Scout is a canoeist.

2. Bill Cook is a baseball player.

Courtesy H. W. Kellogg Company

Practice 3

Complete each sentence with a predicate nominative:

MODELS

1. The commander of the American army in Europe was ——.

The commander of the American army in Europe was General Pershing.

PARTS OF THE SIMPLE SENTENCE 195

2. The Thames is a —— in England.
The Thames is a river in England.

1. The capital of the United States is ——.
2. The Fourth of July is a ——.
3. Longfellow was a ——.
4. Benedict Arnold turned ——.
5. Franklin D. Roosevelt was elected ——.
6. The baby was named ——.
7. One of our greatest living Americans is ——.
8. Mark Twain is the —— of *Tom Sawyer*.

Practice 4

Find the predicate nominatives in these sentences. What does each predicate nominative do in the sentence?

1. Charleston is a city of gardens.
2. The man was a stranger.
3. The first highways were mere trails.
4. Spain was once a world power.
5. Soccer is a game with a great amount of footwork.
6. The usual style of Indian warfare was a surprise attack.
7. It was a moonless night.
8. The jaguar is a stocky animal with a massive head.
9. Foreigners may become citizens of the United States.
10. The inhabitants of ancient Egypt were great builders.
11. For thousands of years man was a hunter.
12. At the age of fifteen Columbus became a sailor.
13. Muscle Shoals is a broad, shallow part of the Tennessee River in northwestern Alabama.
14. Jefferson was elected the third president of the United States.

Practice 5

On one or more of the topics on the next page write ten sentences. Use a predicate adjective or a predicate nominative in each sentence. Draw one line under every predicate adjective and two lines under every predicate nominative.

MODELS

1. Edison's deafness was a great advantage to him in many ways.
2. Standing on the thirty-yard line, James was eager for the kick-off.

1. Games I have played or seen played
2. Camp
3. Summer in the country
4. Fishing
5. Winter sports
6. Heroes I have seen, heard, or read about

Object of a Verb

What does each italicized word do in the sentence?

1. I spread my *bed* on the dry earth.

Bed answers the question "*Spread* what?" (*My* modifies *bed*. The prepositional phrase *on the dry earth* modifies the verb *spread*.)

2. Father put *me* on the horse.

Me answers the question "*Put* whom?"

3. Have you prepared your *homework?*

Homework answers the question "*Have prepared* what?"

4. He waved his *hat* in the moonlight.

Hat answers the question "*Waved* what?"

In each sentence the italicized word or words complete the verb by telling *what* or *whom*. All the verbs — *spread, lifted, have prepared, waved* — express action. In each sentence the subject acts.

PARTS OF THE SIMPLE SENTENCE 197

If the subject acts, a word which answers the question "What?" or "Whom?" after the verb is an object of the verb.

The object of a verb names the receiver or the result of the action. Each picture shows that the object of the verb in the sentence names the receiver of the action.

1. The hunter shot a bear.

Courtesy Canadian Pacific

A GOOD SHOT

2. The boy caught a trout.

Courtesy Canadian Pacific
TROUT FISHING IN LAKE O'HARA

Practice 6

Find the objects of verbs in these sentences:
1. I have a baseball.
2. English boys play cricket.
3. Fire destroys property.
4. Parks provide space for play.
5. The doctor examined me.
6. No one likes selfish people.
7. Trellises improve the appearance of our home.
8. Some people have doubted the story.
9. Pete shrugged his broad shoulders.
10. The two soldiers entered the barn.
11. I roused myself from a sound sleep.
12. The laboratory tests samples of milk.

13. Just then they saw a cloud of dust.
14. The unspoken word never does harm.
15. I filled a bag with camp equipment and supplies.
16. Did you see Commander Byrd's dogs?
17. How many books have you?
18. Loud cries immediately filled the air.
19. In this one garden he has noted one hundred sixteen kinds of birds.
20. Most of them I knew at once.
21. For her birthday my mother received a huge bouquet of beautiful spring flowers.

Practice 7

Write four sentences about the picture on page 206 and five about the picture on page 216. Have an object of a verb in each sentence and draw a line under it.

Predicate Nominative and Object

"Object fever" is a common disease in English classrooms. Without thinking pupils afflicted with it call any word after a verb an object.

What are the differences between the predicate nominative in sentence 1 and the object in sentence 2?

1. Thomas Jefferson became *president*.

(1) *Became* is not a verb of action. (2) *Thomas Jefferson = president*. The subject and the predicate nominative always name the same person or thing.

2. Thomas Jefferson attended *William and Mary College* at Williamsburg, Virginia.

(1) *Attended* is a verb of action. (2) *William and Mary College* is different from *Thomas Jefferson*. The object of a verb, as a rule, does not refer to the same person or thing as the subject.

Practice 8

Copy the following sentences. Draw one line under every object of a verb and two lines under every predicate nominative:

1. Golf is a difficult game.
2. Father plays golf.
3. Ralph knocked the ball over the fence.
4. Ralph is our shortstop.
5. My dog's name is Jerry.
6. Jerry broke his leg.
7. He was always a queer chap.
8. This is a rainy day.
9. I had bought a second-class ticket.
10. A guilty conscience needs no accuser.
11. Newark is the largest city in New Jersey.
12. Vermont produces large quantities of beautiful marble.
13. Rayon has made a great change in the textile business.
14. An honest man is the noblest work of God.
15. America is now the world's largest producer of furs.
16. Find in the dictionary the meaning of *pioneer*.
17. I spied a whole counter of French pastry back there.
18. In 1789 Washington became our first president.
19. How many books have you read this term?
20. Is Marie the president of the Book Club?

Indirect Object

What does each italicized indirect object do in the sentence?

1. I gave *him* some good advice.

Him answers the question "*Gave* to whom?"

2. The bank will lend *us* some money.

Us answers the question "*Will lend* to whom?"

3. I must buy *Mother* some bread.

Mother answers the question "*Must buy* for whom?"

Advice, money, and *bread* are the objects of the verbs, for these words answer the questions "*Gave* what?" "*Will lend* what?" and "*Must buy* what?"

Him, us, and *Mother* are between the verbs and the objects, and name the persons to whom or for whom something is done.

The indirect object tells to or for whom something is done.

What is an easy way to find the indirect object?

1. The salesman offered us a bargain.
2. The salesman offered (to) us a bargain.

As a rule, placing *to* before the indirect object does not change the sense.

1. Mother bought Grace a dress.
2. Mother bought (for) Grace a dress.

After a few verbs, placing *for* before the indirect object does not change the sense.

Practice 9

Find the objects of verbs and the indirect objects:

1. I sold Harold my football.
2. He owes me a dime.
3. Our teacher told us a good story.
4. Give me liberty.
5. I will mail Roland the book tomorrow.
6. I gave Nettie an armful of tulips.
7. Father paid Mr. Penn thirty dollars for the radio.
8. A man's hat in his hand never did him any harm.
9. Why didn't you give Mr. Holmes the message?
10. Did she tell you the joke?
11. Marie brought me some daisies.
12. Mr. Taylor sent us a barrel of apples.

Mastery Test 3A — Predicate Adjective, Predicate Nominative, Object of Verb, Indirect Object

Copy each italicized word on a separate line of your paper. Then place after each word *p.a.* (predicate adjective), *p.n.* (predicate nominative), *o.v.* (object of verb), or *i.o.* (indirect object) to show its use in the sentence.

1. The Ausable River is very *swift*.
2. One day I found a *canoe*.
3. Necessity is the *mother* of invention.
4. Ben gave *me* an *apple*.
5. Fine feathers do not make fine *birds*.
6. The strong man caught the *dog* in his arms.
7. April showers bring *us* May *flowers*.
8. Mother read *us* some *poems*.
9. He was a *prince* among men.
10. A small unkindness is a great *offense*.
11. A fireplace is the *heart* of a forest home.
12. The best preparation for good work tomorrow is good *work* today.
13. After the invention of gunpowder a castle was no longer *safe*.
14. For a number of years Hamlin Garland made his *home* in Wisconsin.
15. A good waiter is always *courteous*.
16. Truthfulness is the *basis* of good character.
17. The whole house was *happy*.

Mastery Test 3B — Predicate Adjective, Predicate Nominative, Object of Verb, Indirect Object

Copy each italicized word on a separate line of your paper. Then place after each word *p.a.* (predicate adjective), *p.n.* (predicate nominative), *o.v.* (object of verb), or *i.o.* (indirect object) to show its use in the sentence.

1. Knowledge is *power*.
2. You are quite *right*.
3. This shark-fishing was great *sport*.
4. Never chew *gum* in public.
5. Such luck was *unbelievable*.
6. He was a big-boned *athlete*.
7. The fall didn't do *me* any *harm*.
8. Dreams of taste are *rare*.
9. George III did not understand the *Americans*.
10. Jack Page is the *owner* of the boat.
11. Father bought *Paul* a *bicycle*.
12. Thirty thousand people filled the *stadium*.
13. In olden days the boar's head was the main *dish* on Christmas Day.
14. I paid *George* twenty-five *cents* for the knife.
15. My hands were *numb* with the cold.
16. A pyramid was always a *tomb* of a king.
17. In the fourth inning Jerry scored a *run*.

Appositive

What does each italicized appositive do in the sentence?

1. Jack Wheat, Carleton's *pitcher*, scored the first run.

Pitcher explains *Jack Wheat*. The two nouns name the same person.

2. Have you seen my sister *Mildred?*

Mildred explains *sister*. The two nouns name the same person.

3. Harrisburg, the *capital* of Pennsylvania, is on the Susquehanna River.

Capital explains *Harrisburg*. The two nouns name the same thing.

A noun added to another noun to explain it and naming the same person or thing is an appositive.

Practice 10

Find the appositives, and tell what word each is in apposition with:

1. My brother James will meet you at the station.
2. Joe Groom, our best catcher, can't play today.
3. Carson City, the capital of Nevada, is a mining center.
4. Mount Vernon, Washington's home, is beautiful.
5. The lion, the king of beasts, has a valuable skin.
6. Cyrus McCormick, the inventor of the reaper, built a factory in Chicago.
7. Have you read about Jim Hawkins, the boy hero?
8. Our next-door neighbors, the Clarks, are away for the summer.
9. Admiral Byrd, the explorer, has had many adventures.
10. Mark Twain, the author of *Huckleberry Finn*, wrote entertaining stories.
11. Halloween, the night of witches and goblins, approaches.
12. Have you read *Greyfriars Bobby*, a story about a dog?
13. Betty's father, James M. Cropsey, paints portraits.
14. Mrs. Helen Wills Moody, the queen of the tennis court, is also an artist.
15. My uncle is now in London, the largest city in the world.
16. Dixon, the gray-haired city editor, leaned back in his swivel-chair.

Do you like number 1 or number 2 better?

1. The "culti-mulcher" is a new farm implement. This machine does four jobs at once.
2. The "culti-mulcher," a new farm implement, does four jobs at once.

Number 1 has 14 words; number 2, 11 words. Appositives save time and make our speech and writing more pleasing.

PARTS OF THE SIMPLE SENTENCE

Practice 11

Combine the two sentences in each group into one sentence containing an appositive. Draw a line under the appositive. How are appositives punctuated?

Model

Mount Kamet is the highest peak ever scaled by man. It is 25,447 feet high.

Mount Kamet, the highest peak ever scaled by man, is 25,447 feet high.

1. Jim Weaver is the tallest pitcher in the American League. He stands six feet six inches.
2. Have you read *Black Beauty?* It is a story about a horse.
3. Daniel Defoe wrote *Robinson Crusoe.* It is a story of adventures on an island.
4. Miss Anita Grew swam the length of the Bosporus. She is an American girl.
5. Danny was the hotel clerk. He had a hard job.
6. St. Paul is the capital of Minnesota. It is situated on the Mississippi River.
7. Even Marion looked serious. She was the giggler of the class.
8. Tom Williams was slightly injured. He is captain of the team.
9. Carol Bird was a little crippled girl. She made a merry Christmas for the nine Ruggleses.
10. James Wolfe was the conqueror of Quebec. He was a gallant soldier.
11. Jim was a Boston boy of eighteen. He had been allowed to join Wolfe's expedition because of his ability to speak French.
12. Have you read about John Paul Jones? He was a naval hero of the Revolutionary War.
13. Marie was a big, bony girl with black hair. She rode a prancing horse.

14. Edith was the lighthouse keeper's daughter. She made coffee for the rescued crew.

15. Miss Amy Johnson flew from London to Tokyo in nine days. She is an English woman.

Courtesy Southern Pacific Railroad

FRIENDS

Nominative of Address

How are the italicized words used?

1. *Mother*, this is Ruth Williams.
2. *John*, take that ink away from the baby.

Mother and *John*, the names of the persons spoken to, are nominatives of address. In sentence 1, *this* is the subject of *is*. In sentence 2, *you* understood is the subject of *take*. A nominative of address is never the subject of the sentence.

The nominative of address is the name of the person spoken to.

Practice 12

Find the nominatives of address and the subjects of the sentences:

1. I can't go this afternoon, Bob.
2. Will you, Fred, help me with this baggage?
3. What do you want, Kate?
4. What do you think of my dog, Jim?
5. I'll be back in the morning, Helen.
6. Will you be home for dinner, Father?
7. Doctor, I didn't sleep a wink last night.
8. This, Mary, is wonderful news.
9. How soon will you be ready, Lillian?
10. Tell me about the game today, Arthur.

Adding Modifiers

A modifier, you know, changes the meaning of the word to which it is attached. Adjectives, adverbs, and prepositional phrases are three kinds of modifiers.

How does sentence 2 differ from sentence 1?

1. Burgoyne had started.
2. Meanwhile Burgoyne had started out bravely with 8000 men.

In both sentences *Burgoyne* is the simple subject, and *had started* the verb. In sentence 2 modifiers of the verb have been added. The modifiers are the adverbs *meanwhile, out,* and *bravely* and the prepositional phrase *with 8000 men.*

1. Bullfrogs croak.
2. The giant bullfrogs in the pond croak hoarsely.

Bullfrogs is the simple subject, and *croak* the verb. *The* (adjective), *giant* (adjective), and *in the pond* (prepositional phrase) modify the simple subject *bullfrogs.* The adverb *hoarsely* modifies the verb *croak.*

Practice 13

Add to the following sentences modifiers of the subject or of the verb or of both:

1. Birds fly.
2. Dogs bark.
3. Coal burns.
4. Roosters crow.
5. Branches wave.
6. Trees grow.
7. Flowers bloom.
8. Lambs play.
9. Boys work.
10. Monkeys chatter.

Practice 14

Complete each sentence with a verb and one or more modifiers. You may insert after the verb a predicate adjective, a predicate nominative, or an object.

1. The express train ——.
2. The big green automobile ——.
3. My kitten ——.
4. Mary and her mother ——.
5. The old man ——.
6. The ducks ——.
7. Franklin D. Roosevelt ——.
8. The basketball game ——.
9. The boys ——.
10. The river ——.

Practice 15

Complete each sentence with a simple subject and one or more modifiers:

1. —— woke me early this morning.
2. —— frightened me on the way home.
3. —— made us all laugh.

4. —— flows past the town.
5. —— did not last long.
6. —— marched down the street.
7. —— is now being built.
8. —— came in.
9. —— waved their flags.
10. —— won the game.

Complete Subject and Complete Predicate

The complete subject is the simple subject with its modifiers. In Practice 14 the complete subject is printed; in Practice 15 you added the complete subject.

The complete predicate includes the verb, its modifiers, and words used to complete its meaning. In Practice 14 you added the complete predicate; in Practice 15 the complete predicate is in the book.

Ordinarily every word in the sentence belongs to either the complete subject or the complete predicate.

1. The <u>flyer</u> | <u><u>hopped</u></u> into his little seat.

The vertical line separates the complete subject from the complete predicate. The simple subject is underscored; the verb has two lines under it. *Hopped* is the verb, because it makes the statement. *Flyer* is the simple subject, because it answers the question "Who or what *hopped?*" *The flyer* is the complete subject; *hopped into his little seat*, the complete predicate.

2. <u>Lindbergh</u> | <u><u>flew</u></u> from New York to Paris in the *Spirit of St. Louis.*

Flew is the verb, because it makes the statement. *Lindbergh* is the simple subject, because it answers the question *"Who or what flew?"* *Lindbergh* is the complete subject; *flew from New York to Paris in the "Spirit of St. Louis,"* the complete predicate.

3. Four <u>sandwiches</u> | <u><u>were put</u></u> into the monoplane.
4. The <u>life</u> of an actress | <u><u>is</u></u> a hard one.

Practice 16

Copy the following sentences. Draw a vertical line between the complete subject and the complete predicate. Draw one line under the simple subject and two lines under the verb.

1. The storm was violent.
2. The master fired guns for help.
3. All hands were called to the pump.
4. We parted soon after.
5. My boat was a very good one.
6. I carried all my provisions into this fortress.
7. The great state of California has a wonderful climate.
8. Harry's roar is still ringing in my ears.
9. Some people are cheerful in spite of sickness.
10. The chief substance in tooth powders is chalk.
11. Tobacco interferes with one's success in class and in athletics.
12. The fourth quarter was much like the third.
13. The lucky boy was thrilled to his toes.
14. The football season came to an end in November.
15. Joe shot the ball over the plate.
16. The two little green turtles often sleep on the alligator's back.
17. Ned Wright sprawled lazily in the stern of his outboard motor boat.
18. The little house on the hillside often seemed lonely.
19. The log schoolhouse lies in a bend of the creek.
20. Many crimes are committed by persons under the influence of alcohol.

Inverted Order

1. Out of the brier patch jumped a rabbit.
(Natural order) A rabbit | jumped out of the brier patch.

When the complete predicate or part of it is before the subject, the order is inverted. In the natural order the subject with its modifiers is placed first.

2. Down the street came one of my pals.
(Natural order) One of my pals | came down the street.

When *there* is used to invert a sentence, it is called an introductory adverb and doesn't belong to either the subject or the predicate.

3. There was a moment of silence.
A moment of silence | was.

4. There were ten thousand people at the baseball game.
Ten thousand people | were at the baseball game.

The inverted order is commonly used in questions.

5. Where is my hat?
My hat | is where?

6. Why should we brush our teeth frequently?
We | should brush our teeth frequently why?

Notice that often the subject is wedged in between the parts of the predicate. In each of the following sentences the complete subject is italicized. The rest of the sentence is the complete predicate.

1. About three o'clock *we* started home.
2. At first *the Indians* fled in fear from Columbus.
3. How narrow *the streets* are!
4. For the first month *my golf* improved.
5. During the summer *these excursion boats* are crowded.
6. In original thought *the beaver* is equaled by few animals.

Practice 17

Arrange these sentences in the natural order. Then draw a vertical line between the complete subject and the complete predicate. Draw a line under the simple subject and two lines under the verb.

MODEL

From the hilltop looks the steeple.
The steeple | looks from the hilltop.

1. Slowly the sun sank.
2. Then I glanced at my watch.
3. Everywhere we hear the tinkle of cowbells.
4. Where are you going?
5. Then Billy snapped his fingers.
6. At that moment the bell rang.
7. There he is!
8. Always the sea was at our door.
9. In front of the house was a small car.
10. In Belfast we visited a linen mill.
11. Down the foul line sailed the ball.
12. At bat was the captain of the Washington team.
13. There are many stones in the cornfield.
14. Near Westminster Abbey in London stands a statue of Abraham Lincoln.
15. Have you ever caught an eel?
16. There is very little water in the creek.
17. Within two minutes he was in the air.
18. The next morning we got up early.
19. There was a loud knock at the door.
20. There is some roast lamb in the refrigerator.

Subject, predicate; subject, predicate; subject, predicate — that's the way many people arrange their sentences. How boresome such sentences become! **A good way to vary sentences is by using the inverted order in some.**

Practice 18

Change these sentences to the inverted order by putting the complete predicate or part of it before the subject. Begin each sentence with a word or words after the vertical line.

Models

1. The soft maples | were among the heaviest sufferers.
Among the heaviest sufferers were the soft maples.
2. I | saw him in London fifteen years ago.
Fifteen years ago I saw him in London.

1. We | then went down the hill.
2. I | was in Rome last year.
3. A blizzard | came with March.
4. The highest peaks | were beyond the valley.
5. A gray-haired man | stood near the dock.
6. Ethel and I | play outdoors after school.
7. We | started home about five o'clock.
8. The soldiers | marched up the street.
9. The small black cattle | plodded across the sands.
10. I | was paddling across a Maine lake a month ago.
11. The icy chill | stopped my breathing for a moment.
12. A picture of Mark Twain | hangs in my classroom.
13. Alexander Graham Bell | patented the telephone in 1876.
14. A small white plane | was in the center of the hall.
15. Platinum | was discovered in the Ural Mountains in the eighteenth century.
16. The plane | dropped down, down to the wild waves.
17. The art of the armorer | was important in the days of knights.
18. General Wolfe | moved up the St. Lawrence River with a large naval force.
19. Steinmetz | studied the causes and effects of lightning for twenty years.
20. The bottle of acid | was unfortunately spilled on the floor.

Simple Sentence Having Compound Subject or Predicate

How many subjects and predicates has each sentence?

1. The <u>French</u> <u><u>are noted</u></u> for their thrift. [One subject and one predicate.]
2. <u>Hotels</u> and private <u>homes</u> now <u><u>have</u></u> electric refrigerators. [Compound subject.]
3. The <u>raccoon</u> <u><u>caught</u></u> a few frogs and <u><u>ate</u></u> them. [Compound predicate.]
4. Then all the <u>boys</u> and <u>girls</u> <u><u>laughed</u></u> and <u><u>cheered</u></u>. [Compound subject and compound predicate.]

A simple sentence has one subject and one predicate, either or both of which may be compound.

Practice 19

In the following sentences either the subject or the predicate is compound, or both are compound. Draw a line between the complete subject and the complete predicate. Draw also a line under every subject word and two lines under every verb.

Model

Then they sat down in the open door and waited for business.

<u>They</u> | then <u><u>sat</u></u> down in the open door and <u><u>waited</u></u> for business.

1. I took the hammer and went to work.
2. Tarkington and Seton are two good writers.
3. I worked and worked on the tenth problem.
4. We returned to our crude camp and ate a cold supper.
5. Father just looked at me and shook his head.
6. Without a word Pinky and Whitey went outside.
7. He and Parker were good friends and always played together.

8. Caroline scratched the frost off the window and looked out.

9. In each Christmas box was a sweater or a pair of stockings.

10. We sat by the window and watched the cars in the rain.

11. There are potatoes, tomatoes, lettuce, and corn in our garden.

12. For ages gold and silver have been precious metals.

13. Along the brook there are forget-me-nots and larks.

14. He was dreaming and did not hear the sound of oars.

15. Carl and Gordon jumped into the river and rescued the child.

Other Compound Parts

What is the compound part in each sentence?

1. Fred is *tall* and *thin*. [Compound predicate adjective.]
2. The United States is English in *customs, language,* and *laws*. [Compound object of a preposition.]
3. Commander Byrd took with him *dogs, food, books, tools,* and *games*. [Compound object of verb.]
4. Washington was a *general* and a *statesman*. [Compound predicate nominative.]

Practice 20

In each sentence what part is compound?

1. Andrew was strong and courageous.
2. Children should not drink tea or coffee.
3. The air was cool and clear.
4. The president is commander-in-chief of the army and navy.
5. Benjamin Franklin was author, inventor, and statesman.
6. The tree had already seen five hundred springs and five hundred autumns.
7. Monday dawned fair and cold.

8. Some of the early castles had secret doors and underground passages.

9. The headache was perhaps caused by indigestion or eyestrain.

10. My favorite games are baseball and croquet.

Courtesy Netherlands Railways

A MILKMAN IN HOLLAND

Game — Parts of the Simple Sentence

Have you forgotten how to play Right-Down? If so, turn to page 187.

Today number 1 on the Blue team will tell the part of speech and the use in the sentence of the first italicized word in sentence 1 following. If his answer is correct, he will be seated, and number 1 of the Reds will take the second italicized word. If this answer is wrong, Blue number 2 will take the same word.

The side that is seated first or has the smaller number standing at the end is the winner.

PARTS OF THE SIMPLE SENTENCE

Model

A *child* early *cultivates* a *taste* for vegetables and *cereals*.

Child is a noun used as the subject of the verb *cultivates*.

Cultivates is a verb and makes a statement about *child*.

Taste is a noun used as the object of the verb *cultivates*.

Cereals is a noun used as object of the preposition *for*.

1. Tom *dangled* his *legs* and *munched* his *apple*.
2. Suddenly there *was* an unusually loud *snort* and a *puff*.
3. Soon *we* found our *way* through the swampy *land*.
4. We are not *red* but have dark *skins*, black *eyes*, and black straight *hair*.
5. Will *you* lend *me* your *knife?*
6. To the song of the north *wind* the *fire added* its *crackle* and *roar*.
7. Up the *street came* the gray-haired *principal*.
8. *Richmond*, the *capital* of *Virginia*, has large locomotive *works*.
9. *Are* you *ready*, *Helen?*
10. Ned Mackey, our third *baseman*, was the *hero* of the *game*.
11. Did *you* send *Louise* a Christmas *gift?*
12. The heart is really a *pair* of force *pumps*.
13. We are *proud* of *you*, *Ruth*.
14. Two hits and an *error* gave the *Athletics* a *run* in the first *inning*.
15. Dave *told us* a good *joke*.
16. For a *moment* the *room* was deathly *still*.
17. *Boys*, I'm *tired* but *happy*.
18. At the *report* of the gun five *figures sprang* into *action*.
19. *Tuck* this little *book* into your *pocket*.
20. Do *you* like Indian *stories* and pirate *yarns?*

Mastery Test 4A — Parts of Simple Sentence

Copy the following sentences. Omit a line after each line you write. Tell the use in the sentence of each italicized word by writing above it on your paper one of these abbreviations. Place only one abbreviation over a name like *Bud Fraser*.

s.s. — simple subject	o.p. — object of preposition
v. — verb	i.o. — indirect object
p.a. — predicate adjective	ap. — appositive
p.n. — predicate nominative	n.a. — nominative of address
o.v. — object of verb	

1. Walter rolled the *ball* in his *hands* and *stared* ahead.
2. The three-horned *giraffes* are the most interesting *animals* in the *building*.
3. My baby alligator, *Spunk*, has a very bad *temper*.
4. *Father*, this is my *classmate*, *Bud Fraser*.
5. Have *you* told *us* the whole *story?*
6. Why *are you* so *slow* this morning, *Edna?*
7. There was no *school* within ten *miles* of us.
8. Occasionally Father sent *us* a *book*.
9. *Are* you *ready?*

Mastery Test 4B — Parts of Simple Sentence

Copy the following sentences. Omit a line after each line you write. Tell the use in the sentence of each italicized word by writing above it on your paper one of the abbreviations in Mastery Test A. Place only one abbreviation over a name like *Mrs. Gates*.

1. Your garden is *wonderful*, *Mrs. Gates*.
2. *Grace*, where are your *books?*
3. I will send *you* the *money* tomorrow.
4. Hazen, our *shortstop*, was a poor *hitter*.
5. That girl is *Nancy Foster*, the tennis *champion* of our school.

6. The new *secretary, Miss Leonard,* was going through the morning *mail.*

7. I threw back the *covers* and *shivered* in the chill of the October *morning.*

8. The Indian gave *me* an *arrow.*

9. *Is* your answer *correct?*

10. From her *father Martha heard stories* of the World War.

Review Questions

1. How does one find the verb in a simple sentence? The simple subject?

2. What is a linking verb? Give five linking verbs.

3. What questions do objects of verbs answer?

4. How does a predicate nominative differ from an object of a verb?

5. What is an easy way to find an indirect object in a sentence?

6. Of what use are appositives?

7. What is the inverted order?

8. What are the simple subject and the verb in this sentence: There are twenty boys in my class?

9. What is one way to vary sentences?

10. Make up a sentence to illustrate each of the following: predicate adjective, object of verb, appositive, predicate nominative, simple sentence with compound subject.

UNIT 12
SENTENCE SENSE
Half-Sentence

Which of these groups of words express complete thoughts?

1. At last back in Galveston, one of the important cotton ports of the United States.
2. At last we *are* back in Galveston.
3. The trees swaying in the breeze.
4. The trees *were swaying* in the breeze.
5. For the center pole a piece of wood two inches square and six feet long.
6. I *cut* a center pole six feet long.
7. A large sailboat on a calm sea under the setting sun.
8. The sailboat *is gliding* over a calm sea.
9. Having selected the cast for the Christmas play.
10. The cast for the Christmas play *was selected* yesterday.

Numbers 2, 4, 6, 8, and 10 are sentences. The italicized verb in each says something about a person, a place, or a thing. The verb is the engine of each sentence and makes it go. In 1, 3, 5, 7, and 9 we do not know what the thoughts of the writer are. These word-groups do not say anything or ask anything. A sentence always has a subject and a predicate and makes complete sense when standing alone.

If a period is used after a part of a sentence that does not make complete sense when standing alone, the fraction of a sentence is called a "half-sentence." **Write and speak sentences, not half-sentences.**

SENTENCE SENSE

Answers to Questions

Sometimes in answer to a question the subject and the predicate are omitted. This is a correct use of the half-sentence.

Where are you going? To the swimming pool. [I am going to the swimming pool.]

How long did the meeting last? An hour. [It lasted an hour.]

Ing and *To*

The *to* form of a verb does not make a sentence. By itself the *ing* form of verb does not make a statement.

(Sentence) The wheat *is ripening* in the broad meadows.
(Half-sentence) The wheat ripening in the broad meadows.

(Sentence) I *am hoping* to see you on Thursday.
(Half-sentence) Hoping to see you on Thursday.

Practice 1

Ten of the following are sentences and ten are half-sentences. Which are the sentences? In each sentence find the word which makes a statement about a person, place, or thing.

1. The newest British battleship at anchor in the harbor.
2. In Algiers we saw the battleship *Rodney*.
3. I hope to hear from you soon.
4. Hoping to hear from you soon.
5. Huge mountains of ice on each side of the tiny ship.
6. The ship was surrounded by icebergs.
7. With the sails and mast and deck covered with ice.
8. The sails and mast and deck were covered with ice.
9. I read in this morning's *Herald-Tribune* your advertisement for an office boy.
10. Having read in this morning's *Herald-Tribune* your advertisement for an office boy.
11. They were all against Silver and Jim.
12. Because they were all against Silver and Jim.

13. A boy who never bragged about his victories.
14. Robert never bragged about his victories.
15. All the way home Harry thought of goblins, ghosts, and witches.
16. Thinking all the way home of goblins, ghosts, and witches.
17. A piece of dry, hard bread and a glass of water.
18. The bread was dry and hard.
19. Father was sitting on a stone.
20. Father sitting on a stone and Mr. Thompson sitting on a box beside him telling him a story.

Some boys and girls incorrectly separate part of a good sentence from the rest and write it with a capital and a period as if it were a sentence.

(Right) Two games will be played, one with Northwest Junior High and another with the alumni.
(Wrong) Two games will be played. One with Northwest Junior High and another with the alumni.

The half-sentence "One with Northwest Junior High and another with the alumni" has no verb and does not make complete sense.

(Right) Mrs. Williams offered me a glass of lemonade, which I gladly accepted.
(Wrong) Mrs. Williams offered me a glass of lemonade. Which I gladly accepted.

The half-sentence "Which I gladly accepted" has a subject *I* and a verb *accepted* but does not make complete sense when standing alone.

Sometimes the half-sentence is the subject, the object, or a modifier of a good sentence.

(Right) You would like it here. Fishing, bathing, boating, tennis, and other sports make life interesting.
(Wrong) You would like it here. Fishing, bathing, boating, tennis, and other sports.

The half-sentence "Fishing, bathing, boating, tennis, and other sports" has no verb and does not make complete sense when standing alone.

(Right) It is snowing today. A heavy rain fell yesterday.
(Wrong) It is snowing today. A heavy rain yesterday.

The half-sentence "A heavy rain yesterday" has no verb and does not make complete sense when standing alone.

Practice 2

What is the half-sentence in each of these? Correct.

Model

Think of the fun you will have. Rowing, swimming, games, and races.
Half-sentence — Rowing, swimming, games, and races.
Think of the fun you will have rowing, swimming, playing games, and running races.

1. One hot day last summer. My uncle and aunt went with us to the beach.
2. There were babies, young and old men. And gray-haired women with long pipes in their mouths.
3. She did many things for the wounded. Such as getting food, bandages, clothing, and beds.
4. Our school has a large auditorium with a balcony and a stage. A swimming pool and two gymnasiums.
5. One afternoon when school was dismissed. The boys spied a large wagon in front of the building.
6. When we were all together. Joe suggested that we find the lost baseball.
7. I was soon surrounded and brought back to camp. Where I was placed in a blanket and tossed up and down.
8. I'm going to give you a program. Before they are all gone.
9. I am enclosing a check for eight dollars. For which please send me a dozen Kroflite golf balls.

10. An experienced bandmaster has been secured. One who plays many instruments.

11. Joan of Arc was a country maiden of France. Very shy and very pretty.

12. The cost of a ticket is only ten cents. A sum so small that no one will hesitate to pay it.

13. At my party there were twelve girls and twelve boys. Twenty-four in all including myself.

14. When he became rich, he didn't really enjoy life. Because he did not have a good education.

15. For sports in the country there are in the summer swimming, golf, tennis, and motoring. In the winter sleighriding, coasting, tobogganing, skating, and snowballing.

Comma Blunder

You know that a sentence begins with a capital letter and usually ends with a period. You know also that when in baseball you are at bat you should strike at a ball if it crosses the plate and is between your knees and your shoulders. But perhaps as you watch the ball coming, you sometimes can't tell whether it is going to be a strike or a ball. Do you when you see a group of words know every time the difference between one sentence and two sentences? One's sentence batting average should be 1000 — that is, he should ALWAYS know a sentence when he sees it.

If a sentence ends with a comma or no punctuation mark and the next one begins with a small letter, the error is called a "comma blunder."

(Right) One of our stops was in Ohio. We saw large cornfields and many cattle.

(Wrong) One of our stops was in Ohio we saw large cornfields and many cattle.

A period should be placed at the end of the sentence "One of our stops was in Ohio." There is one line under the simple subject of each sentence, and there are two lines under each predicate verb.

(Right) But I saw you throw the stone. Why aren't you man enough to admit your guilt?

(Wrong) But I saw you throw the stone, why aren't you man enough to admit your guilt?

A period should be placed after *stone*, because that is the end of the first sentence.

(Right) Jackman, the captain, was the lead-off man. He hit a long fly to the center field for the first out.

(Wrong) Jackman, the captain, was the lead-off man he hit a long fly to center field for the first out.

A period should be placed after *man*, because that is the end of the first sentence.

Practice 3

In each of the following place a period or a question mark at the end of the first sentence, and capitalize the first word of the second sentence. Draw a line under the simple subject of each sentence. Draw two lines under every verb.

1. How would you like a ride down to the beach we can cool off there.
2. Last week I read *Jungle Book*, it is about an Indian boy adopted into a wolf pack.
3. Why shouldn't every pupil buy the school paper it is only five cents a week.
4. The next number was a jig by some girls everyone enjoyed the dancing of this class.
5. *Treasure Island* is a pirate story it was written by Stevenson.
6. After that we shall divide the boys into two groups one half will fetch wood.

226 JUNIOR ENGLISH IN ACTION

7. Yesterday the Bushwicks handed the Yankees their first defeat in ten starts, the score was 5 to 4.

8. I did not have many playmates and on rainy days none at all, I was, however, seldom lonely.

9. We took a bus to Far Rockaway, there we boarded a fishing schooner.

10. The first number was a talk on health by Marjorie Gannon it was enthusiastically applauded by the students.

11. On the left-hand side you will see the clutch pedal and the brake pedal farther to the right is the gasoline throttle.

12. At Laurelton we stopped to eat our oranges then for a half hour we watched two teams of boys playing baseball.

13. What's the matter fellows didn't you sleep well?

14. Marion and I had not seen each other for quite a while that night we talked till eleven o'clock.

15. My sled struck a rock and threw me against an automobile my foot was slightly sprained.

16. Two tables are shown in the cartoon, at one John Bull and Miss Canada are seated.

17. I walked right in front of the automobile of course my injury was my own fault.

18. I am not the only critic of the pupils' behavior on the street cars there are many others.

19. At my first question the class snickered, after that the pupils roared.

20. *Kit Carson* is a very interesting book it tells about a little boy.

Practice 4

Write the following correctly. Begin each sentence with a capital and end it with a period. Do not omit any of the commas in the book.

1. About three o'clock I went down to the beach to look at my rowboat to my surprise the water was very rough

2. It took me about an hour to get home everybody was very happy to see me

3. The flames rose almost to the top of the building the fire engines arrived and tried to put out the fire

4. We shall have dinner at twelve after that we are going to have a treasure hunt and play games

5. Then step on the starter when the engine starts, push the choke in

6. Release the clutch gradually if you let go suddenly, the car will jerk forward

7. A policeman came along and asked me what the trouble was I told him I was lost

8. When I got home, I told my brothers and sisters that my ambition was to be a bareback rider they all laughed at me

9. We heard a queer noise, which seemed to come from the back of the cave that made us want to find out what was there

10. It was about twelve o'clock when I reached home as I neared the house, I started to look for my key

11. I admire Robinson Crusoe's courage although he remained on the island for a long time, he never gave up hope of being rescued

12. After that we walked in silence for a while as we were about to turn the curve, we saw a large bear coming toward us

13. I went to look for a strong stick at last I found one that suited me

14. Someone behind me shouted loudly and frightened me being on the edge of the pier, I lost my balance and plunged headfirst into the water

15. Just as I passed the last house before entering the woods, a black cat crossed my path that, I thought, meant good luck

16. First the magician removed a bowl of goldfish from under a cloth then he borrowed a gentleman's hat and from it took seventeen eggs

17. I decided to continue reading but again heard a noise this time it sounded as if someone were rattling paper

18. The next man up was Del, Brooklyn's first baseman he drove the ball down the first base line for a single

19. My sister took me home and called a doctor when the doctor arrived, he set the bone and put my arm in a sling

20. While I was chopping wood, Walter asked me to go skating with him my mother said that I had worked enough

Practice 5

Write the following correctly. Begin each sentence with a capital and end it with a period. There are twelve sentences. Do not omit any quotation mark, capital, or comma in the book.

"COUNT LUCKNER, THE SEA DEVIL"
By LOWELL THOMAS

An exciting incident of "Count Luckner, the Sea Devil" is Count Luckner's being saved by an albatross the Count had run away from his beautiful home in Germany to become an officer in the German navy and had secured a position as a cabin boy on a fishing schooner
One stormy day the captain ordered some men out to pull down the sails, because the sea was becoming too rough although young Felix, as he was called, was not supposed to go, he went out and tried to help when he had climbed up the rigging and was near the top, the ship gave a lurch and threw him into the sea when he regained his senses, he was far from the boat and could not even see it because of the gigantic waves he called out but to no avail, because he could not be heard above the roar of the wind and waves
Then a flock of albatrosses came around him to feed the biggest one swooped down towards him, and he grabbed it by the leg he held on, and the albatross flapped its wings and kept young Felix from drowning soon a lifeboat with some of the men came up and pulled him out of the water he afterward learned that the albatross not only held him out of the water but also directed the men to where he was — PUPIL

Practice 6

Prepare to tell in class an entertaining or exciting incident in a book you are reading or have recently completed. Practice at home — at the dinner table, for example. Stop for the period at the end of each sentence. Do not tie sentences together with *and, so,* or *ur.*

Perhaps your teacher will have you make this talk at a meeting of the class Book Club.

Practice 7

Prepare to write from dictation the following story. Notice particularly the division into sentences. Make sure that you will be able to put the periods and the capitals in the right places.

A CHILDHOOD ADVENTURE

One day when I was a child about six years old, a Western Union boy ascended the porch steps of my aunt's house in Oklahoma. He handed my aunt a yellow envelope, which I knew was a telegram. We were very much excited, because it was seldom that we received a message of this kind. After my aunt read the telegram, she dropped it on the floor and began to cry. She put her arms around me and told me I was going away from her. Very much bewildered, I asked her to tell me the meaning of all this. She said that I would have to go all the way from Oklahoma to New York alone to meet my father.

The preparation for the trip I do not remember, but I do remember boarding the train, and the trip I shall never forget. I felt like Alice in Wonderland. I can still see the big, good-natured conductor putting me in my berth and chatting with me until I was almost asleep.

My greatest thrill came when I woke up in the morning and looked out of the window. I saw large hills, which I thought were mountains, moving in the opposite direction. Every body of water we passed I thought was an ocean.

The trip lasted two days, and although with my father I have been to the Pacific Coast twice since then, this trip alone was the most thrilling in my life. — PUPIL

Mastery Test 5A — Sentence Sense

Examples

1. Seals feed chiefly on fish that they catch with their sharp teeth they swim with great speed but are clumsy on the land
2. A camp of Arabs near the northern border of the Sahara

Answers

1 — 2
2 — 0

The **1 — 2** shows that number 1 is two sentences. The **0** indicates that number 2 is not a sentence.

The Test

Indicate by 0, 1, 2, or 3 the number of complete sentences in each of the following:

1. The last half of the tenth inning with the score tied
2. When I am near the sea I am happy that is why I enjoy spending my summers at Asbury Park
3. The Indians attacked the white men in their usual way in the first hour's fighting three whites and eight reds were killed when the Indians saw that the whites were getting the best of them they retreated
4. We played all afternoon till supper time when we had finished our supper we went to bed
5. I drew a picture of a ship sailing out of the harbor and a crowd cheering the ship
6. To know plants and animals without destroying them
7. Because he had deceived them before
8. Mrs. Meany ate a spoonful of the strawberries and her face turned white the girls had put salt on them instead of sugar
9. A few years ago when I was at a Halloween party the mother of the boy who was giving the party asked if anyone would like to be hypnotized

SENTENCE SENSE   231

10. When are you planning to start for the lake if I can get ready in time I should like to go with you

11. It was a very attractive little inn the sign was newly painted and the windows had neat red curtains the customers were mostly sailors

12. Wishing you a happy vacation in Florida

13. We went out however and looked around while we were busy examining the lawn a voice behind us ordered us to put our hands up as we did so a shout of laughter greeted our ears

14. Lindbergh discovered that his plane was rapidly nearing the ocean quick as a flash he pulled the stick and the ship went up again

15. I would paint a bride in a colorful dress not a pale-faced creature in white

16. At the dinner table Father told us that he had lost his position the next week I started to work in a department store as a salesgirl it was a very tiresome job but the money came in handy

17. Ovens in which coal is changed to coke

18. The first gold in California was found in gravel in a channel or mill race that was being dug to carry water for a sawmill

19. This job made young Edward Bok want to leave school in those days a boy could leave school at any age

20. A forest of fir trees near the Pacific Coast of the United States

Mastery Test 5B — Sentence Sense

Indicate by 0, 1, 2, or 3 the number of complete sentences in each of the following:

1. Having read your advertisement in the *New York Times* for an office boy

2. My brother has charge of the cows my sister of the chickens

3. I have never had a chance to read *Heidi* did you enjoy it

4. A meeting of several boys from Ralph's camp and some others from a neighboring camp

5. Health education seems to me one of the most important subjects in school a sound mind needs a sound body to dwell in I should like to be a teacher of health education

6. What did I tell you we can beat you any time we feel like it

7. Last summer I had a locker at Broad Channel Pool and went swimming three or four times a week at the end of the season some of us had a beach party which was great fun we toasted marshmallows and ate frankfurters

8. Arguing whether the runner was out at first

9. How did he get the name Washington is he a relative of our first president

10. Although I was absent three weeks on account of sickness I am going to try to pass every subject this term

11. First we rode in one of the Crazy Cars they go around in a circle and bump into each other

12. After the young man had sat there for a half hour

13. We were given back all our tests and composition papers and then were shown how to average our marks

14. A policeman on a motorcycle rode up and asked what we were looking for we said we were hunting for wood

15. When I was in the sixth grade seeds were sold throughout the school I bought a package of marigold seeds when I arrived home I filled an old flower pot with soil and planted the seeds in it

16. The red ants gathered in a huddle then ran over to the army of black ants and attacked them

17. When suddenly a boy yelled to us to look at the ice

18. After my skates were on I was in a terrible hurry to get on the ice as my mother hadn't finished lacing her shoes I thought I'd try to skate without her much to my surprise I felt very wobbly as soon as I stood on the ice

19. After lunch we started to hike through the woods about six o'clock we found a suitable place and pitched our tents

20. Wicked sailors and honest citizens crazed by the hope of finding gold

UNIT 13

PUNCTUATION OF SIMPLE SENTENCES

Why Learn to Punctuate?

How would you like to read letters and books without punctuation marks? Here's an example:

> A funny little man told this to me
> I fell in a snowdrift in June said he
> I went to a ball game out in the sea
> I saw a jellyfish float up a tree
> I found some gum in a cup of tea
> I stirred my milk with a big brass key
> I opened my door on my bended knee
> I beg your pardon for this said he
> But 'tis true if told as it ought to be
> 'Tis a puzzle in punctuation you see [1]

Can you solve this puzzle?

Punctuation marks help the writer to make his ideas clear and save the reader's time by helping him to understand what is meant.

Kinds of Sentences

Practice 1

Which of the following sentences tell something? Which ask something? Which tell someone to do something? Which express strong feeling?

1. I washed my hands before lunch.
2. Did you wash your hands before lunch?

[1] Reprinted by permission of the *Literary Digest*.

3. Wash your hands before lunch.
4. Wash your hands at once!
5. I shall be ready to start at eight o'clock.
6. Will you be ready to start at eight o'clock?
7. Be ready to start at eight o'clock.
8. What, aren't you ready yet!

A declarative sentence tells something. It ends with a period. See sentences 1 (page 233) and 5 (above).

An interrogative sentence asks a question. It ends with a question mark. See sentences 2 and 6.

An imperative sentence expresses a command or a request. It ends with a period. See sentences 3 and 7.

An exclamatory sentence expresses strong feeling. It ends with an exclamation point. See sentences 4 and 8.

Any sentence, whether declarative, interrogative, or imperative, becomes exclamatory when it is spoken with strong feeling.

Practice 2

What kind of sentence is each of the following? How does each sentence begin? Give a reason for the punctuation mark at the end of each sentence.

1. Oh, you don't want to go yet!
2. What would you do in case of fire?
3. Do not fuss about the weather.
4. How has the telephone affected business and trade?
5. What are some of the difficulties of night flying?
6. Do not wear party clothes to school.
7. Here is a puzzle for you.
8. What a good time we had!
9. Keep your teeth white.
10. Missouri ranks first in the production of lead and zinc.
11. What is the largest city in Michigan?
12. Down the road padded a long caravan of camels.

Practice 3

Tell what kind of sentence each of the following is, and write it with the correct punctuation mark at the end. There are three sentences of each of the four kinds.

1. What a thrilling age the boys and girls of today have the good luck to be starting off in
2. Wasn't Tom funny with that big pack of his
3. Don't put a period at the end of a question
4. Niagara Falls is not far from Buffalo
5. Did he bring you many eggs
6. At the first crossroad turn left
7. Practice good table manners three times a day
8. Minneapolis is the largest wheat-milling center in the United States
9. Ah, there you are
10. Why should milk be examined
11. I drink six glasses of water a day
12. How the dogs would sniff along the trail on a trip like this

Practice 4

Name ten cities, and write a sentence about each one. State facts about four of the cities, ask questions about four of them, and write exclamatory sentences about two. Watch your punctuation.

Contest — Question Mark

Imagine yourself the teacher for a day of review, and write three questions about the English you have studied this term. If you place a question mark at the end of each question, you will score three points for your team.

Your teacher will probably have some of the questions answered in class. Be ready to answer your own questions and the questions of other pupils.

The Period after Abbreviations

Notice how abbreviations and initials are punctuated.

P.M.   etc.   N. C.   Mr. L. C. Hodge

The period is used after abbreviations and initials.
Miss and *per cent* are not abbreviations.

The abbreviations in Practice 5 are commonly used. Get into the habit of writing out other words in full.

Practice 5

Place periods after abbreviations and at the end of declarative and imperative sentences:

1. Mr and Mrs Horton, Miss Stilling, and Dr Miles motored to Washington, D C, yesterday
2. They left New York at 6:30 A M and arrived in Washington at 5:30 P M
3. Mr Horton is employed by D C Heath & Co; Dr Miles is secretary of a New York Y M C A
4. Messrs Bing and White sent the bracelet C O D
5. H J Reed Jr lives in St Louis

Comma

Person Addressed

Notice how the name of the person addressed is punctuated. How many commas are there in each sentence?

1. *Jack*, do you remember that blueberry patch?
2. When will you be ready, *Agnes?*
3. I want you, *Janet*, to go with me to Priscilla's cabin tonight.

The comma is used to set off the name of the person addressed.

To set off an expression requires two commas unless the expression comes at the beginning or the end of the sentence.

——————————— , ——————— , ———————————

Practice 6

Punctuate the following sentences:

1. Come right in Mrs Mudge
2. Tom did you see that chipmunk
3. Why are you so late Peg
4. Do you like to travel Dot
5. Can you punctuate this sentence Edward
6. Really Flora you would enjoy *Little Women*
7. Honestly Gladys I couldn't get here a minute earlier
8. Marion would you like to ride with us to the Natural Bridge
9. Joe I don't want you to climb Mount Marcy alone
10. Do you Marie always put a question mark after a question

Appositives

Study the punctuation of the following sentences. What is the use in the sentence of each italicized word?

1. We spent the night in Harrisburg, the *capital* of Pennsylvania.
2. I have a wonderful old dog, a *shepherd*.
3. In 1912 Curtiss built a flying-boat, the *father* of all the seaplanes of today.
4. A great man, in fact *one* of the greatest in American history, was Robert E. Lee, *commander-in-chief* of the Confederate army.

As a rule, an appositive is set off by commas.

5. You'd better telephone your friend *Florence*.
6. I *myself* saw the deer.
7. The year *1931* was a hard one for my uncle *Dick*.

The comma is not used to set off brief, commonly used, closely connected appositives.

Practice 7

What is the appositive in each sentence? With what word is it in apposition? Punctuate the sentences correctly.

1. New Orleans the largest city in Louisiana has great cotton warehouses
2. Monticello the home of Thomas Jefferson is in Charlottesville
3. Mother herself baked the apple pie
4. The crown of a tooth is enamel the hardest substance in the body
5. Jim my cousin is a practical joker
6. The albatross a large bird with a beak like a duck was their daily visitor
7. Paul Revere the Revolutionary War hero was a metal worker and engraver
8. My cousin Ralph was waiting for us at the dock
9. Andrew Jackson the hero of the battle of New Orleans became president
10. My race the 50-yard swim came next
11. The play a fairy tale about a princess was given twice
12. Jack a remarkable dog hunted antelopes with his master
13. The capital cities of the Carolinas Columbia and Raleigh have many beautiful homes
14. Caius the hero of the story is a young shepherd
15. My brother Ned and my uncle Harry are playing golf

Appositives help us to express our thoughts briefly and pleasingly. By practice anyone can form the habit of using appositives.

Practice 8

In sentences of your own, use five of the following as appositives. Punctuate the sentences correctly.

1. the first president of the United States
2. the president of the United States
3. the capital of New York (or another state)
4. the longest river in the United States
5. the largest city in the United States
6. the second largest city in the United States
7. the best book I have read this winter
8. my favorite movie actor
9. the largest state in the United States
10. my favorite author
11. my best friend
12. the pitcher on our baseball team

Practice 9

Combine the two sentences in each group into one sentence containing an appositive. Punctuate the sentence correctly.

1. We spent the night in Germantown. This is a suburb of Philadelphia.
2. Mr. Collins spoke to our assembly. He is the principal of the Lincoln Junior High School.
3. Mr. Jack Bartlett knows about my work. He is head of the sporting goods department at Tracy's.
4. Here comes Jay Parker. He is our number one stunt man.
5. Amy is a spoiled child. She is the baby of the family.
6. Buck was a superb wolf-dog. He was stolen from his home in California.
7. In New York we saw the Empire State Building. It is the tallest building in the world.
8. Kack Ordle lives in that house. He is foreman of a gang of log drivers.

9. Mrs. Stanley Smith gave the party. She is Marjorie's mother.

10. Washington has a population of about a half million. It is the capital of the United States.

11. Ruth Wagner wrote *What Girls Can Do*. This is a book on vocations.

12. Mowgli was an Indian baby. He was adopted into a pack of wolves.

13. Lad was a prize collie. He was devoted to his master.

14. There goes Lefty Irving. He is the captain of our team.

15. Miss Malden spent last summer in England. She is my English teacher.

Series

How are the underlined words used? Notice the punctuation of the sentences.

1. In the United States gold, silver, copper, and lead are mined.

Gold, silver, copper, and *lead* are four subjects of *are mined*. Three commas separate the four subjects. Such a list of words or groups of words used in the same way is called a "series."

2. Long Island is a level, sandy strip of land with market gardens and quaint, old-fashioned houses.

Level and *sandy* are adjectives modifying the noun *strip*. A comma separates them.

Quaint and *old-fashioned* are adjectives modifying the noun *houses*. A comma separates them.

3. You may hide in the barn, behind the barn, or under an apple tree.

In sentence 3 two commas separate the three prepositional phrases.

PUNCTUATION OF SIMPLE SENTENCES

Notice that in sentence 1 a comma is placed before *and* and in sentence 3 before *or*. It is correct to insert these commas or to omit them.

The comma is used to separate items in a series.

When there are only two items and *and* connects them or when two *ands* connect three words, no comma is needed.

Cleveland and *Coolidge* were *wise* and *brave* and *honest*.

Practice 10

Underline the words or groups of words in a series. Punctuate the sentences correctly.

1. James Lewis Archie Otis and I went swimming (Three boys.)
2. James Lewis Archie Otis and I went swimming (Five boys.)
3. Maple pine and white birch shade our cottage in the summer
4. I study history geography science music drawing arithmetic and English
5. Bluefish mackerel flounders and weakfish are sought by the angler
6. A rosy-cheeked bright-eyed boy stood near us
7. A study room should not contain a radio a piano or a victrola
8. Can you keep your head your patience and your poise at all times
9. Horns are worn by both sexes of all bisons buffaloes cattle antelopes and goats
10. We looked for my little brother in the attic under the porch and behind the house
11. Have you ever built a shack got up a circus or organized a secret club
12. Do you know how to meet people to talk with them to take orders without being servile and to give orders without offending

Addresses and Dates

Notice how addresses and dates are punctuated:

ADDRESSES

1. A friend from *Evanston, Illinois,* is visiting me.
2. In *Washington, D. C.,* the younger members of the Y. M. C. A. have formed a camera club.
3. In the November issue the city of *Oxford, England,* is pictured.

Illinois, D. C., and *England* are set off by commas.

DATES

1. Admiral Dewey's victory in *May, 1898,* opened the way for American rule over the Philippines.
2. On *May 5, 1821,* Napoleon died on the island of St. Helena.

1898 and *1821* are set off by commas.

3. Delaware ratified the Constitution in *December, 1787.*

Only one comma is needed to set off *1787.*

In an address or date each item after the first is set off by commas.

Practice 11

Punctuate the following sentences. Tell why each comma is needed.

1. On August 1 1934 we reached Newport Kentucky
2. In Lynn Massachusetts shoes are manufactured
3. In Schenectady New York there are large electric works
4. Benjamin Franklin died in Philadelphia Pennsylvania on April 17 1790
5. On November 7 1934 Father flew to Washington D C
6. On November 11 1918 the Armistice was signed

7. On the night of April 18 1775 British troops arrived by ship in the Charles River

8. George Washington was born on February 22 1732 in Westmoreland County Virginia

Parenthetical Expressions

A side remark which is slipped into a sentence but is not necessary to the thought is called a parenthetical expression and is set off by commas.

1. I, *like many other boys*, enjoy reading detective stories.
2. He is, *or at least seems to be*, rather queer.
3. Pittsburgh, *for example*, is famous for its iron and steel.
4. The next day, *however*, unpleasant rumors began to reach them.
5. There is a second inward curve in the lumbar, *or low-back*, region.

Read the preceding sentences without the italicized words, and you will see that omitting these side remarks would not greatly change the thought of the sentences. Parenthetical expressions are sometimes called "interrupters."

Well, why, or *now* at the beginning of a conversational sentence is commonly set off.

1. *Well*, that's too bad.
2. *Why*, I hardly know.
3. *Now*, what do you think of that?

Practice 12

Punctuate the following sentences. Which expressions are parenthetical?

1. Syracuse like Utica is an important railway center
2. Rebecca however opened her bag and took the two dollars out

3. Our school both grammar and high is one hundred per cent Red Cross
4. I cannot however give you lodging
5. Frances is I think old enough to know her own mind
6. His imitation of an Italian for instance is excellent
7. Well I'll do that particular stunt myself
8. Salem like Boston is an old seaport
9. Have you by the way heard the latest about our play
10. I was to tell the truth getting a little tired of his nonsense
11. Two boys tired and hungry reached home just in time for dinner
12. There is, I think, a card on the house to keep other children away from the disease
13. Like everything great the lion has his share of critics and detractors.

Letter

Use the comma after the greeting of a friendly letter and after the closing of any letter.

Dear Bill,
Dear Mother,

                    Yours truly,
                    Your loving daughter,

Numbers

Notice how numbers written in figures are punctuated:

Italy now counts 60 pussy cats for each 1,000 inhabitants or a total of 40,000,000 men and 2,000,000 cats.

Yes and *No*

Place a comma after *yes* or *no* when used as a part of an answer.

1. *Yes*, I think so.
2. *No*, that's not the answer.
3. *Yes*, it was a close game.

Apostrophe for Contractions

Learn to spell these contractions used in conversation. They are not hard. Then get the habit of spelling them correctly, and you will escape one of the commonest and most serious errors in letters written by people of all ages — the misspelling of such simple words as *it's, doesn't, don't, won't,* and *isn't.*

In a contraction an apostrophe takes the place of an omitted letter.

Are + not = aren't; did + not = didn't; it + is = it's; who + is = who's.

aren't	doesn't	that's	we'll	can't
haven't	he's	what's	I'm	won't
isn't	it's	who's	you've	they're
wasn't	let's	I'll	they've	we're

Practice 13

Punctuate the following sentences and give a reason for each mark you put in. The figure at the end tells how many more marks are needed in each group of sentences.

1. "Are you going straight home from school George"
"No Im going skating" (5)
2. "Will you be at home in time for dinner"
"Yes Ill be there before five o'clock" (4)
3. "Isnt the ice too thin"
"No its about two inches thick" (5)
4. "Is Tom going with you"
"No hes going to work this afternoon for Mr Sullivan" (5)
5. "Doesnt Mother expect you home after school"
"No she gave me permission to go skating" (4)
6. "Arent your gloves too thin for such a cold day"
"No theyre wool" (5)

7. "Havent you a muffler"
"Yes but its at home" (5)
8. "Whats that in your overcoat pocket"
"Why thats my English book" (5)
9. "Shall I take it home for you"
"Yes if you will" (3)
10. "Have you anything else for me to take home"
"Yes heres my geography" (4)

Exclamation Point (!)

Use the exclamation point to mark an expression of strong feeling.

1. The rescuers, alas! were too late.
2. That's great! Tell Mother this instant.
3. Hurrah! Our team has won!
4. Whew! That's over!
5. "And I'm not fat either. I have such big bones."
"Fat!" said Andy. "Fat! Of course you aren't fat. You are merely healthy."
6. Oh, what a shot that was!

Notice the comma after the interjection *oh*. An interjection which is a real exclamation is followed by an exclamation point.

Practice 14

Punctuate the following sentences. Place above each mark the number of the rule on pages 250 and 251. The figure in parenthesis tells how many marks are needed in the sentence.

MODELS

1. Thats a good idea Mr Moss
    15   6 2   1
That's a good idea, Mr. Moss.

2. Yes he is tall lean and gray
  13   8   8   1
Yes, he is tall, lean, and gray.

PUNCTUATION OF SIMPLE SENTENCES 247

1. I dont understand that sentence   (2)
2. Ill be waiting for you Marjorie   (3)
3. The Delaware River like the Mississippi is low this summer   (3)
4. On July 4 1932 a crowd of 35000 saw Ruth hit a home run   (4)
5. Later though we learned better   (3)
6. Milwaukee the chief city of Wisconsin is about eighty-five miles north of Chicago   (3)
7. In Pittsburgh one sees iron furnaces coal barges and trainloads of iron ore and steel   (3 or 2)
8. Yes theyre spending January in Florida   (3)
9. Jane isnt there someone at the door   (3)
10. First of all be prepared for wet weather in camp   (2)
11. Well what do you make of this   (2)
12. Will you buy a magazine Mr Wiggin   (3)
13. Oh Im so glad for you   (3)
14. But Mother arent you going with us to the beach   (4)
15. In Detroit Michigan are a number of large automobile factories (3)
16. Roses marigolds sweet peas and peonies are growing in Mrs Everest's garden   (5 or 4)
17. Everywhere garages signs billboards and dump heaps spoil the roadside   (4 or 3)
18. In his right hand he held a ball and a piece of candy (1)
19. Boston Massachusetts is the largest city in New England   (3)
20. Los Angeles the center of a great fruit region has a delightful climate   (3)
21. Raleigh the capital city of North Carolina is a place of culture education and beautiful homes   (5 or 4)
22. On June 1 1934 Mr Wilson sold his shoe factory for $114000   (5)
23. The honest-to-goodness hitch-hiker is a sort of grown-up Boy Scout a lover of the outdoors the open road   (3)
24. The shortstop perhaps overeager fumbled the ball   (3)
25. Our Fathers' God to Thee
    Author of liberty
    To Thee we sing   (4)

Mastery Test 6A — Punctuation of Simple Sentences

Punctuate the following sentences. Using too many marks is just as bad as using too few. Therefore if you either omit a needed punctuation mark or insert a mark that is not needed, the sentence is wrong. The figure in parenthesis tells how many marks are needed in the sentence.

1. Well whats the trouble (3)
2. Los Angeles on the other hand is a beautiful city (3)
3. Anne this is Kate my friend from Detroit (3)
4. No it isnt far to the library (3)
5. Of course Mrs Earle Ill do the errand (5)
6. With the help of the school nurses the boys and girls are selected given physical examinations and sent to camp (3 or 2)
7. On July 3 1934 Mrs Harris sold her beautiful home for $15000 (5)
8. Miss Wallis answered Mrs Allen's questions easily quickly quietly (4)
9. Mooney fanned seven men walked one and allowed only five hits (3 or 2)
10. Ohio Indiana Illinois the Dakotas Minnesota Nebraska Kansas Missouri and Washington produce millions of bushels of wheat each year (9 or 8)
11. In Grand Rapids Michigan there are many furniture factories (3)
12. Albany the capital of New York is located on the Hudson River (3)
13. Thomas A Edison was born in Milan Ohio on February 11 1847 (5)
14. Take for instance that keen-eyed boy (3)
15. Dont touch that lamp Henry (3)
16. Springfield the largest city of southwestern Missouri is in a mining lumbering and farming section (5 or 4)
17. I like many others enjoyed *Penrod* (3)
18. Whats the answer Fred (3)

PUNCTUATION OF SIMPLE SENTENCES 249

19. Great Scott What a surprise (2)
20. Yes Dr Clark will be at the Y M C A at 1:15 P M today (9)

Mastery Test 6B — *Punctuation of Simple Sentences*

Punctuate the following sentences. If you either omit a needed punctuation mark or insert a mark that is not needed, the sentence is wrong. The figure in parenthesis tells how many marks are needed in the sentence.

1. Well I didnt inquire (3)
2. Margaret can you guess the answer to the puzzle (2)
3. One night for example we were frightened by a noise in the garden (3)
4. Mrs Giles may Katherine come to my home tomorrow for dinner (3)
5. No Jim I cant do that (4)
6. I havent seen Betty for a year (2)
7. On May 7 1934 Mr Arnold bought the News Building for $175000 (5)
8. Im going to wear a blue shirt my hiking breeches and old shoes (4 or 3)
9. Benge held the Cubs to six hits one of them a home run by Hartnett (2)
10. McLaughlin Gaston and Morris pitched for the Red Sox (3 or 2)
11. Omaha Nebraska and Indianapolis the capital of Indiana are meat-packing centers (5)
12. Agricultural implements clothing steel and railroad cars are manufactured in Chicago the second largest city in the United States (5 or 4)
13. The *Mayflower* sailed from Plymouth England on September 16 1620 (4)
14. The schoolmaster usually good-natured was severe in his punishment of lying (3)
15. Yes Mother Ill come home early (4)
16. Why Frances where did you come from (3)

17. Whats Lillian doing this morning (2)
18. Look What a queer airplane (2)
19. Mrs Greeley of Washington D C is spending the week with Miss Spence (6)
20. Bill was rising napkin in hand (2)

Remember that —

A **declarative sentence** tells something.

An **interrogative sentence** asks a question.

An **imperative sentence** expresses a command or a request.

An **exclamatory sentence** expresses strong feeling.

Period (.)

A period is used —

1. At the end of a declarative or an imperative sentence.
2. After abbreviations.

Question Mark (?)

3. The question mark is used after an interrogative sentence.

Exclamation Point (!)

The exclamation point is used —

4. After an exclamatory sentence.
5. To mark any expression of strong feeling.

Comma (,)

The comma is used —

6. To set off the name of the person addressed.
7. As a rule, to set off an appositive.
8. To separate items in a series.

9. To set off each item after the first in an address or date.

10. To set off parenthetical expressions.

11. After the greeting of a social letter.

12. After the closing of any letter.

13. After *yes* or *no* when used as part of an answer.

14. Between hundreds and thousands and between thousands and millions in numbers written in figures.

Apostrophe (')

15. In a contraction an apostrophe takes the place of an omitted letter.

Two Good Habits

1. Punctuate as you write, not after completing a number of sentences or a paragraph. On the typewriter one can't go back to insert punctuation marks.

2. If you punctuate correctly every letter and exercise you write, you will soon form the habit of inserting the needed periods, question marks, and commas, and will not have to think much about these marks.

UNIT 14

NOUNS

Capitalization of Proper Nouns

Would you prefer a history printed in this way?

the commander of the united states forces was general john j. pershing, who, along with foch, the french commander, and haig, the british commander, formed the supreme war council.

Or in this way?

The commander of the United States forces was General John J. Pershing, who, along with Foch, the French commander, and Haig, the British commander, formed the Supreme War Council.

Capitals, like commas and periods, make our sentences easier to read.

What are the two kinds of nouns in these sentences?

1. William Penn, founder of Pennsylvania, paid the Indians friendly visits, ate with them, and took part in their games.

William Penn, Pennsylvania, and *Indians* are proper nouns, because they name one man, one state, and one race.

Visits and *games* are common nouns, because they apply to any visit or game.

2. When Captain John Smith went back to England, he left the colony at Jamestown without a leader.

The proper nouns *Captain John Smith*, *England*, and

Jamestown name one person, one country, and one colony.

The common nouns *colony* and *leader* apply to any colony or leader.

A proper noun is the name of a particular person or thing.

A common noun is a name which applies to any one of its class.

Proper nouns, proper adjectives, and their abbreviations are capitalized.

| John Adams | S. Dak. | United States | Henry Clay |
| English | French | German | Italian |

The names of school subjects except languages are common nouns.

| history | geography | grammar | spelling |
| arithmetic | music | science | hygiene |

Proper nouns include:

1. Names of the days of the week, the months of the year, and the holidays (but not names of the seasons).

| Sunday | August | Fourth of July | summer |
| Wednesday | Christmas | fall | spring |

2. Geographical names — streets, avenues, lakes, rivers, oceans, mountains, countries, states, cities, railroads.

Forty-sixth Street	Lake Michigan	Pacific Ocean
Fifth Avenue	Nile River	Rocky Mountains
Denver	New Hampshire	Union Pacific Railroad

3. The words *North, East, South, Northwest* when they name sections of the country.

Marjorie spent last winter in the *South* and last summer in the *West*.

On Friday we motored *east* a hundred miles to **Albany** and then *south* a hundred fifty miles to New York. [In this sentence *east* and *south* denote directions.]

4. Great events or documents of history.

Revolutionary War   Declaration of Independence
Battle of Bunker Hill   Pure Foods and Drugs Act

5. Names of parts of our government.

Congress   House of Representatives   Police Department
Senate   Altoona Board of Education Fire Department

6. Names of political parties, religious sects, and races.

Democrat   Methodist   Presbyterian   Jew
Republican Catholic   Indian   Negro

7. Names of churches, schools, and buildings.

Lee Junior High School   First Baptist Church
University of Illinois   Woolworth Building
Horace Mann School   Chrysler Building

Junior high school, high school, college, or *school* is capitalized only if the word refers to a particular school.

After completing *junior high school* I expect to attend a *senior high school* in Chicago and a *college* in California.

I attend *Roosevelt Junior High School;* my brother is in *Central High School;* and my sister is in the *University of California.*

8. Titles before proper names and such titles as *the President, the King.*

Judge Burton   Doctor Gray   Captain Jenks
King George   Aunt Marie   Professor Holmes

Mother, Father, Dad, Grandfather, and similar names may be written either with or without capitals.

I'll ask *Mother* and *Father* that question.
I'll ask *mother* and *father* that question.

When a pronoun precedes *mother, father, dad,* or *grandfather,* no capital is used.

I'll ask my *mother* and *father* that question.

9. Titles of books, poems, stories, and compositions.

"The Star-Spangled Banner"   *Tales from Shakespeare*
"The Lady or the Tiger?"   *Story of My Life*
Book of the Camp Fire Girls   *Days and Deeds*

Notice that prepositions (*of, from*) and conjunctions (*or, and*) are not capitalized. *A, an,* and *the* are capitalized only when they begin titles.

10. Names given to God and names for the Bible and divisions of the Bible.

Old Testament   Psalms   Lord   Father Almighty

Practice 1

Capitalize the following. Give a reason for each capital. The figure in parenthesis tells how many capitals have been omitted.

1. Have you ever read hamlin garland's *boy life on the prairie?* (5)
2. An engineer in the woolworth building called the fire department. (4)
3. After graduating from wilson junior high school, everett entered a senior high school in cleveland. (6)
4. Last spring we lived for a month at the statler hotel in boston. (3)
5. Washington irving was born in william street, new york, on april 3, 1783. (6)
6. William penn sailed for england, august 12, 1684, having spent not quite two years in pennsylvania. (4)

7. The largest college in the city of new york is columbia university. (4)

8. Other english captains set out to trade with the rich spanish settlements in the west indies. (4)

9. The united states gained by the louisiana purchase of 1803 a large area west of the mississippi river. (6)

10. In 1681 the quakers settled pennsylvania. (2)

11. How many french were in the forts lying between lake erie and the ohio river? (5)

12. Mr. arthur, colonel roosevelt, and professor simpson are the guests of governor davis. (7)

13. My title is "a tragedy of my childhood." (4)

Practice 2

Copy from your history, arithmetic, or other books ten sentences in which proper names are capitalized. Be ready to explain why each capital is used.

Practice 3

Prepare to write from dictation the following letter. Turn to page 43 to find out how to study for a dictation. Think why each capital is needed.

16 Walnut Place
Rochester, New York
September 19, 1934

Dear Helen,
Here we are home again! Last Tuesday the "Baltic" brought us safely into New York harbor.
While in the city, we stayed at the Pennsylvania Hotel on Seventh Avenue and Thirty-second Street. We were there but three days but had time to go to the top of the Empire State Building — one hundred two stories, I think. The view of the Hudson River, the New Jersey shore, and Central Park was wonderful.
On Wednesday we took a Fifth Avenue bus about town.

Father pointed out to us Lord and Taylor's, Altman's, the public library, the French Building, and Columbia University. Such beautiful things in the windows! The library, a fine building, made me think of Venice, because there were so many pigeons about. At Forty-second Street and Fifth Avenue the streets were crowded with people, and we had to wait a long time for the green light. Finally we moved slowly north in a perfect sea of cars. At Grant's Tomb we turned around, and came back along Riverside Drive.

On Friday we went to the Bronx Park. One needn't go to Africa to see the jungle animals. They are all here.

On Saturday morning the New York Central Railroad brought us home. The time seemed long, in spite of the fact a friend had given me an interesting book, " Men of Iron," by Howard Pyle.

I'm just now getting started in Washington Junior High School. Geography, arithmetic, history, and English are my regular subjects. Since seeing Paris, I am eager to begin the study of French.

Mother and Aunt Kate send love. We all hope to see the dear Briggs family at Christmas time.

Can't you, Helen, run up your first vacation? Do you have school on Columbus Day? Is it any inducement to say I bought you some Venetian beads?

I'm saving my trip to tell you about when I see you.

Lovingly,
Grace E. Tucker

Mastery Test 7A — Capitalization

Capitalize the following sentences. If you omit a needed capital or insert a capital that is not needed, the sentence is wrong. The figure after a sentence tells how many capitals have been omitted.

1. In senior high school judge reed studied history, english, typewriting, geometry, and german. (4)
2. Father went west by the canadian pacific railroad and lived in the west all winter. (4)

3. The empire state building is on thirty-fourth street and fifth avenue, new york. (9)

4. For christmas professor williamson gave me *jan of the windmill* and *story book of science.* (8)

5. After a year in the george washington junior high school josephine last fall entered a junior high school in san francisco. (8)

6. The topic of my composition for tomorrow is "how to bathe a dog." (3)

7. The colorado river rises in the rocky mountains. (4)

8. This year christmas comes on sunday. (2)

9. In the battle of long island general howe missed a chance to capture the american forces. (6)

10. Have the democrats or the republicans a majority in congress? (3)

Mastery Test 7B — Capitalization

Capitalize the following sentences. If you omit a capital that is needed or insert a capital that is not needed, the sentence is wrong.

1. My course in junior high school includes social science, english, french, algebra, and general science. (2)

2. Last winter major allen spent a month in the south. (3)

3. The metropolitan building is on twenty-third street and fourth avenue. (6)

4. On the fourth of july I began to read lewis carroll's *alice in wonderland.* (6)

5. After graduating from elementary school jerry entered boys' high school. (4)

6. For tomorrow we are to write on the topic "a story for a camp fire." (4)

7. The susquehanna river cuts its way through the allegheny mountains. (4)

8. The constitution divides congress into the senate and the house of representatives. (5)

9. After the boston tea party general gage was made governor of massachusetts. (6)

10. We spent august in the yellowstone national park. (4)

Plural

Which of these nouns refer to one? Which mean more than one?

boy, boys
city, cities

ax, axes
bench, benches

If a noun names one person, place, or thing, it is singular: *boy, city, ax, bench.*

If a noun refers to more than one, it is plural: *boys, cities, axes, benches.*

1. Plurals are commonly formed by adding *s* or *es* to the singular.

pencil, pencils
day, days
wave, waves

girl, girls
table, tables
garage, garages

After *s, x, z, sh,* and *ch, es* is added and forms a separate syllable.

grass (one syllable), grasses (two syllables)
watch (one syllable), watches (two syllables)
gas (one syllable), gases (two syllables)
wish (one syllable), wishes (two syllables)
fox (one syllable), foxes (two syllables)
Jones (one syllable), Joneses (two syllables)
bench (one syllable), benches (two syllables)

Practice 4

Write the plural of each word:

1. horse
2. author
3. box
4. glass
5. church
6. dish
7. Burns
8. radish
9. sailor
10. pupil
11. peach
12. lass
13. birch
14. guess
15. ranch
16. brush
17. tax
18. rule

260   JUNIOR ENGLISH IN ACTION

19. door   23. desk   27. mother
20. mattress   24. book   28. father
21. match   25. class   29. year
22. loss   26. aunt   30. bush

2. Six frequently used words ending in *o* add *es* to form the plural.

    hero, heroes   potato, potatoes
    mosquito, mosquitoes   tomato, tomatoes
    Negro, Negroes   motto, mottoes

Note these four plurals formed by adding *s* to words ending in *o*:

    auto, autos   solo, solos
    piano, pianos   soprano, sopranos

3. Nouns ending in *y* preceded by a consonant change *y* to *i* and add *es*.

    fly, flies   story, stories
    baby, babies   army, armies
    lady, ladies   city, cities

Nouns ending in *y* preceded by a vowel — that is, in *ay, ey, oy, uy* — add *s* regularly.

    monkey, monkeys   donkey, donkeys
    chimney, chimneys   turkey, turkeys
    boy, boys   day, days

4. Some nouns ending in *f* or *fe* change the *f* to *v* and add *es*.

    calf, calves   self, selves
    elf, elves   sheaf, sheaves
    half, halves   shelf, shelves
    knife, knives   thief, thieves
    leaf, leaves   wharf, wharves
    life, lives   wife, wives
    loaf, loaves   wolf, wolves

Other nouns in *f* and *fe* add *s* regularly.

 chief, chiefs   dwarf, dwarfs
 roof, roofs   hoof, hoofs
 handkerchief, handkerchiefs   proof, proofs

5. A few words have a plural in *en*.

 child, children   ox, oxen

6. Some words change the vowel.

 man, men   foot, feet
 woman, women   goose, geese
 tooth, teeth   mouse, mice

7. In compound words the noun that tells about whom or what you are talking is usually made plural.

Son-in-law is a kind of *son;* hence the plural is *sons-in-law.* *Editor-in-chief* is a kind of *editor;* hence the plural is *editors-in-chief.*

 teacup, teacups   hanger-on, hangers-on
 Englishman, Englishmen   newsboy, newsboys

Exceptions are:

a. Nouns ending in *ful: spoonfuls, cupfuls.*

b. A few words which make both parts plural: *menservants, women servants.*

8. The plurals of letters, figures, and signs are formed by adding *'s*.

 Your *n*'s look like *u*'s and your *i*'s like *e*'s.
 Cancel the *6*'s and *7*'s.
 Change the +'s to −'s

9. Some nouns have the same form in the singular and the plural.

 deer   salmon   shad   Chinese
 sheep   trout   heathen   Japanese

(Singular) That rainbow *trout* is a foot long.
(Plural) There are many *trout* in this stream.

(Singular) There is a *sheep* in the yard.
(Plural) There are fifty *sheep* in the field.

10. Some nouns are used only in the plural.

| scissors | pincers | ashes | (golf) links | thanks |
| trousers | shears | riches | goods | spectacles |

The scissors are dull.
His trousers are too short.

11. A few nouns ending in *s* are singular in meaning.

| news | measles | civics | mathematics |
| physics | mumps | the United States | |

Many nouns that are singular in form have a plural meaning. **The name of a group is a collective noun.**

army	class	company	flock
committee	team	crew	couple
family	club	herd	jury

Collective nouns have plural forms: *armies, committees, families, classes.*

Practice 5

Write the plural of the following:

1. grass
2. potato
3. family
4. knife
5. bookcase
6. 4
7. apple
8. manservant
9. trout
10. gas
11. hero
12. wolf
13. chief
14. class
15. reply
16. daughter-in-law
17. ax
18. fairy
19. fisherman
20. lass
21. heathen
22. tomato
23. company
24. fly
25. carpenter
26. auto
27. roof
28. pony
29. army
30. stitch

31. woman	38. thief	45. guess
32. mouthful	39. Burns	46. tooth
33. committee	40. dish	47. calf
34. navy	41. monkey	48. sheep
35. journey	42. handkerchief	49. turkey
36. deer	43. half	50. radish
37. daisy	44. solo	51. baby

Practice 6

Prepare to write from dictation the following sentences:

1. Farmers sell tomatoes, potatoes, apples, radishes, peaches, turkeys, and donkeys.
2. Fishermen catch trout, salmon, shad, and weakfish.
3. The ladies are gathering daisies and lilies in the valleys.
4. Buses and autos keep policemen busy.
5. In stories we find wolves, thieves, old women, young wives, enemies, babies, chiefs, and fairies.
6. There are three Alices and two Joneses in my classes.
7. His *6*'s look like *0*'s and his *k*'s like *h*'s.
8. Did the Negroes fight like heroes against the mosquitoes?
9. The hunters shot with their rifles two wolves, two bears, and three deer.
10. Do monkeys take long journeys under clear skies to pick berries?

Gender

Nouns denoting males are in the masculine gender: *boy, man, bachelor, husband, uncle.*

Nouns denoting females are in the feminine gender: *girl, woman, maid, wife, aunt.*

Names of things that are neither male nor female are in the neuter gender: *star, tree, house, pond, mountain.*

Some words may be either masculine or feminine:
pupil, child, parent, friend, cat, teacher, musician, baby.

My cousin invited me to her commencement. [*Cousin* is feminine.]

Dick is my cousin. [*Cousin* is masculine.]

My cousin is in Maine. [*Cousin* is either masculine or feminine.]

Generally different words are used for masculine and feminine.

Masculine	Feminine	Masculine	Feminine
drake	duck	bull	cow
gander	goose	monk	nun
buck	doe	sir	madam

Many feminine nouns end in *ess*.

Masculine	Feminine	Masculine	Feminine
actor	actress	host	hostess
god	goddess	lion	lioness
master	mistress	prince	princess
heir	heiress	waiter	waitress

Practice 7

Write the following words in two columns headed *masculine* and *feminine:*

uncle, aunt; maid, bachelor; goose, gander; doe, buck; sir, madam; heroine, hero; Francis, Frances; Joseph, Josephine; widow, widower; deaconess, deacon; duke, duchess; nun, monk; heiress, heir; mother, father; prince, princess.

How to Form the Possessive

How are the italicized words used?

Oh! say, can you see, by the *dawn's* early light,
What so proudly we hailed at the *twilight's* last gleaming?

NOUNS

Each noun with an apostrophe shows ownership or possession and is in the possessive case.

The possessive case denotes ownership or possession.

The possessive of a noun always has an apostrophe. (These six possessives of pronouns end in s but do not have an apostrophe: *his, hers, its, ours, yours, theirs.*)

Possessive Singular

To form the possessive singular of a noun, add 's. Although this rule looks easy, many boys and girls find it hard to learn to spell the possessive correctly in their writing. Don't change the word. Don't add a letter or omit a letter. Just write the word and then quickly put *'s* AT THE END of it.[1]

```
year + 's        = year's
child + 's       = child's
lady + 's        = lady's
monkey + 's      = monkey's
woman + 's       = woman's
Jones + 's       = Jones's
enemy + 's       = enemy's
boy + 's         = boy's
fox + 's         = fox's
policeman + 's   = policeman's
Dickens + 's     = Dickens's
father + 's      = father's
```

Practice 8

Write the possessive singular of each of the words on the next page. First write all the words just as they

[1] Nouns ending in *s* may take the apostrophe only: *Moses', James', Dickens', Burns', Jones'*. The easy way is always to add *'s* at the end of the word. Stabbing the name by putting the apostrophe before the *s* (*Dicken's*) is a serious blunder.

are in the book; don't change a letter. Then quickly place 's AT THE END of each word.

1. girl
2. day
3. summer
4. boy
5. man
6. donkey
7. officer
8. mouse
9. bird
10. thief
11. horse
12. baby
13. soldier
14. cousin
15. pupil
16. ox
17. Burns
18. mosquito
19. wife
20. fisherman
21. goose
22. hero
23. teacher
24. dog
25. woman

If you get into the habit of spelling the possessive singular correctly, you will avoid in your letters the common and serious error of misspelling words like *boy's*, *girl's*, *man's*, *dog's*, *horse's*, *John's*.

Practice 9

Prepare to write from dictation the following sentences:

1. Jim's home is an hour's walk from Newport.
2. Please send me a catcher's glove and a first baseman's glove.
3. Philip's father walked up to the doctor's door.
4. Is that a cat's tail or a dog's tail?
5. Do you prefer a sailor's or a farmer's life?
6. After an hour's ride we arrived at Uncle Ralph's home.
7. In a tree in my uncle's yard I saw a bird's nest.
8. After an hour's search I found Helen's watch.
9. Julia's mother is staying at a friend's cottage.
10. Is that your mother's or your sister's dress?

Practice 10

Prepare to write from dictation the following paragraphs. Be sure to spell the possessives correctly.

ON MY UNCLE'S FARM

During my month's stay on my uncle's farm swimming, eating, and sleeping made up many a day's work. Each morning I was awakened by a rooster's crowing. Rover's barking, Dobbin's neighing, a duck's quacking, a turkey's gobbling, and a cow's mooing were sounds I liked to hear. A cricket's chirping and a katydid's shrill song lulled me to sleep each night. Once a mosquito's buzzing woke me up in the night.

One day Cousin James and I found a crow's nest in Mr. Holmes's tall tree. There weren't any eggs or little crows in it.

One of James's jobs was to drive the cows to pasture. I often helped him. We had to drive them through Mr. Clark's woods. Under a tree near the road I found a snake's skin, a boy's whistle, and a man's pipe.

I shall not forget Aunt Jane's pies, cookies, fried chicken, and ice cream.

Practice 11

Write sentences containing the possessive singular of these words:

year	girl	bird	Mr. Adams	woman
child	boy	man	brother	fox
lady	teacher	Ralph	sister	enemy
baby	hour	father	farmer	month

Possessive Plural

There are two steps in forming the possessive plural. If you try to do two things at a time, you are likely to do both badly. In learning the possessive plural, save time by taking one step at a time.

1. To form the possessive plural, first write the plural.

Singular	Plural	Singular	Plural
year	years	Jones	Joneses
child	children	enemy	enemies
lady	ladies	man	men
monkey	monkeys	fox	foxes
woman	women	policeman	policemen

2. **Then add 's to the plurals of words that do not end in s and an apostrophe to the plurals that end in s.** Do not change the plural in any other way. Do not omit a letter. Just add 's or an apostrophe.

The plurals that end in s are checked.

Plural				Possessive Plural
√ years	+	'	=	years'
children	+	's	=	children's
√ ladies	+	'	=	ladies'
√ monkeys	+	'	=	monkeys'
women	+	's	=	women's
√ Joneses	+	'	=	Joneses'
√ enemies	+	'	=	enemies'
men	+	's	=	men's
√ foxes	+	'	=	foxes'
policemen	+	's	=	policemen's

Practice 12

Write the plural of each of the words in Practice 8. Then change the plural to possessive plural by adding an apostrophe or 's. Don't change a letter in the plural. Just add an apostrophe or 's.

Practice 13

Write sentences containing the possessive plural of these words:

girl	woman	day	horse
boy	teacher	month	thief
man	lady	week	brother

Mastery Test 8A — Possessive

Complete each sentence by filling the blanks with the correct forms of the words in parentheses:

1. In your class are the —— marks higher than the ——? (boy) (girl)
2. The —— patrol keeps order in the —— lunch room. (boy) (pupil)
3. I like —— and —— stories. (Barbour) (Clemens)
4. Is —— baseball in —— desk? (Harry) (Ralph)
5. Mr. Andrews sells —— and —— suits. (man) (boy)
6. Please send me a —— mask and a first —— glove. (catcher) (baseman)
7. After an —— search I found my —— knife. (hour) (brother)
8. A —— burden is often heavy, and in an —— time he does not go far. (donkey) (hour)
9. —— and —— shoes are sold in that department store. (lady) (child)
10. My —— cottage is a —— throw from the lake. (grandfather) (stone)

Mastery Test 8B — Possessive

Complete each sentence by filling the blanks with the correct forms of the words in parentheses:

1. In your class are the —— books cleaner than the ——? (girl) (boy)
2. My sister sells —— and —— dresses. (woman) (child)
3. —— geography is on —— desk. (Alice) (Father)
4. That —— pay for a —— work is twenty dollars. (man) (week)
5. I like that —— hat better than ——. (girl) (Nellie)
6. After painting my —— house Mr. Baldwin took a —— rest. (uncle) (week)
7. The —— club is giving the plan a three —— trial. (woman) (month)

8. At a —— house I saw a —— nest. (friend) (robin)
9. The science book is ——, and the book on aviation is ——. (Tom) (Ned)
10. Have you read —— *Biography of a Grizzly* or —— *Oliver Twist?* (Seton) (Dickens)

Distinction Exercise

Use each of the following words or expressions correctly in a sentence:

1. year's, years
2. ladies, ladies'
3. boys, boys'
4. teachers, teachers'
5. baby's, babies
6. woman's, women's
7. day's, days
8. city, cities
9. Burns, Burnses
10. Francis, Frances
11. waiter, waitress
12. brother's, brothers
13. captain, Captain
14. west, West
15. junior high school, Junior High School

UNIT 15

PRONOUNS

A pronoun is a word used instead of a noun. This definition you know, and you have had some practice in finding pronouns in sentences. But do you always use pronouns correctly when you speak and write?

Personal Pronouns

Which of the following pronouns refer to the person speaking? Which to the person spoken to? Which to the person or thing spoken of?

1. My brother and I went to visit our uncle.

My, *I*, and *our* refer to the person or persons speaking. They are pronouns of the first person.

2. You left your hat in the dining room.

You and *your* stand for the person spoken to. They are pronouns of the second person.

3. He and his sister went with their aunt to her summer home.

He, *his*, *their*, and *her* refer to the person or persons spoken of. They are pronouns of the third person.

All these pronouns of the first person, the second person, and the third person are personal pronouns.

A personal pronoun shows by its form whether the person speaking, the person spoken to, or the person or thing spoken of is referred to.

Practice 1

Make a list of the personal pronouns in the following sentences. In your list place (1) after a pronoun in the first person, (2) after a pronoun in the second person, and (3) after a pronoun in the third person. The figure in parenthesis tells how many personal pronouns there are in the sentence.

1. My sister and I decided to ask two of our friends to go with us on a picnic. (4)
2. Over the telephone my sister said to one of her friends, "Will you and your brother Joe go with my brother and me on a picnic tomorrow?" (6)
3. "Joe and I would hate to miss it," said Marjorie. "Are you taking your bathing suits?" (4)
4. "Yes, we're taking them," said my sister. (3)
5. Mother prepared the lunch for us and drove us to Sunken Meadow Park. (2)
6. Joe is a wonderful swimmer; he can swim much faster than I. (2)
7. Marjorie is an excellent cook; she fried the potatoes and kept them piping hot. (2)
8. A maple tree dropped some of its leaves on our picnic table. (2)
9. A thrush sang its song to us. (2)
10. When we reached home, Marjorie said, "We've thoroughly enjoyed your picnic." (3)

Case

Both *I* and *me* are personal pronouns of the first person; both *he* and *him*, personal pronouns of the third person. In the following sentence what is the difference in use between *I* and *me?* Between *him* and *he?*

I saw him, but he didn't see me.

I, the subject of the verb *saw*, is in the nominative case; *me*, the object of the verb *did see*, is in the objective case. *Him*, the object of the verb *saw*, is in the objective case; *he*, the subject of the verb *did see*, is in the nominative case.

The case of a pronoun depends upon its use in the sentence.

Subjects of verbs and predicate nominatives are in the nominative case.

    (Predicate nominative)   It is *I*.
    (Predicate nominative)   Was it *she* or her sister?

Objects of verbs and of prepositions and indirect objects are in the objective case.

    (Object of verb)   I saw *him* yesterday.
    (Object of preposition)   Harry gave the book to *me*.
    (Indirect object)   Harry gave *me* the book.

Only seven commonly used English words have different forms for the nominative and the objective case.

Nominative	I	we	he	she	they	who	whoever
Objective	me	us	him	her	them	whom	whomever

The possessive case of a pronoun shows ownership or possession.

His cap is new, but *mine* is old.

Practice 2

Tell the use and case of each personal pronoun in the following sentences:

Model

I gave him my book.
I — subject of *gave*, nominative case
him — indirect object of *gave*, objective case
my — modifier of *book*, possessive case

1. He and I went with her.
2. It was they.
3. Will you go with him and me?
4. Father gave him and me bicycles.
5. They are my friends.
6. She and I need your help.
7. Harry and I saw your rabbits.
8. Father climbed the mountain with her and me.
9. It was she and I.
10. He and Jack won the first tennis game from Henry and me.

The Personal Pronouns Grouped

First Person

	Singular	Plural
Nominative	I	we
Possessive	my, mine	our, ours
Objective	me	us

Second Person

	Singular and Plural
Nominative	you
Possessive	your, yours
Objective	you

Third Person

	Singular			Plural
	Masculine	Feminine	Neuter	
Nominative	he	she	it	they
Possessive	his	her, hers	its	their, theirs
Objective	him	her	it	them

Old forms of the second person, *thou, thy, thine, thee,* and *ye,* are found in the Bible and are sometimes used in poetry.

Correct Case

Which forms are correct?

1. Who is there? —— (I, me)

The correct pronoun is *I*, because *I* is the subject of *am* understood.

2. Is it ——? (he, him)

He is the predicate nominative of the verb *is*. The predicate nominative of a verb is in the nominative case.

3. My aunt had sleeping quarters for all except Louise and ——. (I, me)

Me is the object of the preposition *except*. The object of a preposition is in the objective case.

4. —— were the winners. (he and I, him and me)

He and *I* are subjects of the verb *were*. The subject of a verb is in the nominative case.

Errors in case are commonest in compound subjects and compound objects. Everyone says, "*He* was the winner" and "*I* was the winner." For that reason it should be easy to get into the habit of saying "*He* and *I* were the winners." Everybody says, "Mother sent *me* to the store." Why should anyone have trouble with "Mother sent Jean and *me* to the store"?

Practice 3

Fill the blanks with the correct pronouns. Explain the use in the sentence of each pronoun selected.

1. Are you and —— going? (he, him)
2. —— are reading *Up from Slavery*. (John and I, me and John)

3. Is that ——? (her, she)
4. —— two sat in the rumble seat. (us, we)
5. Grace went with Mother and ——. (I, me)
6. —— and —— can't swim. (her, she) (I, me)
7. John and —— went to the game yesterday. (I, me)
8. My scoutmaster called another tenderfoot and —— to his desk. (I, me)
9. —— and —— are going to play baseball. (he, him) (I, me)
10. Every week my father and —— went to the beach. (I, me)
11. Father sent Jerry and —— for the cattle. (I, me)
12. The principal will select either —— or ——. (he, him) (I, me)
13. —— and —— have been friends for years. (her, she) (I, me)
14. It was neither —— nor ——. (he, him) (her, she)
15. Let us divide the Christmas candy between you and ——. (I, me)
16. —— went for a walk. (he and I, me and him, him and me)
17. Are you and —— in the same class? (he, him)
18. Edith invited —— and ——. (her, she) (I, me)
19. —— and —— went to the store for Mother. (her, she) (I, me)
20. I like to play with Marion and ——. (her, she)
21. The director of the camp invited another boy and —— to his cottage for dinner. (I, me)
22. Let Miriam sit between you and ——. (I, me)
23. The teacher told —— girls a good story. (us, we)
24. Who is making that noise? —— (I, me)
25. Everyone but —— and —— had gone to the movies. (her, she) (I, me)

Practice 4

Read aloud three times the correct sentences in the preceding exercise. Choose quickly. This practice will help you to get into the habit of using correct pronouns.

Practice 5

Why is each italicized word correct? Repeat these correct expressions until you form the habit of using them.

1. *He* and *I* like to skate.
2. Will you go skating with *him* and *me?*
3. *She* and *I* like to sew.
4. Will you sew with *her* and *me?*
5. *We* girls are forming a sewing club.
6. Mother gave *us* girls a sewing basket.
7. Is the box of candy for *him* or *me?*
8. *He* and *I* will divide the candy.
9. It wasn't *she.*
10. Was it *he?*
11. Father gave *her* and *me* a pup.
12. Where were you and *he* yesterday afternoon?
13. Why aren't you and *she* going to the game?
14. Shall I send for *him* or *her?*
15. The winner was neither *he* nor *I.*
16. Mother saw my brother and *me* in the boat.
17. *We* boys won the spelling match.
18. Catherine asked my sister and *me* to her party.
19. Frank and *I* have not missed a day.
20. No one but *him* knew the answer.

Practice 6

In sentences of your own, use correctly —

1. He and I
2. Him and me
3. My brother and I
4. My brother and me
5. She and I
6. Her and me
7. You and I
8. You and me
9. My uncle and I
10. My uncle and me
11. He and Edwin
12. She and Charlotte

Word Order

When speaking about yourself and another, as a matter of courtesy mention the other person first.

1. —— went to the Yale-Harvard football game. (I and my father, my father and I)

My father and I is correct and shows the speaker well-bred, because he mentions his father first and himself last. *Father and I* is the compound subject of *went*.

Practice 7

In each sentence select the courteous expression:

1. —— are going to cook our supper in the woods on Thursday. (I and some other girls, some other girls and I)
2. Come with ——. (Jimmy and me, me and Jimmy)
3. —— went to the game. (a friend and I, I and a friend)
4. Neither —— thought of the fire extinguisher. (I nor my mother, my mother nor I)
5. Last Saturday —— had lunch in a Chinese restaurant. (I and my sister, my sister and I)

Double Subject

(Right) Mr. Hyde was a small man. [*Mr. Hyde* is the subject.]

(Wrong) Mr. Hyde he was a small man. [*Mr. Hyde he* is a double subject.]

(Right) My opponent made an inaccurate statement. [*Opponent* is the simple subject.]

(Wrong) My opponent she made an inaccurate statement. [*Opponent she* is a double subject.]

(Right) Sherlock Holmes walked around the house. [*Sherlock Holmes* is the subject.]

(Wrong) Sherlock Holmes he walked around the house. [*Sherlock Holmes he* is a double subject.]

Practice 8

What is the double subject in each sentence? Correct the sentence.

1. Mary she went to get a drink.
2. One man he crawled up the ladder.
3. The stranger he walked down the road.
4. Louise she is a brave girl.
5. Jim Hawkins he never forgot his mother.
6. The pitcher he couldn't put the ball over the plate.
7. Wolf he asked for some food.
8. One boy he suggested playing punch ball.
9. Billy Bones and Black Dog they had a fight.
10. Rachel and Mary they went to see *The Silver Candlesticks*.

Them, Those

Which is correct?

1. —— are mine. (them, those)

Those is the correct subject. *Them* is in the objective case; a subject is in the nominative case.

2. —— shoes hurt my feet. (them, those)

The adjective *those* modifies the noun *shoes*. A pronoun in the objective case never modifies a noun.

Practice 9

Fill each blank with *them* or *those* and give a reason for your choice:

1. I have read all —— books.
2. —— flowers are artificial.
3. —— Giants are good hitters.
4. One of —— boys has my ball.
5. Throw away —— papers.
6. —— girls are in my class.
7. Are —— chickens yours?
8. Where did you find —— rubbers?
9. —— are my books.
10. —— big fellows won't let us play here.

Practice 10

If you ever use the double subject or *them* for *these* or *those*, read aloud three times the correct sentences in Practice 8 and Practice 9.

Compound Personal Pronouns

Compound personal pronouns end in *self* in the singular and *selves* in the plural. The following are the compound personal pronouns:

	SINGULAR	PLURAL
First Person	myself	ourselves
Second Person	yourself	yourselves
Third Person	himself herself itself	themselves

There are no such words as *hisself* and *theirselves*.

Practice 11

In each sentence select the correct word:

1. Joe's brother enjoyed —— in the mountains. (himself, hisself)
2. Milton played by ——. (himself, hisself)
3. All the boys enjoyed —— on the trip. (theirselves, themselves)
4. He is master of ——. (himself, hisself)
5. Bob hurt —— in the gymnasium. (himself, hisself)

Interrogative Pronouns

How are the italicized words used?

Who is captain?
Which do you like best?
What is the answer?

The interrogative pronouns, *who*, *which*, and *what*, are used in asking questions.

Case

Who, the nominative case, is used as the subject; *whom*, the objective case, is used as the object of a verb or a preposition.

It is easier to find the use of a word if the sentence is arranged in grammatical or natural order: (1) subject and modifiers; (2) verb; (3) object, predicate adjective, or predicate nominative.

Which pronoun in each sentence is correct?

1. —— is it for? (who, whom)

The grammatical order of the sentence is, "It is for (who, whom)?" *Whom* is object of the preposition *for*. ("Who is it for?" is, however, good conversational English.)

2. —— is your geography teacher?

The grammatical order is, "Your geography teacher is (who, whom)?" *Who* is the predicate nominative of the verb *is*.

Practice 12

Fill each blank with the correct or preferred word. Tell how each pronoun selected is used in the sentence.

1. —— was elected president of the Book Club? (who, whom)
2. —— did the pupils elect president of the Book Club? (who, whom)
3. —— saw you in the post office? (who, whom)
4. —— did you see in the post office? (who, whom)
5. —— is the captain? (who, whom)

6. With —— did Harry go skating? (who, whom)
7. For —— does Mr. Clemson work? (who, whom)
8. —— are these men? (who, whom)
9. —— do you know in Santa Barbara? (who, whom)
10. For —— are you going to vote? (who, whom)

Indefinite Pronouns

Other troublesome pronouns are the indefinites.

1. *Neither* is present today.
2. *Both* are sick.
3. *One* was sick yesterday.
4. *Many* are going to the fair.

In these sentences *neither, both, one,* and *many* are indefinite pronouns.

Indefinite pronouns point out less clearly or definitely than *this* and *that*. (The pronouns *this* and *that* are called "demonstrative pronouns.")

Although there are only five frequently used personal pronouns (*I, you, he, she, it*), three interrogative pronouns (*who, which, what*), and two demonstrative pronouns (*this, that*), there are about forty in the indefinite pronoun family. Some of them are: *each, either, neither, anyone, anybody, anything, everyone, everybody, everything, someone, somebody, something, no one, nobody, one, some, any, many, few, all, both, none, such, other, each other, another, one another, several.*

One, other, and compounds of *one, body,* and *else* form the possessive singular by adding *'s*.

Practice 13

Prepare to write the following sentences at dictation. Be sure to spell the possessives correctly.

1. Everybody's answer is wrong.
2. Everybody else's cottage has electric lights.

3. We corrected each other's compositions.
4. Everyone's work is neat.
5. One's friends are valuable.
6. Everybody's story was handed in on time.
7. One should take advantage of one's opportunities.
8. We marked each other's spelling papers.

Pronouns and Adjectives

Do you always know the difference between an adjective and a pronoun? What are the italicized words?

1. *This* is a torn book. [*This* is a pronoun used as the subject of the verb *is*.]
2. *This* book is torn. [*This* is an adjective modifying the noun *book*.]
3. *Each* did his share of the work. [*Each* is a pronoun used as the subject of the verb *did*.]
4. *Each* boy did his share of the work. [*Each* is an adjective modifying the noun *boy*.]
5. *One* was lost. [*One* is a pronoun used as the subject of the verb *was lost*.]
6. *One* baseball was lost. [*One* is an adjective modifying the noun *baseball*.]

Practice 14

In sentences of your own use the following words as pronouns and as adjectives:

this	other	some	few
that	either	any	all
one	neither	many	both

Agreement with Antecedent

The noun for which a pronoun stands is called its antecedent.

1. Danny is training *his* dog.

His is used instead of *Danny; Danny* is the antecedent of *his*.

2. Has Mildred completed *her* story?

Her is used instead of *Mildred; Mildred* is the antecedent of *her*.

In number, person, and gender a pronoun agrees with its antecedent.

We need to watch the number of our pronouns, especially if the antecedents are words like *each, everybody,* and *anyone*.

***Each, every, either, neither, anyone, anybody, everyone, everybody, someone, somebody, no one, nobody, one, many a,* and *a person* are singular.**

To decide whether a singular or plural pronoun is correct, find the antecedent and notice its number; then use a pronoun in the same number.

Which is the correct pronoun in each sentence?

1. Everyone was in a hurry to get to —— classroom. (his, their)

His is correct, because the antecedent *everyone* is singular.

2. Every boy has —— own ideas about the best way to spend the summer vacation. (his, their)

His is correct, because the antecedent *boy* is singular.

3. Everyone is expected to do —— bit for the unemployed. (his, his or her, their)

His is correct. *His or her* calls attention to the fact that men and women are included. It is correct but clumsy.

4. One can spend happy evenings in —— own home. (his, one's, their)

Either *his* or *one's* may be used to refer to *one*.

Practice 15

Fill each blank with a suitable pronoun and tell the antecedent of each pronoun used:

1. After dinner everyone took off —— coat. (his, their)
2. Everybody did —— homework. (his, their)
3. Everybody ran to —— own seat. (his, their)
4. Did everyone prepare —— speech? (his, their)
5. Everybody studied —— English lesson. (his, their)
6. Any member may bring —— friends. (his, their)
7. Everyone should take —— hat off in the school building. (his, their)
8. Every girl did —— best. (her, their)
9. My mother bought some nuts and gave —— to the squirrel. (it, them)
10. Each girl had been guilty of some neglect of —— health. (her, their)
11. Everybody should be careful of —— pronunciation. (his, their)
12. Everyone tried to persuade Kak to remain with ——. (him, them)
13. Everyone did —— best to straighten the logs. (his, their)
14. Each pupil had to go to the front of the room and tell the class about —— book. (his, their)
15. Everybody must bring —— book. (his, their)
16. Everyone had —— chance. (his, their)
17. Everyone may choose —— own topic. (his, their)
18. Everyone desires to look —— best. (his, their)
19. Each one had a chance to show —— skill in the tournament. (his, their)
20. What radio fan doesn't enjoy seeing pictures of —— favorite radio entertainers? (his, their)
21. One should learn how to speak —— language correctly. (his, one's, their)

22. Each runner put —— foot on the mark. (his, their)
23. Everyone there enjoyed ——. (himself, themselves)
24. Any girl going with us has to take —— books. (her, their)
25. One can be successful in —— own town. (his, one's, their)

Practice 16

Read the correct sentences in Practice 15 aloud three times. Supply the correct word quickly.

Error Box

Jot down all the errors you hear in the use of pronouns, and bring them to class. Do not include errors made by boys and girls in grades below the seventh. After the sentence write the name of the person who made the mistake; or if the speaker was a stranger, tell where you heard it.

EXAMPLE

Jessie will drive up and take we girls along. (Jane Rollins)
That isn't her on the front seat. (Movie)
Between you and I he must be mistaken. (Street car)

Be ready to correct the errors you hand in. The teacher may have the wrong sentences placed in the Error Box every day for a week or two, and then open the Error Box for a period of class correction.

Mastery Test 9A — Pronouns

Select the correct or preferred word or expression to complete each sentence. On your paper write this answer after the number of the sentence. (Right − Wrong = Score)

1. It is ——. (he, him)
2. Frank and —— went home. (I, me)

3. —— will go. (he and I, him and me, me and him)
4. —— girls belong to the Story Club. (them, those)
5. —— girls are going. (us, we)
6. We shall meet you and —— at the game. (her, she)
7. Between you and —— I don't believe that story. (I, me)
8. The bull chased Henry and ——. (I, me)
9. My —— is spending the winter in California. (uncle, uncle he)
10. Has anyone lost —— coat? (his, their)
11. Each may take —— pencil. (his, their)
12. Is everyone in —— place? (his, their)
13. —— is the governor of this state? (who, whom)
14. The boys found some old tin cans and tied —— to the fence. (it, them)
15. Everybody should be careful of —— English. (his, their)
16. Nobody may leave —— seat without permission. (his, their)
17. Theodore and Albert went to New York by ——. (theirselves, themselves)
18. —— took the oversea railroad to Key West. (I and my brother, my brother and I)
19. Uncle Will gave the candy to Elizabeth and ——. (I, me)
20. No one but —— escaped. (he, him)

Mastery Test 9B — Pronouns

Select the correct or preferred word or expression to complete each sentence. On your paper write this answer after the number of the sentence. (Right − Wrong = Score)

1. It is ——. (she, her)
2. My brother and —— went for a ride. (I, me)
3. —— went to the store. (her and me, me and her, she and I)
4. He asked for John and ——. (I, me)

5. —— boys have formed a club. (us, we)

6. My —— caught sixteen flounders. (father, father he)

7. Are you going swimming this afternoon with Ralph and ——? (I, me)

8. Where did you buy —— books? (them, those)

9. The flag belongs to Frank and ——. (I, me)

10. Everyone must do —— own work. (his, their)

11. Each player may select —— partner. (his, their)

12. Everybody is to bring —— own pencil and paper. (his, their)

13. —— is the president of the Better Speech Club? (who, whom)

14. The author of these plays did not want to have —— published. (it, them)

15. Everybody should put —— things away. (his, their)

16. One of the boys lost —— book. (his, their)

17. Sidney decided to publish the paper by ——. (himself, hisself)

18. Mother sent Grace and —— for a quart of ice cream. (I, me)

19. —— saw pineapples growing in Florida. (Helen and I, I and Helen)

20. Boys like —— are respected. (he, him)

UNIT 16
VERBS

A verb is as necessary in a sentence as an engine is in an automobile, an airplane, or a motor boat. A group of words without a verb does not go, does not say or ask anything, does not express a complete thought.

Some verbs, like some engines, are very simple: "Yesterday I *saw* a baby raccoon." Others resemble an eight-cylinder engine: "Edward *should have been elected.*" In this sentence the verb *elected* and the helpers *should have been* together say something about Edward.

Transitive and Intransitive

Transitive means "going over." If the action is received by some person, animal, or thing, the verb is **transitive.** Other verbs are **intransitive.**

1. Babe Ruth *hit* the ball.
2. The ball *was hit* by Babe Ruth.

Ewing Galloway
BABE RUTH AT BAT

Hit and *was hit* are transitive verbs, because the action was received by the ball.

1. The girl *fed* the woodchuck.
2. The woodchuck *was fed* by the girl.

Fed and *was fed* are transitive verbs, because the action was received by the woodchuck.

FEEDING A WOODCHUCK

Courtesy Union Pacific System

That is one way to tell a transitive verb. A better way often is to apply this test: **A verb is transitive if it has an object or if the subject is acted upon. Other verbs are intransitive.**

Which of these verbs are transitive? Which are intransitive?

1. I *have* two dogs.

Have is transitive, because *dogs* is its object.

2. Skippy *can run* fast.

Can run is intransitive, because it does not have an object and the subject is not acted upon.

3. The aviator *flew* a tiny plane.

Flew is transitive, because *plane* is its object.

4. The aviator *flew* over the mountain.

Flew is intransitive, because it does not have an object and the subject is not acted upon.

5. The farmer *shot* a deer.

Shot is transitive, because *deer* is its object.

6. The farmer *shot* at a deer.

Shot is intransitive, because it does not have an object and the subject is not acted upon.

7. Harold *was elected* captain.

Was elected is transitive, because the subject *Harold* is acted upon.

8. Harold *is* captain.

Is is an intransitive verb, because it does not have an object and the subject is not acted upon.

Sentences 3, 4, 5, and 6 show that a verb may be transitive in one sentence and intransitive in another.

The verb *be* (*am, is, are, was, were, has been, have been, had been, may be, might be*) NEVER TAKES AN OBJECT, hence is always intransitive.

Practice 1

Which of the transitive verbs in the sentences on page 292 have objects? Which have subjects that are acted upon? In the exercise there are five of each kind.

Model

1. Barnaby Lee was captured by pirates.

The subject, *Barnaby Lee*, was acted upon.

2. A group of men discovered an ancient treasure city in the mountains of Mexico.

City is the object of the transitive verb *discovered*. *City* answers the question "*Discovered* what?"

1. We saw your play.
2. English is used by nearly twenty-five per cent of the population of the world.
3. I have your book.
4. Tad was thrown overboard in the night.
5. Soils are moved by wind, water, and glaciers.
6. She brought the teapot and the pitcher of cream.
7. Miriam knew practically everyone in the village.
8. Coach Barnum was injured in an automobile accident.
9. Augusta has large cotton mills.
10. Jacques, a French lad, is taken as cabin boy on board a boat.

An intransitive verb which joins a predicate adjective or a predicate nominative to the subject is called a linking verb. *Be, seem, appear, remain, become, look, grow, feel, smell, taste,* and *sound* are often used as linking verbs.

I *am* sorry. He *looks* happy. He *seems* strong.

Practice 2

Which of the following intransitive verbs are linking verbs? How do you tell? In the exercise there are five linking verbs.

Model

This apple tastes sour.

Tastes is a linking verb, because it joins the predicate adjective *sour* to the subject *apple*.

1. Walter is seven years old.
2. Father is in Milwaukee.
3. Look at the camera.
4. Mother looks tired.
5. How tall you have grown!
6. These peanuts grew in North Carolina.
7. There is much level land in Louisiana.
8. Detroit is an important railroad center.
9. Does the rose smell sweet?
10. Boats were gliding from shore to shore.

Practice 3

Which of the transitive verbs in the following sentences have objects? Which have subjects that are acted upon? Which verbs are intransitive?

1. Last summer Mr. Dunn traveled in England and France.
2. In Pittsburgh there are large railroad shops.
3. A wolf cub was given to Dusty Star.
4. Above Harrisburg we crossed the Susquehanna River.
5. Gatty and Post flew around the world in eight days.
6. Cole dived headfirst from the wing of the airplane.
7. Thirty thousand saw the game between the Yankees and the Athletics.
8. Gar Wood won the speed boat championship.
9. Davis slid right over second base.
10. Walter Berger drove a home run into the left field seats.
11. Johnson batted for Davis in the ninth inning.
12. The corn was eaten by an army of grasshoppers.
13. Governor Ross rode on horseback through the Sawtooth Mountains of Idaho.
14. Vast deposits of iron ore are found in Michigan.
15. Nashville is the capital of Tennessee.
16. Much sugar cane is raised in Louisiana.
17. The famous Mammoth Cave is in the southern part of Kentucky.
18. Rice grows only in a warm climate.

19. I'll not take it.
20. Eighteen kinds of turtles are found in the Carolinas.
21. When did you arrive in Chicago?
22. When were you weighed last?
23. Are those scales accurate?
24. How many pounds have you gained?
25. Rome was made a beautiful city during a time of peace.

Practice 4

In sentences of your own use each of the following as a transitive and as an intransitive verb: *hear, shoot, read, speak, ask, call, run, taste, sing, study.*

Model

(Transitive) I heard the President's speech over the radio.
(Intransitive) I was not at the game but heard about it.

Tense

Which of the verbs in the following sentences refer to the present time? To past time? To future time?

1. I *see* a mountain now.
2. I *saw* a mountain yesterday.
3. I *shall see* a mountain tomorrow.
4. Mary *is* happy now.
5. Mary *was* happy yesterday.
6. Mary *will be* happy tomorrow.
7. Father *plays* golf often.
8. Father *played* golf yesterday.
9. We *shall play* golf tomorrow.

The verbs in sentences 1, 4, and 7 refer to present time and are in the present tense.

The verbs in sentences 2, 5, and 8 refer to past time and are in the past tense.

The verbs in sentences 3, 6, and 9 refer to future time and are in the future tense. Notice that in these sentences *shall* is used with *I* and *we* and *will* is used with other subjects.

Tense means time. The present tense is used for present time; the past tense, for past time; the future tense, for future time.

Present Tense	Past Tense	Future Tense
Now I *go*	Yesterday I *went*	Tomorrow I *shall go*
Now I *speak*	Yesterday I *spoke*	Tomorrow I *shall speak*
Now I *write*	Yesterday I *wrote*	Tomorrow I *shall write*

Practice 5

Tell the tense of every verb in the following sentences:

1. Gehrig knocked the ball over the fence.
2. Mrs. Helen Wills Moody will play tennis at Forest Hills.
3. Mrs. Moody is a great tennis player.
4. The President spent Saturday at his camp.
5. When will your cousin arrive in Louisville?
6. I enjoy *Boys' Life* every month.
7. General Pershing commanded the American army in France.
8. Ten motor boats are ready for the Gold Cup contest, which will be held at Montauk on Saturday.
9. Memphis is a lumber center and has cottonseed oil mills.
10. Girls' hats will be larger this winter.

The Perfect Tenses

Although time is divided into the lengthy past, the brief present, and the future, three tenses are not enough to express all our thoughts. We often need the three perfect tenses to express action completed or perfected at some time.

If one, for example, wishes to say that he has just finished bathing the dog, he can't say,

(Present) I *bathe* (or am bathing) the dog,

because the present is used for action that is going on. Likewise he can't say,

(Past) I *bathed* the dog,

because that sentence might refer to a bath last month. He must say,

(Present perfect) I *have bathed* the dog.

The present perfect tense is used if the action is completed in the present time or extends to the present time.

How is the present perfect tense formed?

He *has gone*. They *have come*. We *have hurried*.

Gone, *come*, and *hurried* are the past participles (see page 300) of the verbs *go*, *come*, and *hurry*. The present perfect tense of a verb is always made up of *have* (or *has*) and the past participle of the verb.

The past perfect tense is used if the action was completed before some past time. It consists of *had* and the past participle of the verb.

He *had gone*.
They *had come*.
We *had hurried*.

The future perfect tense is used if the action will be completed before some point in future time. It is formed by joining *shall have* or *will have* and the past participle of the verb.

He *will have gone*.
They *will have come*.
We *shall have hurried*.

The Six Tenses

	FIRST PERSON SINGULAR OF *BE*	THIRD PERSON SINGULAR OF *GO*
Present	I am	he goes
Past	I was	he went
Future	I shall be	he will go
Present Perfect	I have been	he has gone
Past Perfect	I had been	he had gone
Future Perfect	I shall have been	he will have gone

Practice 6

Write in list form the six tenses of *say*, *see*, and *go* in the first person singular. Write also the six tenses of *be*, *do*, and *break* in the third person singular.

Practice 7

Find all the verbs in the following sentences and tell the tense of each. The figure in parenthesis tells how many verbs there are in the sentence.

1. How long have you lived in San Francisco? (1)
2. How long had you lived in Seattle before you moved to San Francisco? (2)
3. We shall have raised all the potatoes by next Friday. (1)
4. Lincoln's mother told her children all the Bible stories she had ever learned. (2)
5. Butte is the center of a tract of land that has produced more copper than any other equal area in the world. (2)
6. "I'll answer the telephone," said George. (2)
7. "Stop a little till I load again," warned Livingstone, for he saw the big lion. (4)
8. Mother had said to me, "Walls have tongues, and hedges ears." (2)
9. "What have I done?" cried Agnes. (2)

10. No one knows who he is. (2)
11. Have you guessed the answer to the puzzle? (1)
12. By that time I shall have saved enough money for college. (1)
13. It had been years since I had last seen them. (2)
14. "I have done my homework," said Dick. (2)
15. "Shall I fire again, sir?" asked the chief mate. (2)

Correct Use

Which is correct?

The repairman —— and charged three dollars. (came, comes)

Because *charged* is in the past, *came*, the past tense of *come*, is correct. To shift from the present to the past or the past to the present without a good reason is an error.

How are the past tense, the present perfect tense, and the past perfect tense used?

(Past) The car *ran* six years.

The car no longer runs. The running took place entirely in the past.

(Present perfect) The car *has run* six years.

The car still runs. The running extends to the present.

(Past perfect) The car *had run* six years before it was smashed to pieces in a wreck.

The accident took place in past time, and the running was completed prior to the wreck.

Practice 8

Select the correct word or expression. Give a reason for each choice.

1. I —— him yesterday. (ask, asked)
2. Last term I —— on the front seat. (sat, sit)
3. Yesterday Arthur —— me this knife. (gave, give)
4. Maurice —— to sell the apples last evening. (help, helped)
5. We —— to live in Trenton. (use, used)
6. I —— that trick better years ago. (did, have done)
7. I —— to America five years ago. (came, have come)
8. I —— Washington Junior High School last September. (entered, have entered)
9. Oliver's mother dies and —— Oliver an orphan. (leaves, left)
10. Mr. Raiman's term as sheriff —— last year. (expired, has expired)
11. I heard a noise and —— behind me. (look, looked)
12. Then the cabin boy —— to Larsen and called him a coward and a murderer. (goes, went)
13. *The Deerslayer* by Cooper —— an entertaining book. (is, was)
14. The old man stopped me and —— telling about his adventures. (start, started)
15. Mr. Brocklehurst believes in equality and once a week —— a party for his servants. (gave, gives)

Principal Parts

Three forms of the verb are so important that they are called the principal parts. They are: (1) the present tense, (2) the past tense, and (3) the past participle.

Practice 9

Many junior high school boys and girls make mistakes in using the thirty troublesome verbs on pages 300 and 301. If you don't know these principal parts, time yourself while you are learning them.

The present perfect tense is made up of *have* or *has* and the past participle.

Study first these four groups:

PRESENT TENSE	PAST TENSE	PAST PARTICIPLE
1		
I *begin*	I *began*	I have *begun*
I *ring*	I *rang*	I have *rung*
I *run*	I *ran*	I have *run*
I *sing*	I *sang*	I have *sung*
I *sink*	I *sank*	I have *sunk*
2		
I *break*	I *broke*	I have *broken*
I *freeze*	I *froze*	I have *frozen*
I *speak*	I *spoke*	I have *spoken*
I *tear*	I *tore*	I have *torn*
3		
I *grow*	I *grew*	I have *grown*
I *know*	I *knew*	I have *known*
I *throw*	I *threw*	I have *thrown*
4		
I *drive*	I *drove*	I have *driven*
I *ride*	I *rode*	I have *ridden*
I *write*	I *wrote*	I have *written*

Principal Parts of Other Verbs

PRESENT TENSE	PAST TENSE	PAST PARTICIPLE
beat	beat	beaten
become	became	become
bring	brought	brought
burst	burst	burst
come	came	come
do	did	done
draw	drew	drawn
eat	ate	eaten
fall	fell	fallen
go	went	gone
give	gave	given

Present Tense	Past Tense	Past Participle
see	saw	seen
show	showed	shown
take	took	taken
teach	taught	taught

Practice 10

Give the present tense, the past tense, and the present perfect tense of all the words in the preceding table in this way:

Present Tense	Past Tense	Present Perfect Tense
Now I *am*	Yesterday I *was*	I *have been*
Now I *bring*	Yesterday I *brought*	I *have brought*

Practice 11

Complete each sentence with the verb form named. The past perfect tense consists of *had* and the past participle of the verb.

See

1. I (past tense) her only yesterday.
2. The Indian boy (past tense) the water spout first.
3. I (past) my mother in the crowd.
4. I (past) about twenty-five battleships.
5. Last Thursday evening my father and mother went to the movies to see a picture that I (past perfect) that afternoon.
6. I (past) a good animal picture yesterday.
7. Jack promised not to tell anybody that he (past perfect) Oliver.
8. They (past) a boy in a sixth-floor window.
9. I (present perfect) four robins this spring.
10. We soon (past) what was wrong.
11. It is the prettiest dress I (present perfect) this spring.
12. His father (past) that Ralph had told the truth.
13. When I (past) the bill, I almost fainted.

14. Yes, I (past) her in a German film.
15. In a minute I (past) a light ahead.

Do

16. Elizabeth (past) the wrong examples.
17. The first thing I (past) was to put the candle on the table.
18. The boy's mother thanked us for what we (past perfect).
19. I (past) all the problems on page 48.
20. He (past) a good deed that day.
21. He (past) the same thing again.
22. After listening to Amos and Andy I (past) my homework.
23. See what I (present perfect).

Come

24. When he (past) back, he was crippled.
25. I (past) home last week.
26. Another traveler (past) in all worn out.
27. When the pirates (past) back, they handed Silver the black spot.
28. Then the War of 1812 (past) on.
29. A burglar (past) into the room.
30. Then Jimmy (past) up to the car.

Run

31. I (past) all the way here.
32. The young calf (past perfect) away from its mother.
33. George, seeing the accident, (past) all the way down the hill to my assistance.
34. This summer I (present perfect) errands for Mr. Jensen.
35. Then the little boy (past) as fast as he could.
36. Our Studebaker (present perfect) for six years.

Go

37. The camel (past perfect) across to the other side of the road.

38. Marietta (present perfect) with them.
39. They (present perfect) without Marion and me.
40. I wish I (past perfect) with them.
41. After I (past perfect) to bed, Carl called for me.

Take

42. Mother (past perfect) the baby from me.
43. I (present perfect) upon myself to find the owner of the pen.
44. The thief (past perfect) my ring and pin.

Eat

45. The guests (past perfect) all the food offered them.
46. I (past) two dishes of ice cream and three pieces of chocolate cake.
47. After we (past perfect) dinner, we got out the car for a ride to Silver Lake.

Break

48. I (present perfect) my knife.
49. Elwood (present perfect) his mother's heart.

Beat

50. Our team (past) yours 6 to 0.
51. Our baseball team (present perfect) Roosevelt Junior High twice this year.

Become

52. George suddenly (past) very jealous of Peter.
53. After passing all the tests Jack (past) an Eagle Scout.

Write

54. I (present perfect) three letters this evening.
55. I (present perfect) a story for the school paper.

Fall

56. Jim (past perfect) down the back stairs.
57. The horse (present perfect) on the ice.

Give

58. I (present perfect) Alice my ring.
59. He (past) a cry of surprise.

Sing

60. We then (past) the school song.
61. The thrush (past) to us while we were eating our lunch.

Show

62. I want to thank you for the interest you (present perfect) in me during my year in junior high school.
63. I (present perfect) Harry how to do the trick.

Other Verbs

64. John (past of *ring*) the bell.
65. I (present perfect of *ride*) many horses.
66. Alfred (present perfect of *speak*) twice to the club.
67. Count Luckner (past of *sink*) fourteen British and American steamers, sailboats, schooners, and cruisers.
68. All the pipes in the kitchen (present perfect of *freeze*).
69. Winifred (past of *begin*) to take music lessons last summer.
70. Just then the balloon (past of *burst*).
71. Eileen (present perfect of *grow*) very rapidly.
72. I (past of *know*) the answer to the question but couldn't think of words to express my thoughts.
73. When I (past of *throw*) the snowball, I didn't see the window.
74. When I reached home, I discovered that I (past perfect of *tear*) a hole in my stocking.
75. Since Monday Father (present perfect of *drive*) eight hundred miles.

Practice 12

Read aloud three times the sentences in Practice 11. Supply the correct verb quickly; don't pause before it. Read distinctly.

Practice 13

Use in sentences of your own the past tense of *see, come, begin, do, give, run, sing, bring, burst, throw, know, ring, teach, draw, grow;* the present perfect tense of *go, do, see, come, eat, ring, write, give, take, drive, fall;* and the past perfect tense of *run, ride, sing, break, speak.*

Ain't and Other Errors

I am not = *I'm not*	*has + not* = *hasn't*
is + not = *isn't*	*have + not* = *haven't*
are + not = *aren't*	

Get into the habit of saying *I'm not, he isn't, it isn't, they aren't, I haven't, he hasn't*. *Ain't* is always incorrect.

May have seen, might have seen, must have seen, could have seen, would have seen, **and** *should have seen* **are correct verbs.** The preposition *of* is never part of a verb.

The past participle is used after *have*.

I could have *driven* to Williamstown that day.
I might have *gone* with Harold to Plattsburgh.

Practice 14

Complete each sentence with the correct word or words:

1. I would —— gone, but no one would go with me. (have, of)
2. I should —— got up a half hour earlier. (have, of)
3. —— going to worry about that. (I ain't, I'm not)
4. I should —— let you know sooner. (have, of)
5. There —— any seats in this car, Bill. (ain't, aren't)
6. That's wrong, —— it? (ain't, isn't)

7. Frank could —— been here by this time. (have, of)
8. I should —— phoned her sooner. (have, of)
9. I should have —— more surprise in the second scene. (past participle of *show*)
10. We should have —— by way of Ticonderoga. (past participle of *go*)
11. I would like to have —— Oliver Twist. (past participle of *know*)
12. I —— seen him for a long time. (ain't, haven't)
13. I should have —— when I was told. (past participle of *go*)
14. —— you going to the game? (ain't, aren't)
15. —— sure of the answer. (I ain't, I'm not)
16. Your coat —— here. (ain't, isn't)
17. The answer —— on this page. (ain't, isn't)
18. She might —— asked some questions in our social science class. (have, of)
19. Marvin —— going on the hike tomorrow. (ain't, isn't)
20. I could —— had a ride to school if I had wanted it. (have, of)
21. —— going to wait any longer. (I ain't, I'm not)
22. There —— any game today. (ain't, isn't)

Practice 15

Read aloud three times the correct sentences in Practice 14. Choose quickly. Pronounce *have* correctly. Say *would have* (not "woulda"), *could have* (not "coulda"), and *should have* (not "shoulda").

Mastery Test 10A — Verbs

Which of the following verbs are transitive? Which are intransitive? On your paper number your answers 1, 2, 3, 4, 5, and write *Transitive* or *Intransitive* after each number.

1. What difference does it make?
2. We sat down at the counter.

3. I'll have a roast pork tenderloin with apple sauce and mashed potato.

4. The news was flashed by radio, telephone, telegraph, and cable to all parts of the world.

5. The highest elevation in Michigan is about two thousand feet above the sea.

Complete each sentence. On your paper write the correct word or words after the number of the sentence.

6. I (past of *come*) in to ask you a question.

7. I (past of *see*) him break the window.

8. Cyrus (past of *do*) the trick twice.

9. Aunt Miriam (present perfect of *go*) to Miami for the winter.

10. Bruce (present perfect of *run*) many races.

11. I (present perfect of *take*) care of the baby all summer.

12. Billy (present perfect of *break*) his engine.

13. Booth Tarkington (present perfect of *write*) many entertaining stories.

14. We soon (past of *become*) tired of his boasting.

15. My uncle (past of *bring*) me a string of beads from Cairo.

16. —— that right? (ain't, isn't)

17. You should —— tried the experiment again. (have, of)

18. It must —— been dark before you reached Bennington. (have, of)

19. You should have —— to the championship game. (gone, went)

20. There —— any books in the closet. (ain't, aren't)

21. When Watson heard this, you could —— knocked him over with a feather. (have, of)

22. If I could —— got my hands on him, he would have been sorry. (have, of)

23. I recited the rule and —— examples. (gave, give)

24. I —— that problem yet. (didn't solve, haven't solved) [*Didn't solve* is the emphatic form of the past tense.]

25. I —— to school six years ago. (started, have started)

Mastery Test 10B — Verbs

Which of the following verbs are transitive? Which are intransitive? On your paper number your answers 1, 2, 3, 4, 5, and write *Transitive* or *Intransitive* after each number.

1. Have you ever made a visit by telephone?
2. Good golfers of the future come from boyhood ranks.
3. In the Spanish-American War, Pershing was promoted for gallantry in action.
4. Fargo is the largest city of North Dakota.
5. Downstairs the kitchen door slammed.

Complete each sentence. On your paper write the correct word or expression after the number of the sentence.

6. I (present perfect of *show*) Rodney how to take care of the furnace.
7. Mother (past of *come*) to the door.
8. I never (past of *see*) you dance before.
9. I (past of *do*) exactly what I was told to do.
10. I should have (past participle of *go*) to the city yesterday.
11. I (past of *run*) till I was out of breath.
12. The bridge (past perfect of *fall*) into the river.
13. Then everybody stood up and (past of *sing*) "The Star-Spangled Banner."
14. Harry (past of *throw*) the snowball.
15. Then it (past of *begin*) to rain.
16. My clock —— slow. (ain't, isn't)
17. I could have —— along to Los Angeles. (gone, went)
18. Clara Barton must —— had a big heart. (have, of)
19. She should have —— the name of the author of the book. (gave, given)
20. They —— going until tomorrow. (ain't, aren't)
21. I would —— won the race if I hadn't stumbled. (have, of)

22. You must —— had a queer sensation when you discovered that you had lost the key. (have, of)

23. The bell —— yet. (didn't ring, hasn't rung)

24. I rang Mr. Eastman's bell and —— him to buy a *Saturday Evening Post*. (ask, asked)

25. My family —— to California in 1932. (moved, have moved)

Review Questions

1. What is the best way to tell a transitive verb?

2. Is the verb in the following sentence transitive or intransitive: "The donkey brayed at the top of his lungs"? How do you know?

3. Give five words which are often used as linking verbs.

4. Use *ride* as a transitive verb and as an intransitive verb.

5. What is the difference in use between the past tense and the present perfect tense?

6. How is the present perfect tense formed? The past perfect tense?

7. Use in sentences of your own the past tense of *see, come, begin,* and *do.*

8. What are the contractions of *I am not, is not, are not, has not,* and *have not?*

9. What are the principal parts of a verb?

10. Give the principal parts of five troublesome verbs.

UNIT 17

THE RIGHT WORD

Putting Thoughts into Words

John had been the first to raise his hand when Miss Jackson asked who knew any stories about birds that were helpful to farmers. He knew several interesting stories about flickers destroying harmful insects. But his speech was hesitating, and he made a poor recitation because he did not have the right words to express himself.

What about your vocabulary? Can you explain things clearly, or do you, too, hesitate and stumble for lack of words? Do you use the same word over and over? Vary your vocabulary. Try to use words which express exactly what you mean.

Vocabulary Test A

In each of the following sentences one word is in italics. Under each sentence are five words or expressions. Select the one of the five which means the same or nearly the same as the word in italics. Write this word or expression on your answer paper after the number of each sentence. Do not copy the sentences.

1. The chest *contained* many treasures.
   furnished, held, raised, hid, contributed
2. A *famous* artist visited the school.
   handsome, strange, favorite, natural, noted

THE RIGHT WORD

3. Some people have no *regard* for other people's property.
    respect, anxiety, regret, eagerness, room

4. The boy built a model of an *ancient* ship.
    foreign, anchored, old, pirate, trading

5. The boys *observed* strange tracks in the snow.
    followed, hunted, drew, discussed, noticed

6. He took this *opportunity* to win their sympathy.
    petition, friend, hard luck story, occasion, opposition

7. She *descended* the stairs hurriedly.
    scrubbed, went down, pounded, examined, climbed

8. American Indians have strange *habits*.
    customs, tepees, totems, moccasins, features

9. The ground seemed *moist* when we sat on it.
    rough, soft, damp, uneven, dry

10. Dorothy knew she was a *lucky* girl.
    studious, tired, frightened, fortunate, frivolous

11. *Fables* teach us good lessons.
    books, plays, stories, movies, failures

12. The view from this rock is *gorgeous*.
    magnificent, blurred, ordinary, extensive, trivial

13. That kind of citizen is *undesirable*.
    well-liked, unsteady, useful, practical, not wanted

14. He boasted to the other boys about his *bravery*.
    brilliancy, courage, stamp collection, skill, courtesy

15. The soldiers hurried to the *trench*.
    mess hall, train, parade, ditch, attack

16. I am *positive* they will come.
    afraid, glad, hoping, doubtful, sure

17. The woman told the crowd about the *incident*.
    danger, fun, happening, accident, runaway

18. The hoot of the owl is a *mournful* sound.
    sad, cheerful, funny, frequent, sweet

19. Theodore Roosevelt Jr. inherited an *illustrious* name.
    peculiar, famous, disgraceful, ordinary, difficult
20. Frank showed us his hiking *outfit*.
    shoes, plans, pictures, equipment, staff

Vocabulary Test B

1. He *completed* the work in a short time.
   corrected, finished, criticized, erased, copied
2. The *object* of the meeting was announced to everyone.
   purpose, place, time, result, president
3. She *succeeded* where others had failed.
   climbed, tried, chuckled, wrestled, won
4. Which do you *prefer*, roast beef or chicken?
   eat, purchase, dislike, choose, suggest
5. Each had his *opinion* about the robbery.
   story, excuse, warning, idea, orders
6. He *obtained* his license several days later.
   lost, discovered, returned, removed, secured
7. The carpenter *accomplished* more than we expected.
   achieved, complained, requested, donated, attempted
8. In India the cow is a *sacred* animal.
   savage, holy, petted, troublesome, frightened
9. Everett had great *confidence* in his father's word.
   faith, dislike, experience, annoyance, doubt
10. The warm room made the children *drowsy*.
    noisy, sleepy, active, discontented, talkative
11. Anne's friends thought that she seemed more *liberal* than her brother.
    bitter, sarcastic, comfortable, generous, healthy
12. Helen Wills Moody is an *expert* tennis player.
    clumsy, quick, serious, reliable, skillful
13. Our little dog leads a *joyous* life.
    active, lazy, merry, sheltered, miserable
14. He has a *gruff* manner of speaking.
    pleasing, funny, harsh, happy, hesitating

15. The snow was *dazzling* in the sunlight.
    glaring, dirty, deep, slippery, beautiful
16. Friends received *tidings* of his safe arrival.
    maps, news, tokens, sketches, descriptions
17. Her mother tried to *suppress* a smile.
    describe, ignore, force, check, create
18. Charles Lindbergh proved that he was *fearless*.
    clever, well-trained, reckless, patient, brave
19. I pledge *allegiance* to the flag of the United States of America.
    strength, loyalty, happiness, greatness, patriotism
20. The principal stopped to *ponder* the question.
    ask, read, consider, quarrel about, talk about

Why Learn New Words?

How strange it would be if we had no words with which to express our thoughts! If we could talk only with signs, how difficult it would be to make our desires known! Imagine yourself traveling through villages in Russia where English is not spoken. How would you get food? How would you find your friends if you were lost? You would have to use signs, and then perhaps you would not get what you wanted. All your life you will be traveling through a world in which you will need words. You can learn these by hearing them, by seeing them in books, magazines, and newspapers, and especially by using them.

Notebook Work

Begin at once your Vocabulary List in your notebook and add to it regularly. You will enjoy watching it grow. This device may help you remember to learn new words, to avoid overworking words, and to use more descriptive expressions.

New Words

Date	Word	Meaning	Sentence Illustrating the Use
Apr. 1	excel	surpass	He wanted to *excel* in baseball.
Apr. 2	alert	watchful	By being *alert*, he learned the game more quickly than his brother.
Apr. 3	courageous	brave	He proved to be a *courageous* fireman.

The Dictionary

The most important book to use in building your vocabulary is the dictionary. If you are not accustomed to using one, you do not realize how much you can learn about each word. The dictionary gives not only the meaning, but the pronunciation, spelling, part of speech of each word, and even the language from which it comes. You should become so familiar with it that you can find words quickly.

Try opening your dictionary as near the middle as possible. What letter do you find? Try opening it in the middle of the first half. What letter do you find? Try opening it in the middle of the second half. What letter do you find? You will discover that the middle is between *k* and *l*; the end of the first quarter in the *d*'s; the end of the third quarter about the last of the *r*'s. Repeat this procedure until you can open the dictionary quickly at these divisions.

Practice 1

Keeping these divisions in mind, tell in which quarter you will find the following words:

house	swallow	fright	observe
noun	pumpkin	trick	queer
diet	chimney	valuable	bureau

Practice 2

As the teacher pronounces each of the preceding words, locate it quickly and with as little fumbling as possible. As soon as you find it, raise one hand, keeping a finger of the other hand on the word. See how often you are the first to locate it.

Game

You will be given ten minutes for this game. Copy the following words. Find each in the dictionary. Write after each the number of the page on which you find it. At the end of ten minutes a check will be made to see who has found the most words.

arrange	hoard	bargain	finance
pamphlet	twelve	kerosene	endorse
wither	wistful	gasoline	smallpox
contempt	marble	vocation	paragraph
event	division	rainbow	legend
investigate	puncture	arithmetic	immortal

Alphabetizing

Learning to arrange words in alphabetical order will help you to locate words more quickly in the dictionary. In case the words begin with the same letter, it is necessary to consider the next letters in order.

Practice 3

Arrange the words in each group in alphabetical order:

1

mission	never	worry	everybody
because	heart	caution	know
storm	physician	friendly	valid
accurate	jump	object	receive

2

definite	arrest	dictate	accident
dwarf	avenge	dike	domino
duchess	dark	attract	applause
admirable	absolute	drought	among

3

bold	bail	belief	bitter
boat	bystander	bought	beat
buckle	bind	broken	butterfly
bright	blast	barrier	blood

Use of Guide Words

The guide words at the top of each page in the dictionary are additional help in locating words quickly. The arrangement of the guide words differs somewhat according to the dictionary. In Webster's *New International Dictionary* and in the *Winston Simplified Dictionary* the guide words at the top of the page are the first word and the last word on the one page; in the *Standard Dictionary* the guide words are the first and last words on both pages.

Practice 4

If *cow* and *crayon* are the guide words on one page, which of the following words would you find on that page?

crash	coward	carver	confess
church	circulate	cradle	crab
crook	crawl	coyote	cranberry

List five words which would be found on a page if *frequent* and *from* were the guide words.

Finding Out How Words Are Pronounced

Last week a new boy came into the class. When the teacher called on him, everyone was surprised at his peculiar pronunciation. The pupils wondered why he made mistakes in pronouncing such easy words.

Presently the class learned that he had lived in another country the greater part of his life and that English was still a strange language to him. As the pupils listened with amusement to his awkward pronunciation, few realized how often they mispronounced words which they have used all their lives.

Are you satisfied with your own pronunciation? Just because you have always pronounced a word a certain way, does that make your way correct? Get the habit of consulting the dictionary every time you are in doubt. Yet you cannot tell how a word is pronounced unless you are familiar with the important marks of pronunciation which the dictionaries use.

Diacritical Marks and Key Words

To pronounce a word correctly one must know the sounds of the letters in it. Signs called "diacritical marks" give the sounds of the vowels and of a few consonants. In the front of every dictionary will be found a page entitled *A Guide to Pronunciation*, and at the top or bottom of every page of the dictionary will be found an abbreviated key. Because the diacritical marks in dictionaries vary somewhat, one needs to study those in his own dictionary.

The pronunciation of some words is shown by marks, of others by the use of other letters. When the letter *s* has the sound of *z*, the word is respelled in parenthesis to show the pronunciation; as, *rise* (rīz). When *k* is silent, the dictionary shows it by the spelling in the parenthesis; as, *knot* (not).

Practice 5

Study these markings given by several dictionaries:

a — ā (date); ḁ (desperate); â (dare); ă (at); ȧ (sofa); ȧ (after); ä (arm)
e — ē (even); ė (event); ĕ (net); ě (recĕnt); ẽ (cover)
i — ī (fine); ĭ (fin)
o — ō (cold); ŏ (sob); ȯ (oblige); ô (organ); o̊ (loft); ǒ (confess)
oo — o͞o (soon); o͝o (stood)
u — ū (use); ŭ (tub); u̇ (unite); û (turn); ŭ (circus)
th — t̶h̶ (they); th (think)

Practice 6

Which word in each line has in the dictionary a letter marked like the one at the beginning of the line? Refer to the above table or to the dictionary.

ā — rate, dart, hat, cast, surface
ē — left, erase, cent, over, me
ĭ — sin, dine, time
ô — obey, sob, sober, contract, soft, order
o͞o — food, wood, root
û — rudder, burn, up, unjust, unit
th — thin, that, though, whether

Practice 7

Copy the following words, marking the vowels. Then pronounce them correctly. Read down, then across.

ape	at	ask	arm
lay	lag	last	lark
slate	slam	slant	salve
clay	clap	class	cart
paste	pat	path	park
tame	tan	task	tar
game	gap	glance	garb

Syllabication and Accent

The dictionary shows how words are divided into syllables and indicates which syllable should receive the greater stress or accent. When you say the word *wisdom*, you put more emphasis on the first part — that is, you accent the first syllable.

You will find these words divided and accented as follows: *fa'vor-ite*, with the emphasis on the first syllable; *in-ven'tive*, with the emphasis on the second syllable; *il'lus-tra'tion*, with a slight emphasis on the first syllable, indicated by a light mark ('), and the greater stress on the third syllable, indicated by a heavy mark ('). Some dictionaries use two marks ('') for the light accent and one mark (') for the main accent — *il''lus-tra'tion*.

Practice 8

Copy the following words and place the accent marks correctly:

di-rect	re-gret	ve-hi-cle	com-mu-ni-ty
u-nit	ter-race	un-just	ath-let-ic
ac-cept	spir-it	at-tempt	o-ver-alls
fre-quent	o-bey	twi-light	pa-tri-ot
pic-ture	traf-fic	pi-an-o	the-a-ter

Practice 9

Copy the following words, divide them into syllables, and place the accent correctly. Use the dictionary when you are in doubt.

character	electricity	courteous	Saturday
mechanic	recreation	conjunction	hospital
material	beautiful	apricot	necessary
familiar	additional	irrigation	positively
government	congratulation	superintendent	particularly

Practice 10

Copy the following words in your notebook. After each word write in parenthesis the pronunciation given in the dictionary. Learn to pronounce each word correctly.

arctic	forehead	heroine	Tuesday
salmon	column	sieve	mortgage
yolk	weapon	drowned	heiress
leisure	often	calm	apparatus
toward	corps	antique	attacked

Practice 11

The following words are frequently mispronounced. Look them up, copy them in your notebook, and indicate the correct division into syllables and the accent. Then study them until you have mastered the correct pronunciation.

poem	mischievous	deaf	address
history	recognize	theater	municipal
library	museum	drowned	Italy
geography	evidently	photographer	February

Practice 12

Good English speech requires that the final *ng* and the *th* in words be sounded distinctly. Do not say *comin'* for *coming*, *doin'* for *doing*, *seein'* for *seeing*, *tru* for *through*, *dis* for *this*, *tot* for *thought*. Pronounce the following words, paying special attention to *ng* sounds:

flinging	saying	bring	finger
bringing	cunning	king	linger
singing	playing	ring	singer
beginning	going	sing	anger

THE RIGHT WORD

Pronounce these, watching the *th* sounds:

eighth	throw	thousand	strength
depth	three	throat	length
twelfth	think	through	farther
with	thirst	thorough	rather

Practice 13

Have you ever heard conversations like the following? Avoid such careless speech. Translate the following conversations into correct English.

1

"Wat'cha goin' t'do now?"
"I'm goin' t'the libery."
"Take dis book wit'cha."
"Awright."

2

"Wy're you goin' this way?"
"'Cause this way's shorter'n I'm late agin."

Practice 14

Study the following sentences in preparation for reading them correctly:

1. He took part in athletics regularly.
2. Under the big elm were heaped innumerable pumpkins.
3. Hundreds listened to his patriotic address on Washington's Birthday.
4. Do you realize that those mischievous children have torn their clothes?
5. There is an old saying that when the winter days begin to lengthen, then the cold begins to strengthen.
6. Her description was so vivid that it gave an accurate picture.
7. The boy was calm, unemotional, and courteous.
8. Are salmon deaf?
9. One sunny Saturday in autumn the boys hunted in the bushes along the creek for cocoons.

10. I positively refuse to accept your assistance.

11. Evidently you found the film interesting.

12. Correct pronunciation and enunciation require constant practice.

13. Chocolate is considered a valuable food for explorers in the arctic region.

14. The first Tuesday after the first Monday in November is election day.

15. The subject of a sentence is always in the nominative case.

16. A comfortable laboratory is an ideal place on a cold February day.

17. The sword hanging in the library belongs to an Italian who fought with the allies.

18. In Russia the government controls all theaters.

19. I made inquiry at the Information Bureau regarding my Southern trip.

20. The architect has submitted plans for the new municipal museum.

Practice 15

Copy the words in italics, divide them into syllables, and place the accent correctly:

1. The *entire audience* agreed with the speaker's *opinion*.

2. You *probably* lost your *handkerchief* in the subway.

3. The coach made *practical suggestions* for improving the team's play.

4. She kept the *appointment regularly* each *Wednesday* at *eleven* o'clock.

5. Many *grammatical errors* are made in using *singular* pronouns.

6. The *aviator's ambition* was to make a transatlantic flight.

7. The *president* of the *university* was installed with fitting *ceremony*.

8. A happy frame of mind has a *beneficial* effect upon one's health.

Studying a Word

Study the definition of the word *honor* as it is given in Webster's *Secondary School Dictionary:*

> **hon′or, hon′our** (ŏn′ẽr), *n.* [fr. OF., fr. L. *honor, honos.*] **1.** Esteem due or paid to worth; manifestation of respect or reverence; hence, fame; reputation. **2.** That which rightfully attracts esteem, respect, or consideration, as dignity, courage, fidelity; esp., high moral worth; nobleness; specifically, in men, integrity; uprightness; in women, purity; chastity. **3.** A nice sense of what is right, just, and true, with strict conformity thereto. **4.** Distinguished position; high rank. **5.** A token of esteem paid to worth; a mark of respect. **6.** A title given to the holders of certain honorable civil offices. **7.** A cause of respect and fame; a glory; an ornament. **8.** *pl.* Academic distinctions. **9.** *pl. Whist.* Ace, king, queen, and jack of trumps. — **Syn.** See REPUTATION, HONESTY. — *v.t.* **1.** To regard or treat with honor, esteem, or respect; also, of God, to adore, worship. **2.** To bestow honor on; elevate in rank; dignify; hence, to treat in a complimentary manner or with civility. **3.** To accept and pay when due; as, to *honor* a draft.

The word *honor* may be spelled in two ways. The spelling which is preferred always comes first. The form in parenthesis is a guide for pronunciation and should not be confused with the spelling of the word.

Several abbreviations are used. The *n.* after the parenthesis is an abbreviation of *noun.* Those in the brackets tell that *honor* comes from the Latin (*L.*) words *honor, honos.* Other abbreviations which are given are *pl.* for *plural; Syn.* for *synonym* (a word of the same or nearly the same meaning); *v.t.* for *transitive verb.* Additional abbreviations which are sometimes used are —

a. — adjective
adv. — adverb
v.i. — intransitive verb
pron. — pronoun

conj. — conjunction
prep. — preposition
sing. — singular
Obs. — obsolete (no longer in use)

Practice 16

Copy the following words, and, consulting your dictionary, write after each word its part of speech:

to	hardly	remember	and
perhaps	anecdote	forbid	from
happy	merrily	never	pickpocket
believe	moment	shrink	not

Many words are used as more than one part of speech.

Example:

Play as a verb (*v.i.*) may mean *to frolic;* as a verb (*v.t.*) may mean *to engage in;* as a noun (*n.*) may mean a *dramatic performance.*

Practice 17

Copy the following words and tell the parts of speech each may be:

honor	autumn	which	reply
sure	fancy	sting	white
far	still	such	trim
but	race	report	prime

Finding a Definition That Fits

As a noun the word *honor* has nine different meanings. In the sentence "Bob has a strong sense of honor" the meaning of *honor* is the third given or *a nice sense of what is right, just, and true.* None of the other meanings would fit the sentence.

Practice 18

Find in your dictionary at least two different meanings of the following words. Use each word in sentences that will show these different meanings.

| stamp | yoke | walk | batter |
| stage | frog | labor | wrap |

Writing a Definition

You may think that you know what a word means, and yet find that you cannot give an exact definition. A boy defined a school as a building where people study. That is not a good definition, as one studies at home, in a library, or even on a train.

In giving the meaning of a word, avoid using *when* and *where;* as, *A store is where goods are kept for sale,* or *Winter is when it is cold.*

Examples of correct definitions:

A store is a place where goods are kept for sale.
Winter is the coldest season of the year.

Practice 19

Write your own definitions of the following common words. Check your definitions with those given in the dictionary, correct errors, and rewrite if necessary.

a box	a chair	a hem	a helmet
a needle	a valley	a table	a house
a pond	a circus	a pencil	a ditch

Use of Hyphen

The dictionary shows whether or not a word is spelled with a hyphen. The hyphen is the long heavy dash and should not be confused with the short light dash which divides the syllables. For example, in *top–heav′i-ness*, the mark after *top* is a hyphen.

Practice 20

Find out from your dictionary which of these words need hyphens. Can you work out a rule for words combined with *self?* For *any, every, some,* combined with *body, thing, where?* For words like *northeast, southwest?*

anybody	northwest	selfsacrifice	toothache
something	northeast	selfpraise	upstairs
nobody	southeast	hightoned	almost
everybody	himself	grandson	goodbye
anywhere	oneself	halfmoon	tomorrow

When to Use Capitals

One may know that a proper name begins with a capital, and yet not be sure whether a word is a proper name. Names of important persons, places, and things will be found in a dictionary. Some dictionaries place such names at the back of the book in a list called "Dictionary of Proper Names." Others include them in the main part.

Practice 21

Look up the following names of people and places. Find out who or what each is and how to pronounce it. This study will give you an idea of the varied information which may be found in a dictionary.

Buddha	Winnipeg	Trinidad	Socrates
Sir Galahad	Cairo	Lansing	Manhattan
Bluebeard	The Hague	Charles Dickens	Napoleon
Malay	Pierre	Madame Curie	Moor
Shanghai	Chopin	Sherwood Forest	Zeus

Practice 22

Find out from your dictionary which of the following words begin with capitals. Copy the corrected list in your notebook.

street	latin	bible	easter
english	europe	history	college
terrier	robin	april	mayflower
mathematics	palm sunday	june bug	halloween

Finding the Plural of Nouns

Generally, the singular of a noun is given in the dictionary. Unless the plural is given also, it may be understood that it is formed by adding *s* or *es* to the singular. For example, the plural of *hammer* is *hammers*, and is not given; but the plural of *child* is *children*, and is given: **child** (chīld), *n.; pl.* CHILDREN (chĭl′drĕn).

Practice 23

Find in your dictionary the plural form of the following words:

woman	secretary	chimney	manservant
elf	ally	ox	mosquito
alley	half	cupful	banjo
potato	sheep	brother-in-law	goose
echo	solo	wolf	lady

Common Abbreviations

Abbreviations which are used commonly may be found in the dictionary. Some dictionaries list them separately at the back of the book. In others they may be found in alphabetical order in the dictionary itself.

Practice 24

Find the meanings of the following abbreviations. Copy the list and the meanings in your notebook.

Mr.	Mrs.	A.M.	P.M.
St.	Ave.	U.S.A.	M.D.
C.O.D.	P.S.	B.C.	A.D.
Sr.	Co.	bal.	vol.
pkg.	pp.	lb.	vs.

Words Often Misused

Accept, except. *To accept* means *to receive*. As a verb *to except* means *to leave out*, but the word is more generally used as a preposition.

The leader *accepted* all the boys *except* Jim.

Cute. Use *pretty, lively, amusing, attractive*, or some other word in good usage and of definite meaning.

Good, well. Do not confuse *good*, the adjective, with *well*, the adverb.

He sings *well*.

Learn, teach. *To learn* is *to acquire knowledge*. *To teach* is *to instruct*.

He *learned* German in order to *teach* his brother.

Let, leave. *To let* means *to permit*. *To leave* is *to go away*, or *allow to remain*.

Let me *leave* my car in your garage.

Most, almost. *Most* means *greatest in quantity, number, or size*. *Almost* means *nearly* or *very nearly*.

We had *almost* reached the camp when the rain began.
He found the *most* chestnuts.

THE RIGHT WORD

Principal, principle. *Principal* as an adjective means *main* or *chief;* as a noun means the *chief person* or *head of a school or institution.* *Principle* means a *rule* or *law of conduct.*

Mr. Bennett is the *principal* of our junior high school. He is a man of strong *principles*.

Quiet, quite, quit. These words are annoying because of similar spelling. *Quiet* means *silent, free from noise.* *Quite* means *completely, wholly.* To *quit* means *to stop* or *to abandon.*

He was *quite* embarrassed that he had not *quit* talking when the room became *quiet*.

To, two, too. *To* is a preposition; *too* is an adverb meaning *more than enough* or *also;* *two* is an adjective or noun meaning the number *2*.

The *two* boys were *too* excited *to* listen attentively.

Mastery Test 11A — Correct Word

Select the correct or preferred word to fill each blank. (Right − Wrong = Score)

1. I —— always drink a glass of milk for lunch. (most, almost)
2. The boys did their work ——. (good, well)
3. The house was —— after he went away. (quite, quiet, quit)
4. —— everyone has read about Lindbergh. (most, almost)
5. I am glad that I can —— your invitation. (except, accept)
6. Father —— him to play golf. (taught, learned)
7. Sam wouldn't —— his little brother go with him. (let, leave)
8. If you —— him go now, he will return before noon. (let, leave)

9. He was —— pleased with the gift. (quiet, quite, quit)
10. Her dream came true ——. (to, too, two)
11. This experience will —— him a lesson. (teach, learn)
12. Marion bought a —— hat. (cute, becoming)
13. Don't use —— many conjunctions. (too, to, two)
14. John's father agreed with the —— decision. (principal's, principle's)
15. Mother told him to hurry, as it was —— time for school. (most, almost)
16. Elizabeth does her work ——. (good, well)
17. All were willing —— Mary and Joan. (accept, except)
18. Miss Brown —— us the rules for capitalization. (learned, taught)
19. Bob plays the game —— for a beginner. (good, well)
20. We saw —— beavers along the bank of the stream. (too, to, two)
21. Mary's mother asked us to be ——, as the baby was asleep. (quiet, quite, quit)
22. No one was late —— me. (accept, except)
23. Ruth took the —— part in the play. (principal, principle)
24. Wouldn't your mother —— you go? (let, leave)
25. In science we study about the —— of nature. (principals, principles)

Mastery Test 11B — Correct Word

Select the correct or preferred word to fill each blank. (Right − Wrong = Score)

1. —— everybody likes candy. (most, almost)
2. Tom was —— ill yesterday. (quite, quit, quiet)
3. My sister —— me how to make candy. (learned, taught)
4. Mary knew only —— rules of the game. (to, too, two)
5. Fred worked —— when the teacher was watching. (well, good)
6. Our car runs ——. (well, good)

THE RIGHT WORD

7. Harry was hoping that he could earn some money ———. (to, too, two)

8. The ——— made an announcement about the game. (principal, principle)

9. Will you ——— me go this afternoon, Mother? (let, leave)

10. Oscar tried to ——— the cat a trick. (teach, learn)

11. I cannot ——— your explanation. (accept, except)

12. My ears were ——— frozen yesterday. (most, almost)

13. You can ——— some animals more easily than others. (learn, teach)

14. All did well in the test ——— Donald. (accept, except)

15. The little girl looked ——— in her new pink dress. (cute, pretty)

16. ——— us go to the movies tonight. (let, leave)

17. Several men have ——— already. (quite, quit, quiet)

18. The storm ——— ruined our garden. (most, almost)

19. The candy looked ——— enough to eat. (good, well)

20. It was against his ——— to permit such actions. (principals, principles)

21. The boys were ——— when they realized the danger. (quiet, quit, quite)

22. The coach praised all the boys ——— Dick. (accept, except)

23. The doctor said Betty had eaten ——— much candy. (to, too, two)

24. Please ——— the door open for me. (let, leave)

25. Helen's fancy skating was the ——— part of the exhibit. (principal, principle)

First find out which words in the lesson you can't spell. Perhaps your teacher will test you before you begin to study. If he doesn't, have someone at home pronounce for you all the words in the lesson.

How to Learn to Spell a Word

1. Pronounce the word correctly. Say each syllable distinctly, and look at each syllable as you say it. Use both your voice and eyes.

2. Close your eyes and think how the word looks. See every letter. Use your mind's eye.

3. Look at the word to find out whether your spelling is right. If it isn't, go through steps 1 and 2 again.

4. Use your hand. Without looking at your book write the word. Compare with the book.

5. With the word covered, write it again and check with the book.

6. In the same way write it a third time and compare.

7. If you misspelled the word on any one of the three trials, copy it in your spelling notebook.

8. After studying all the words, write them as a parent, brother, sister, or friend pronounces them for you.

UNIT 18

SPELLING

Why You Should Be a Good Speller

A good business house does not send out misspelled letters. Rarely does one find a misspelled word in a book, a magazine, or a good newspaper. In school, misspelling is severely penalized. Out of school — in a social letter or letter of application, for example — an error in spelling is more surely discovered than any other error and is commonly considered a sign of carelessness or ignorance.

How the Words Were Selected

A number of people have studied thousands of compositions and letters written by seventh-grade pupils and have found out what words boys and girls in your grade use and which ones they misspell. The spelling lists in this book are based on these studies and contain only words which you are likely to need in your writing and which are commonly misspelled.

Notebook

Keep in your notebook a NEVER AGAIN list of all the words you misspell in letters, compositions, spelling and other tests, and other writing. Study these words until you are sure you can spell every one. Have someone test you. Check the words missed. A few days later study the list again, have someone pronounce the words for you, and check the ones you miss. Then cross off the words spelled correctly both times. Start a new list with the words missed.

The Ten Hardest Words

The ten words most frequently misspelled by high school students are —

too	together	committee	separate
its	their	therefore	pleasant
believe	principal		

Notice the **ie** in *belie*v*e*. Note that all the letters of *together* are together. There is no hyphen to separate them.

Watch the three doubles, **mm, tt,** and **ee,** in *com-m*i*ttee.*

Separate, *pleasant*, and *grammar* are 2a words. *Principal* is a 1a word. Notice the **pa** in *sepa*r*ate* and *princi*p*al.*

Exercise 1 (*Dictation*)

1. I **believe** the **committee** has handed in **its** report.
2. **Their** hats are **too** small.
3. **Their principal** is a **pleasant** man.
4. The **committee** is **too** large to do **its** work quickly.
5. The **principal believed** the boys; **therefore** he did not **separate** them.
6. **Its** hair is **too** long.
7. I **believe** the **principal** actors will eat **their** lunch **together.**
8. Did you study **separately** or **together?**
9. It was not **too** cold; **therefore** we had a **pleasant** trip.
10. **Its** front feet are **together.**

Exercise 2

Write sentences containing the ten hardest words. You may use two of them in one sentence.

SPELLING

Four Groups

o	al	aid	*per*
lose	almost	laid	perhaps
whose	already	paid	perform
move	altogether	said	person
prove	always		perfect
forty			

Exercise 3 (Dictation)

1. **Whose move** is it?
2. I had **already paid forty** cents.
3. **Perhaps** he can **prove** what he **said.**
4. I **almost always lose** my pencil.
5. He **performed** the trick **perfectly.**
6. Has any **person laid** the carpet?
7. My work was not **altogether** lost.

Exercise 4

Write sentences containing the sixteen words in the four groups. You may use two of them in one sentence.

Adding *s* and *ed* to Verbs

THIRD PERSON SINGULAR

	Present Tense	Past Tense
ask	he asks	he asked
show	he shows	he showed
turn	he turns	he turned
appear	he appears	he appeared

Final *y*

Final *y* preceded by a consonant is changed to *i* before any suffix that does not begin with *i*. (A suffix is a syllable or syllables added at the end of a word. The vowels are *a, e, i, o, u,* and sometimes *y*. The other letters are consonants: *b, d, x, g, h, s,* etc.)

Verbs

THIRD PERSON SINGULAR

	Present Tense	Past Tense
copy	he copies	he copied
carry	he carries	he carried
study	he studies	he studied
supply	he supplies	he supplied
cry	he cries	he cried
try	he tries	he tried
marry	he marries	he married

Exercise 5

In the way just shown write the third person singular of the present tense and of the past tense of these verbs: *cry, fry, spy, dry, deny, reply, hurry, apply, bury, defy, baby, modify, multiply, occupy, satisfy, accompany, justify, pity.*

Plural of Nouns

lad*y*(i) + es = ladies   pupp*y*(i) + es = puppies

Singular	Plural	Singular	Plural
country	countries	city	cities
enemy	enemies	party	parties

Exercise 6

Write the plural of these nouns: *fly, copy, berry, lily, body, company, century, activity, library, courtesy, family, pony, salary, difficulty, secretary, duty, story, baby, reply, inquiry, county, worry, delivery, memory, opportunity.*

Nouns ending in *y* preceded by a vowel — in *ey*, for example — add *s* regularly.

monkey, monkeys	attorney, attorneys
turkey, turkeys	donkey, donkeys

SPELLING

Exercise 7

Write the plural of these nouns: *chimney, valley, pulley, trolley, kidney, turkey, alley, attorney, monkey.*

Adding **ness**

busy(i) + ness = business
friendly(i) + ness = friendliness

Exercise 8

Change each adjective to a noun by adding *ness:* lonely, wordy, heavy, cozy, worldly, dreary, crazy, dizzy, kindly, lovely, happy.

Adjectives and Adverbs

pretty, prettier, prettiest
lively, livelier, liveliest
lovely, lovelier, loveliest
happy, happier, happiest, happily
heavy, heavier, heaviest, heavily
steady, steadily
easy, easily
necessary, necessarily
hearty, heartily
pity, pitiful
plenty, plentiful

Three Nouns

carry, carriage
marry, marriage
modify, modifier

Exercise 9

Write sentences containing: (1) five verbs ending in *ies;* (2) five verbs ending in *ied;* (3) five nouns ending in *ies;* (4) three nouns ending in *iness;* (5) two adjectives ending in *ier;* (6) two adjectives ending in *iest;* (7) two adverbs ending in *ily;* (8) two nouns ending in *iage*.

Possessive Singular

To form the possessive singular of a noun, add *'s*. Don't change the word. Don't add a letter or omit a letter. Just write the word and then quickly put *'s* AT THE END of it.

baby + 's = baby's   farmer + 's = farmer's
boy + 's = boy's   father + 's = father's

Exercise 10

Write the possessive singular of these words: *brother, child, company, country, customer, day, dealer, grandma, hour, lady, life, mamma, man, master, moment, month, morning, mother, night, one, papa, people, president, secretary, sister, teacher, today, treasurer, uncle, wife, week, woman, world, writer, year, yesterday.*

Exercise 11 (*Dictation*)

You have just had the forty most frequently used possessive singulars and probably can spell every one correctly.[1] That is not enough. Have you formed the habit of writing *'s* at the end of a possessive singular? Do you write *'s* when you are not thinking about spelling?

1. A boy's ball broke a window in the doctor's house.
2. The secretary's report is on the teacher's desk.
3. After an hour's wait we heard a horse's hoofs.
4. James's mother saw him cutting the baby's hair.
5. In Grandma's garden I saw a bird's nest.
6. Andrew spent his week's vacation at his uncle's home.
7. After an hour's search I found my father's knife.

[1] Ernest Horn's *A Basic Writing Vocabulary.*

8. Is that your **mother's**, your **brother's**, or **your sister's** book?

9. The **treasurer's** report is in **yesterday's** paper.

10. We went home pleased with our **day's** outing.

Exercise 12

Write sentences containing the possessive singular of ten nouns in Exercise 10 on page 338 and of five other nouns.

One Hundred Demons [1]

Probably these demons do not frighten you a bit. You can spell most of these short words and can easily learn to spell the rest. But do you ALWAYS spell them correctly when you write? Easy words cause most spelling errors.

Exercise 13 (*Dictation*)

1. **Some** time has passed **since their** house was **built**.
2. Your **guess** is as good as **any**.
3. **Won't** you **write** your **dear** mother asking her **whether** she is **ready** to come.
4. I looked for a **whole** day for berries but found **none** until I was **coming** home.
5. The glass top has long been **loose,** and this morning I **heard** it **break**.
6. Mr. Melvin is **busy** because he is trying to **raise sugar** on his plantation.
7. A **business** letter should go **straight** to the point and usually should end with "Yours **truly**."
8. **Tonight** I am **tired** and my bones **ache,** so I am going to bed at **half** past eight.
9. It is not **very easy** to find flowers in the **early** spring **among** the wet leaves, but I **used** to search for them daily.
10. Last night she was **hoarse** and today she has a **cough**.

[1] Dr. W. Franklin Jones's *A Concrete Investigation of the Material of English Spelling.*

11. He does not **believe** it will rain **much, though** the sky is dark.

12. **Which** boys **knew** the **answer?**

13. Cheap **shoes** don't **wear** well.

14. On **Wednesday** the **women** held a meeting to **choose two** officers.

15. **February** is not a cold month in **every country** along the **blue** Mediterranean.

16. George **seems** to have **done** his work for next **Tuesday.**

17. The **doctor wrote** something on a **piece** of paper.

18. **Too many** cooks spoil the broth.

19. I **hear** you **could** not match the **color.**

20. My **friend says** he is **beginning** to train for the games but **does** not **know** when **they** begin.

21. I have **read forty** pages of *Birds' Christmas Carol.*

22. I **often** spend a **week** in our camp, **where** we have **been** building **separate** sleeping cabins.

23. After we had driven an **hour,** the **trouble** began **again.**

24. **Having just laid** the stones in the water, I walked on them **through** the stream **instead** of crossing the bridge.

25. **Here** are **writing** materials with which to prepare your **grammar** lesson.

26. I **once** stopped a **minute** by that stream and had to **tear** myself away.

27. He **said** he **would always buy enough** food for camp.

28. Are you **sure** you did not **lose** your compass in the woods?

29. In the room **there** are forty girls **making** hats.

30. I **meant** to return the book today but **can't** find it.

New York State Spelling List for the Seventh Year [1]

abundant	acknowledge	additional
accomplished	acquaint	administration
accordance	acquainted	admission
accordingly	activity	advancement
accurate	actual	advertising

[1] Taken by permission from the Spelling Syllabus of the State of New York.

SPELLING

affair
agency
agreement
agriculture
alfalfa

allowed
almonds
altogether
ambitious
ambulance

announce
announcement
annual
anxious
applicant

application
arrival
article
assembly
assistant

association
assortment
assurance
attain
attitude

attorney
attract
auditor
auditorium
authorized

autumn
available
baggage
bandage
barely

based
bashful
beggar
beginning
behavior

believed
berth
billed
biscuit
blizzard

booster
bracelet
brief
British
business

calves
canned
carriage
cartoon
castle

cedar
chapel
character
choosing
cigarette

circumstance
circumstances
civilization
closing
colonies

column
combination
commercial
companies
compelled

completion
concerning
concert
conference
confidence

confirming
congress
constitution
contemplate
contemplated

contemplating
convince
convinced
cordial
coupon

courtesy
culture
curious
cushion
custom

customer
daddy
data
debate
decide

decrease
deliveries
delivery
democrat
democratic

departments
dependent
description
desert
desire

destination
detective
determined
develop
development

difficulty
disagreeable
discontinued
disgusted
disposal

distinguish
divide
Dr.
drawer
duly

duplicate
elaborate
electrical
elsewhere
endurance

energy
engineer
engineering
enrollment (*or*
 enrolment)
envelope (*or*
 envelop)

equally
equipment
errand
establish
established

estimate
estimated
etc.

evidence
evidently

examination
examine
examined
excursion
exercise

exercised
existing
expensive
experience
extreme

fabric
fashionable
favorable
favorably
federation

ferry
filing
finally
foliage
folks

foreign
formerly
fortunate
frequently
furniture

genuine
germ
glorious
government
governor

gradually
graduation

gratitude
grower
haste

hauled
heir
hereby
hire
hitched

honorable
hug
hurriedly
hustling
hygiene

identify
illustrated
illustrating
illustration
imagine

impression
inclined
influence
inside
install

institute
institution
instructor
instrument
interrupt

investigate
investigation
invitation
involved
irrigate

irrigation
issued

SPELLING

item	notified	profession
janitor	obedient	profitable
jewel	obligation	proposition
	occupy	prosperous
jobber	occur	publish
journal		
junior	odor	publisher
knee	official	purchased
lawyer	operate	qualities
	operating	questions
liable	operation	raised
library		
lining	opinion	realize
literary	orchestra	realizing
literature	ordinary	really
	organized	receiving
lovingly	parade	recognize
lying		
maintain	partner	reference
majority	pear	regardless
management	pears	registered
	personality	regularly
manual	pleasant	relations
meant		
medal	policy	reliability
mental	political	relief
merchandise	politics	relieve
	population	religion
mere	possession	remedy
millionaire		
mining	possibly	removal
missed	postscript	requirement
mistress	poultry	resign
	practice	resigned
moisture	prairie	respectfully
mosquito		
neighboring (*or*	prefer	responsible
neighbouring)	premium	rinse
nephew	prevail	sacrifice
ninth	previous	safely
	principal	salesman

samples	stomach	type
sandwich	stopped	umbrella
sanitary		unanimous
satisfactory	strawberries	unfortunate
satisfy	stretch	universal
	strictly	
scatter	studying	university
scene	submitted	urge
scratched		usual
secretary		usually
senate	subscription	valuable
	substitute	
senior	suburb	various
series	succeed	vary
serious	suggest	vicinity
services		village
shipped	suggested	volunteer
	superior	
signature	surplus	voyage
sincere	surrender	wherever
source	tact	whether
spear		wholesale
speech	telegraph	worn
	terrible	
squeeze	territory	worrying
stationary	theater (*or* theatre)	wrap
stationery	transit	yield

Mastery Tests 12A and 12B

For Mastery Tests 12A and 12B your teacher will select words or sentences from this unit.

INDEX

A, an, 255
Abbreviations, 78, 115, 236, 252, 253, 323, 324, 327, 328
Accent, 319
Acceptance, 82, 83
Address, change of, 125, 126
Address, nominative of, 206, 207, 236
Address, of letter, 114, 117; of envelope, 78, 122; return, 78, 122
Addresses and dates, punctuation of, 242, 243
Adjectives, 172–174, 191, 192, 207, 337; predicate, 191–193, 292; proper, 253; pronouns and, 279, 283
Adverbs, 176–179, 207, 337; confusion with prepositions, 184, 185
Agreement, of pronoun with antecedent, 283
Ain't, 305
Akeley, Carl, 59
Alcott, Louisa M., 6, 47, 60, 70
Alphabetizing, 315
American Circus, The, 66
An, a, 255
And, 186, 241, 255; overuse of, 8, 24, 29, 31, 34
Anecdote, 47, 48
Answers, complete, 110, 111; to questions, 221
Antecedent of pronoun, 283, 284
Anybody, anyone, 282, 284
Apostrophe, 245, 251, 265

Appear, 192
Appositive, 203–206; punctuation of, 237–240

Barter, 146
Be, predicate adjective after, 191, 192, 291
Become, 192
Big Boy and Tar Baby, 68
Block style, 114–117, 119, 120, 122
Body of letter, friendly, 71, 75; business, 114, 119
Borrowing, 47
Both, 186, 282
"Bread-and-Butter" letter, 84
Browning, Robert, 33
Building something, 103–105
Business letter, 114–133; parts, 114–121; envelope, 122, 123; paper and folding, 123; change of address, 125–127; request for catalog, 127; order, 128–131; correction of an error, 131–133
But, 186; overuse of, 8, 29, 31, 34

Capitalization, 222, 224–226, 252–259, 326, 327; composition title, 24; letter, 73, 74, 118, 120; outline, 97
Carroll, Lewis, 69
Case, possessive of nouns, 264–268, 338; objective, 273, 275, 279, 281; nominative 273, 274, 275, 279; of personal pronouns, 272–277; of pronouns, 273, 274; of interrogative pronouns, 281; correct, 275

Causes of Forest Fires, 99, 100
Change of address, letter of, 125, 126
Chase, Mary Ellen, 70
Childhood Adventure, A, 229
Clearness, in speech, 7, 31, 32, 34, 106; in letters, 81, 119, 128; in explanation, 91, 93–95, 105, 106
Climax, story-telling, 52, 142; in news story, 142
Collective noun, 262
Colon, 118
Comma, 250; direct quotation, 40; direct address, 236, 237; appositives, 237–240; series, 240, 241; addresses and dates, 242, 243; parenthetical expressions, 243, 244; numbers, 244; *yes* and *no*, 244; after *oh*, 246; salutation and complimentary close of letter, 73, 74, 115, 117, 244
Comma blunder, 224–230
Common noun, 253
Comparisons, in a paragraph, 64
Complete definitions, 109, 110, 324, 325
Complimentary close, friendly letter, 71, 74, 244; business letter, 114, 120
Composition reminders, 49
Compound object, 275
Compound personal pronouns, 280
Compound predicate, 214, 215
Compound subject, 214, 215, 275, 278
Conjunctions, 185, 186, 255
Contractions, 245
Conversation, each one's share, 12, 13; accuracy and clearness in, 14; over the telephone, 18; in stories, 39–43, 68

Conversing, 3–22
Correction of an error, letter of, 131, 132
"*Count Luckner, the Sea Devil,*" 228
Courtesy, 5, 12, 18, 33, 119

Daily Trip to School, My, 97, 98
Dates and addresses, punctuation of, 242, 243
Declarative sentence, 234, 250
Definitions, complete, 109, 110; that fit, 324, 325
Demonstrative pronouns, 282
Details in a paragraph, 64
Development, paragraph, 63–65
Diacritical marks, 317, 318
Diagrams, 93, 94
Dictation, 43–47, 86, 256, 257, 334, 335, 338, 339; how to prepare, 43, 44; rules, 44
Dictionary, use of, 314–328
Didn't See Him Steal, 48
Direct address, punctuation of, 236, 237
Direct quotations, 40–43
Directions, accuracy in, 14, 93–95; letters giving, 83; how to read, 144–146
Doing something, 101–103
Double subject, 278, 279

Each, 282, 284
Either, 186, 282, 284
Elliot and Forbush, 106
Enunciating, 7, 8, 18, 31–34
Envelope, 79, 80; how addressed, 78, 122
Error, correction of, 131–133
Error box, 286
Every, everybody, everyone, 282, 284
Exclamation point, 234, 246, 250
Exclamatory sentence, 234, 250
Experiences, telling, 50–57

Explaining, 91–113; clearness, 14, 91–95; accuracy, 14, 95; outlining, 96–101; how to do something, 101–103; how to make something, 103–105; how to play games, 105–109; meaning of words, 109–110; proverbs, 112, 113

Fable: Uncle Mitya's Horse, A, 35
Fainting, 144
Feel, 192
Feminine gender, 263, 264
Ferriter, Captain John P., 135
Figures, plural of, 261
Flying Sticks, 135
Folding of a letter, 80, 123
Friendly letter, parts, 71–76; envelope, 78–80; informal notes, 81–86; postcards, 86, 87; of travel, 87, 88
Future perfect tense, 296, 297
Future tense, 295, 297

Games, 166, 174, 187, 216, 217, 315
Gender, of nouns, 263, 264; of pronouns, 284
Getting Off for School, 42
Grammar, 9–12, 151–219, 233–286; parts of the simple sentence, 151–165, 191–218; parts of speech, 165–190; sentence sense, 220–232; simple sentences, 223–251; nouns, 252–270; pronouns, 271–288; verbs, 289–309
Grow, 192

Half-sentence, 220–224
Handwriting Scale, A, 26, 27
Heading of letter, 71, 72, 73, 114–116

Horn, Ernest, 338
How to Make Baking-Powder Biscuits, 103
How to Pack a Blanket Roll, 104
Hunting a Coon, 37
Hunting in the Days of Daniel Boone, 99
Hyphen, 24, 325

If You Are Lost in the Woods, 91
Illustration, use of in a paragraph, 64
Imperative sentences, 234, 250
Indefinite pronouns, 282
Indention, 24, 68, 80, 119
Indians and the Wolves, The, 34
Indirect object, 200, 201, 273
Informal notes, 81–86
Initials, period after, 236
Ink, 23, 79
Interjections, 187, 246
Interrogative pronouns, 280, 281
Interrogative sentence, 234, 250
Intransitive verbs, 289–295
Introductory adverb, 211
Inverted order, 211–213
Invitation and reply, 82, 83

Jones, Dr. W. Franklin, 339

Kick-The-Stick, 106

Letters, friendly, 71–90, 244; business, 114–133
Letters, plural of, 261
Lincoln, Abraham, 88
Linking verb, 192, 193
Listener, good, 5, 33
Longfellow, Henry W., 90
Look, 192

McNair, J. B., 98
Magazine Story, 135

INDEX

Making a Will, 107, 108
Making something, 103–105
Many, 282; *many a*, 284
Margin, 23, 24, 58; letter, 80, 119
Marks, diacritical, 317, 318
Masculine gender, 263, 264
Meeting the Indians, 35
Memorize, how to, 146–148
Mills, Edward C., 26
Modifiers, 171, 172, 207, 208, 209, 222
Most Exciting Christmas I Ever Had, The, 56

Natural order, 210, 211
Neither, 186, 282, 284
Neuter gender, 263
News Stories, 141–143
Nicolay, Helen, 88
No, yes, punctuation of, 244
Nobody, no one, 282, 284
Nominative, predicate, 193–196, 199, 216; of address, 206, 207
Nominative case of pronouns, 273, 274, 275, 279
Nor, 186
Notes, informal, 81–86
Note-taking, 100, 101
Nouns, 165–167, 192, 193, 203, 204, 252–270; capitalization of proper nouns, 252–259; common, 253; formation of plural, 259–263, 336; collective, 262; possessive form, 264–268, 338; gender, 263, 264
Now, misuse of, 8
Number, of nouns, 259–263; of pronouns, 284
Numbers, 244

Object, of verb, 196–200, 216, 222, 273, 274, 290, 291; of preposition, 215, 273; indirect, 200, 201, 273

Objective case, 273, 274, 275, 279, 281
On My Uncle's Farm, 267
One, 282, 284
Only Seven, 189
Or, 186, 241, 255
Order, natural, 210, 211; inverted, 211–213; word, 277, 278
Order letter, 128–131
Outlining, 96–101

Paper, 23; letter, 79, 123
Paragraph, 58–70; topic sentence, 59–61; unity, 62, 63; how built, 63–65; beginnings and endings, 65–67; conversation, 39–43, 68
Parenthetical expressions, punctuation of, 243, 244
Parker, Arthur C., 34
Participle, past, 299, 300, 305
Parts of speech, 165–190; same word as different, 167, 168
Parts of the simple sentence, 191–219
Past participle, 299, 300, 305
Past perfect tense, 296, 297
Past tense, 295, 297, 299, 300, 335, 336
Penmanship, 23–28; handwriting scale, 26, 27
Perfect tenses, 295–299
Period, 224, 225, 250; in outline, 97; after declarative or imperative sentence, 234; after abbreviations and initials, 236
Person, 271, 272, 274, 284
Person, a, 284
Personal pronouns, 271–280
Phrase, prepositional, 179, 207; beginning sentences with, 182, 184
Plural, of nouns, 259–263, 327, 336, 337; possessive, 267, 268

Poison Ivy, 98, 99
Possessive case, of nouns, 264–268, 338; of personal pronouns, 273, 274
Postcards, 86, 87
Posture, 31
Predicate, 151, 191; simple, 151, 152; complete, 209, 210; compound, 214, 215
Predicate adjective, 191–193, 215, 292
Predicate nominative, 193, 194, 199, 216, 273, 275, 292
Preposition, 179–182; object of, 179–182, 184, 215, 273, 275; adverbs and, 184, 185; conjunctions and, 185, 186
Prepositional phrases, 179, 207; beginning sentences with, 182, 184
Present perfect tense, 296, 297
Present tense, 295, 297, 299, 300, 335, 336
Principal parts of verbs, 299–301
Pronouns, 169–171, 192, 271–286; and adjectives, 174, 176, 283; personal, 271–280; interrogative, 280, 281; demonstrative, 282; indefinite, 282; agreement with antecedent, 283, 284
Pronunciation, 7, 8, 30–33, 316–323
Proper nouns, 252–257
Proverbs, explanation of, 112, 113
Punctuation, in title of composition, 24; of conversation, 40, 41; in letters, 73, 74, 78, 115, 117; of simple sentences, 233–251

Question mark, 225, 234, 235, 250
Questions, complete answers to, 110, 111
Quotations, direct, 40–43

Reading and memorizing, 134–148; reading for pleasure, 134–141; for information, 142–146; memorizing, 146–148
Regret, letter of, 82, 83
Reminders, composition, 49
Request for catalog, letter of, 127, 128
Return address, 78
Right word, 310–331
Robin Hood and the Bishop, 40

Said, overuse of, 8, 40
Sales talks, suggestions for, 16
Salutation of letter, 71, 73, 114, 118, 119, 244
Sarah Ann's Ride, 50
Seem, 192
Sentence, definition of, 151; topic, 59–61; parts of simple, 191–219; simple with compound parts, 214, 215; punctuation of simple, 233–251; declarative, 234, 250; exclamatory, 234, 250; imperative, 234, 250; interrogative, 234, 250
Sentence outline, 96, 97
Sentence sense, half-sentence, 220–224; comma blunder, 224–230
Series, punctuation of, 240, 241
Seton, Ernest Thompson, 37
Shaw, Anna Howard, 35
Signature, 71, 74, 114, 120
Signs, plural of, 261
Silent reading, 134–141
Simple predicate, 151, 152
Simple sentence, 151–163; parts of, 191–219; punctuation of, 233–251
Simple subject, 160, 161
Slant style, 114, 116, 117, 118, 120, 122
Smell, 192

So, overuse of, 8, 29, 34
Somebody, someone, 282, 284
Something to say, 4
Sound, 192
Speaking distinctly, 7, 34
Speech campaign, 22
Spelling, 259–263, 267, 268, 332–344; one hundred demons, 339; list of words, 340–344
Story, magazine, 135
Story, news, 141, 142
Story-telling, 29–57
Stuck in the Mud, 53
Subject, simple, 160, 161, 191; complete, 209, 210, 222; compound, 214, 215; case of, 273; double, 278, 279; phrase before, 182, 184
Syllabication, 24; and accent, 319, 320

Talks, sales, 16
Taste, 192
Teasdale, Sara, 147
Telephone conversation, 18
Tense, 294–299
Tests, 25, 69, 124, 141, 164, 190, 202, 218, 230, 248, 257, 269, 286, 306, 310, 312, 329, 344
Thanks, notes of, 84
That, 175, 282
The, 255
Them, 279
There, introductory word, 162, 211
This, 175, 282
Those, 279
Title of compositions, how to write, 24

Titles of books, poems, stories, and compositions, 255
Tolstoi, Leo, 35
Topic sentence, 59–61
Topical outline, 96, 98
Transitive verbs, 289–295
Travel, letters of, 87
Twins, The, 66

Unity, paragraph, 62, 63

Verbs, 151–160, 192, 223, 289–309; two-word, 153, 154; of three words, 157, 158; separated, 155; in questions, 156, 157; linking, 192, 193; object of, 196–200; indirect object of, 200, 201; transitive and intransitive, 289–295; tense, 294–299; principal parts of, 299–304; past participle of, 299, 300, 305; troublesome, 299, 300, 301; *ain't* and other errors, 305
Vocabulary, 310–331
Voice, 7, 18, 29, 30

Weathercocks, 106, 107
What, 281
What I Like to Do, 66
Which, 281
Which Was Right? 48
Who, 281
Why, misuse of, 8
Word order, 277, 278
Words, overworked, 8, 40; pet, 8; right, 310–331; often misused, 328–331
Wrong Room, The, 54

Yes and *no,* punctuation of, 244

MASTERY TESTS A AND B

NUMBER	PAGE
1. Subject and Verb	164
2. Parts of Speech	190
3. Predicate Adjective, Predicate Nominative, Object of Verb, Indirect Object	202
4. Parts of Simple Sentence	218
5. Sentence Sense	230
6. Punctuation of Simple Sentences	248
7. Capitalization	257
8. Possessive	269
9. Pronouns	286
10. Verbs	306
11. Correct Word	329
12. Spelling	344